Mission in the Twenty-first Century

Mission in the Twenty-first Century

Exploring the Five Marks of Global Mission

Andrew Walls and Cathy Ross, Editors

ORBIS BOOKS

Maryknoll, New York 10545

Founded in 1970, Orbis Books endeavors to publish works that enlighten the mind, nourish the spirit, and challenge the conscience. The publishing arm of the Maryknoll Fathers and Brothers, Orbis seeks to explore the global dimensions of the Christian faith and mission, to invite dialogue with diverse cultures and religious traditions, and to serve the cause of reconciliation and peace. The books published reflect the views of their authors and do not represent the official position of the Maryknoll Society. To learn more about Maryknoll and Orbis Books, please visit our website at www.maryknoll.org.

First published in Great Britain in 2008 by
Darton, Longman and Todd Ltd
1 Spencer Court
140-142 Wandsworth High Street
London SW18 4JJ

FSC
Mixed Sources
Product group from well-managed
forests and other controlled sources
Cert no. SGS-COC-2953
www.fsc.org
© 1996 Forest Stewardship Council

First published in the USA in 2008 by
Orbis Books
P.O. Box 308
Maryknoll, New York 10545-0308

Printed and bound in Great Britain.

Library of Congress Cataloging-in-Publication Data

Mission in the twenty-first century : exploring the five marks of global mission / Andrew F. Walls and Cathy Ross, editors.
   p. cm.
 ISBN-13: 978-1-57075-773-0
 1. Missions. I. Walls, Andrew F. (Andrew Finlay) II. Ross, Cathy, 1961-
 BV2061.3.M57 2008
 266.009'0511--dc22

                              2007038386

Contents

Contributors

Dr Cathy Ross works for the Church Mission Society in Oxford, where she oversees the Crowther Centre for Mission Education. She is also J. V. Taylor Fellow in Missiology at the University of Oxford. Prior to this she taught for seven years at the Bible College of New Zealand and has been a mission partner with NZCMS in Rwanda, Congo and Uganda.

Dr Ken Gnanakan is one of India's well-known educators, environmentalists and theologians. After completing PhD studies in London in 1979, he and his wife Prema returned to India to set up the ACTS Institute, a vocational training school, which also imparted spiritual values to young people. This gradually grew to become a large network of education, health and environmental projects, all under the banner of ACTS. He is also an accomplished musician and he has published widely in the areas of theology and environmental issues.

Rt Rev. Dr D. Zac Niringiye is a theologian, pastor, Bible teacher, counsellor, trainer and organisational development consultant. He is currently Assistant Bishop of the Diocese of Kampala, a position he assumed after four years as Regional Director of the Church Mission Society's work in Africa and 20 years of ministry among students in Uganda and all over English- and Portuguese-speaking Africa, initially with the Fellowship of Christian Unions (FOCUS) Uganda and then with the International Fellowship of Evangelical Students (IFES).

Rt Rev. Emmanuel Egbunu is the Bishop of the Diocese of Lokoja in the Church of Nigeria. He had served previously as Suffragan Bishop to the Most Rev. Peter Akinola in the Diocese of Abuja, and as Director, Global Inter-Anglican Relations, Church of Nigeria. He is passionate about teaching the Bible faithfully and relevantly, and nurturing young Christians to a fuller understanding of Christian discipleship. His research interest is in the area of inculturation and he is presently working towards a doctorate in Church History.

Rt Rev. Ande Georges Titre is Congolese (Democratic Republic), and is currently the Bishop of the Diocese of Aru, Democratic Republic of Congo. He is a former principal of the Anglican Theological College, IsThA, at Bunia. He has a PhD from the University of Birmingham.

Dr Melba Padilla Maggay is a writer and a social anthropologist, and holds a doctorate in Philippine Studies, a masters degree in English Literature, and a first degree in Mass Communication. She has lectured on intercultural communication and other cross-cultural issues world-wide. As founder and long-time director of ISACC (Institute for Studies in Asian Church and Culture), she has been cited for her outstanding leadership in organising the evangelical Protestant presence at the EDSA barricades during the February People Power Uprising in 1986. In 1991 she stepped down from ISACC leadership and hands-on management to specialise in the more technical aspects of its work in cross-cultural and social transformation studies. Since the year 2000 she has come back to the leadership of ISACC as President and Chief Executive Officer.

Sam (Haami) Chapman has been married to Thelma for 35 years. They have four adult children and 7 grandchildren. Together, they have worked in community development for over 30 years in Aotearoa/New Zealand. Their home in Auckland has always been their base and a haven for many. In 1987, Sam and Thelma established *Houhanga Rongo* Trust (HHR). HHR's vision, and Sam and Thelma's life work, is to enable and empower individuals, *whanau* (extended family) and communities to discover and develop their God-given potential. They are also very committed to encouraging community development projects that support regional and local initiatives throughout Aotearoa/NZ and the South Pacific. Sam is of *Ngati Tuwharetoa* and *Whakatohea* descent and Thelma is of English and Irish heritage.

Dr Valdir Steuernagel is Brazilian and is World Vision International Vice President for Christian Commitments. He also serves as a global minister-at-large and author. Dr Steuernagel has been married to Sileda for 30 years and they have four sons. Being an ordained Lutheran Minister, Dr Steuernagel graduated from the Theological School of the Evangelical Church of Lutheran Confession in Brazil and holds his master and doctoral degree from the Lutheran School of Theology in Chicago, Illinois.

Dr Beverley Haddad is Senior Lecturer in the Theology and Development Programme, School of Religion and Theology, University of KwaZulu-Natal, South Africa. She is an ordained priest in the Anglican Church of Southern Africa and a member of the Circle of Concerned African Women Theologians. She has published widely in the field of HIV and AIDS, gender and development, and the role of the church in social transformation.

Professor Calvin B. DeWitt is Professor of Environmental Studies at the University of Wisconsin-Madison where he is a member of the graduate faculties of Land Resources, Conservation Biology and Sustainable Development, Water Resources Management, and Limnology and Marine Science. He is also President Emeritus of Au Sable Institute. His research and writing integrates Christian belief with science, ethics, and praxis in addressing environmental issues.

Rev. Dave Bookless is National Director of *A Rocha* UK and a CMS Mission Partner. Dave has a national and international role writing and speaking on a

Christian approach to environmental issues, and has contributed to several books. With his wife Anne he founded *A Rocha* UK in 2001, with a major project in multicultural Southall, West London, where they live with their four daughters.

Rev. Professor Kwame Bediako holds doctorates from the Universities of Bordeaux (French Literature) and Aberdeen. He is an ordained minister of the Presbyterian Church of Ghana. He is Founder/Director of the Akrofi-Christaller Memorial Centre for Mission Research and Applied Theology, Akropong-Akuapem, Ghana, and Founder Secretary of the Africa Theological Fraternity. He is a member of the International Board of the Oxford Centre for Mission Studies.

Dr Jehu J. Hanciles was born in Sierra Leone. He is Associate Professor of Mission History and Globalization in the School of Intercultural Studies and Director of the Global Research Institute at Fuller Theological Seminary in USA. He came to Fuller as a scholar with the Global Research Institute in 1998, and joined the faculty full time in 2000 after serving in an adjunct capacity. His current research is focused on the impact of migration on the spread of world religions, notably Islam and Christianity.

Professor Lamin Sanneh was a professor at Harvard University for eight years before moving to Yale University in 1989 as the D. Willis James Professor of Missions and World Christianity, with a concurrent courtesy appointment as Professor of History at Yale College. He has been actively involved in Yale's Council on African Studies. He is an editor-at-large of the ecumenical weekly, *The Christian Century*, and serves on the editorial board of several academic journals. He is an Honorary Research Professor at the School of Oriental and African Studies in the University of London, and is a life member of Clare Hall, Cambridge University. He serves on the board of Ethics and Public Policy at Harvard University, and the Birmingham Civil Rights Institute in Birmingham, Alabama. He is the author of over a hundred articles on religious and historical subjects, and of several books. For his academic work he was made Commandeur de l'Ordre National du Lion, Senegal's highest national honour.

Dr Moonjang Lee is originally from Korea and is Associate Professor of World Christianity at Gordon Conwell Theological Seminary in USA. Dr Lee served five years (2001–2006) at Trinity Theological College, Singapore and three years (1997–2000) at the University of Edinburgh, Scotland as a Lecturer in Asian Theology. As the Christian centre of gravity shifts to the South, Dr Lee endeavours to articulate an authentic Asian understanding of Christianity from within the Asian epistemological framework that will be both faithful to the Bible and relevant to the multi-religious Asian context. His research areas include examining the issues related to the interface between the Gospel and Asian cultures; working out a viable methodology for Christian studies in the Asian religious milieu; articulating a new approach in the world mission and finding a way to utilise the traditional Asian reading method(s) in the study of the Bible.

Dr Ken Christoph Miyamoto is Associate Professor of Christian studies at Kobe Shoin Women's University, Kobe, Japan, a college affiliated with Nippon Sei Ko Kai. He was awarded the PhD in Mission and Ecumenics by Princeton Theological Seminary in 1999 for a dissertation on Asian contextual theology. His publications include *God's Mission in Asia: A Comparative and Contextual Study of This-Worldly Holiness and the Theology of* Missio Dei *in M. M. Thomas and C. S. Song* (Pickwick Publications, 2007).

Professor Gerald Pillay is thought to be only the second ethnic minority vice-chancellor to be appointed in Britain. Pillay is an Indian from South Africa where he lectured in Durban and Pretoria. From 1997 to 2003 he was Foundation Professor and Head of the Department of Theology and then Head of Liberal Arts at the University of Otago in New Zealand. In 2003 he was appointed as Vice-Chancellor at Liverpool Hope University.

Canon Tim Dakin came to lead the Church Mission Society into its third century at Easter 2000, succeeding Canon Diana Witts as General Secretary. Tim, his wife Sally and their two children lived for the previous six years in Nairobi, Kenya, where Tim was Principal of Carlile College. Tim finds being General Secretary of CMS a challenging privilege, and one that provides outlets for his interests in theology, teaching, world mission and organisational change.

Professor Andrew Walls, formerly Director of the Centre for the Study of Christianity in the Non-Western World at the University of Edinburgh, worked in Sierra Leone and Nigeria and has since taught in Europe and North America. He is currently Honorary Professor in the University of Edinburgh and a regular visiting Professor at the Akrofi-Christaller Institute of Theology, Mission and Culture in Ghana. He is founding editor of the *Journal of Religion in Africa*.

Foreword

There is a sense in which the classical missionary movement, from the sixteenth to the twentieth century, was bound up with what more than one of the contributors to this book calls the great 'migration' of Europeans to other regions of the world (and saying that reminds us of the difference between early Christian mission and the movements of the more recent past). It would be wrong to pass the simple judgement that this was such a deeply compromised phenomenon that we can write off its achievements: far from it, as these pages fully acknowledge. But the world is no longer the sort of place where you can take it for granted that there is a natural centre, or a natural 'flow' of resource and information and wisdom from one part to another. The old adage of the most far-sighted of mission thinkers has come true: mission must now be from all and to all.

If we are to think about migration today, and it is a recurring theme here, we have to recognise that the 'West' is the destination, not the point of origin. And if this is so, we are not in a position to say that this or that Western trend or assumption is self-evidently the path of the future. Even when the old colonialisms have vanished, we in the Western world are still prone to think as if there were one *narrative* for Christianity, in which we continue to set the pace. But this can no longer be assumed. In some ways, this is profoundly encouraging – there is no fixed and foreordained narrative of decline or secularisation, whatever may be true of the 'European exception', as it has been called. In other ways, it will be uncomfortable: what has been assumed as the steady progress of Christian thinking towards certain broadly 'liberal' conclusions (about ethics or society, intellectual pluralism or interfaith relations, for example) can't be taken as inevitable and unchallengeable. If anyone wants to defend these conclusions, they have to argue from basic theological principle, not simply by appeal, explicit or implicit, to the march of history.

But the greatest positive thing in all this, as several of these essays point out, is that we are being called to recognise that we (we in the 'developed' world) have not by any means finished reading the Bible – or, to put it more strongly, the Bible hasn't finished with us. Read afresh in new contexts, it delivers more of God's challenge and promise. Read to us and with us by those who are now 'migrating' in our direction, it becomes new for us too. And it is sound theology to say that there are things we shall never know about Jesus Christ and the written Word unless we hear and see what they do in ever-new contexts. Mission is not only the carrying of good news; it is the willingness to hear good news as the Word goes abroad and is embedded in culture after culture. We see more and more of its depths as we see more and more of what it does in diverse lives and worlds. If, as St Paul says in 2 Corinthians, we give what we have been given so that those to whom we give may become givers to us, the new pattern of theological and missional migration is exactly in accord with what Scripture might encourage us to hope for.

So this is a book to welcome very warmly, introducing us as it does to the new landscape of global mission, a landscape which even ten years ago it would have been hard to imagine (think only of the accelerating situation of evangelism in China!). It is not a summons to any kind of uncritical submission to a new reverse colonialism, but it is a summons to serious, hopeful, and humble engagement with what God is doing and saying in the growth of faith outside Europe and the North Atlantic, and in the new mobility of populations as boundaries come down. The global economy of our age is by no means a benign thing; yet, like the empires of the ancient world, it is a fact that changes what is possible. And when facts change what is possible, we may expect to see God creating new possibilities at the heart of them. This book will help us to pray intelligently that we may have the courage to respond to them as God wills, for his Kingdom's sake.

+ Rowan Cantuar:
Lambeth Palace
Advent 2007

Introduction:
Taonga

Cathy Ross

Taonga is a Māori word that comes from Aotearoa/New Zealand and means a treasured thing – whether tangible or intangible. It is difficult to define a *taonga*. It is a word associated with wisdom, with something precious and cherished; an heirloom perhaps, land in the family for generations, a beautiful garment, a valued piece of jewellery, a grandparent. To call something or someone a *taonga* is an accolade. In many ways this book is a *taonga*. It tells us vivid stories and brings us moving reflections from many different contexts in our world. It brings years of accumulated wisdom, years of pain and suffering, years of faithful service into its pages. It brings story and scholarship, anecdote and contemplation, the burden of history and the hope for the future before our eyes. To be granted a glimpse into how other people follow Jesus in their contexts and to listen and learn from other travellers along the Way – this is indeed a *taonga*.

This book is also a risky undertaking and calls into question all sorts of assumptions. A disparate set of authors from around the world invited to contribute on selected topics. Who issues the invitations? Who chooses the topics? Who accepts and who refuses? We can immediately see that this is indeed a risky undertaking, but an undertaking ripe with both potential and compromise.

Let me say at the outset that one such compromise is the use of English. English is not the first language of the majority of our contributors and yet we are writing and publishing in English. I cannot emphasise enough the injustice of this. The hegemony of the English language means that the world is a different shape from what it could be. We all know and are diminished by the experience of the globalising and totalising tendencies of one language to rule them all. It is not fair but because of the need for communication we accept this compromise. Such is the way of the world. Or such is the world as we have made it.

Another compromise, and one I feel keenly, is the lack of gender balance – fewer than one third of the articles are by women. I can neither explain nor excuse this. We know that women form the majority and are the backbone of the

Christian church but once again, when it comes to conversations like this, in the public arena, men do most of the talking. Such is the world as we have made it. I am tempted to reflect that while men are doing the talking, women are working it out, but I do not think that is completely fair either. Somehow we need to ensure that women's voices are heard in the public square as well as at home and hearth.

A final compromise is scope and representation. Choices have to be made. Some places are not represented. Some important themes are not discussed. Some voices are not heard – or perhaps just dimly through other speakers. Everything is not yet possible – such is the world as we have made it. But one day all will be possible and we anticipate this day with longing.

May this book be a preview of that in a modest fashion as we hear from these voices from the majority world, for that is the context of most of our contributors. These really are some of the representative voices in mission today. Yes, we as editors are from the West, and perhaps we are like beachcombers, searching the seashore for treasures, presented and delivered in English at present. Yes, there are compromises but let us also celebrate the rich diversity displayed before us in this *taonga*. Let us be challenged by the stories told and the conversations started – conversations around the 'Five Marks' and some contemporary issues in mission.

The Five Marks of Mission

1. To proclaim the Good News of the Kingdom
2. To teach, baptise, and nurture new believers
3. To respond to human need by loving service
4. To seek to transform unjust structures of society
5. To strive to safeguard the integrity of creation and sustain and renew the life of the earth

The Five Marks are neither a perfect nor a complete definition of mission. They do not say everything we might want to say about mission in today's world. Compromise again. However, they are also rich with potential and they do form a good working basis for a holistic approach to mission.

You will see that the articles on the Five Marks are in pairs. They are intended to be two types of articles and are not privileged or prioritised in any way. They are different sorts of articles to express different approaches. The first article of the pair is a more reflective, theological article, which explores the mark in some depth. The second article is more descriptive and has more of a praxis orientation. So together these articles explore how this particular mark is worked out on the ground in the writers' particular contexts. In this way we hope to draw out the missiological depth and practical engagement that each mark implies.

These essays are not intended to be either sleek or slick. Reflective practitioners have taken time out of busy lives to produce these articles – in English – usually their second, third or maybe even fourth language. These essays do have a smell of the earth about them and this is as it should be. These essays are supposed to be grounded and applied. Their voices urge us, disturb us, encourage us and challenge us. The voices are not uniform – some speak in narrative, some in poetry, some in a tight prose, some in an English less familiar to our ears. I believe this is the beauty and the power of the book for this is the reality of our world – the world as we have made it. We live in a world of migrants and strangers, of friends and familiar faces, of the streets and of the academy; and this selection of essays grants us a taste of our world – with all its beauty and potential as well as its despair and compromise.

Listen to their voices and hear their stories. Rejoice with their situations as you read of a street mission in urban Kampala; of a bishop struggling to empower Christians in Congo; of the gift of lace curtains to provide dignity in Aotearoa/NZ; of a Brazilian middle-class pastor falling in love with the God of justice; of a London wasteland being turned into a green space and a place of beauty. Empathise with them as you read of a Nigerian bishop trying to contextualise theological curricula suffering from Western legacies and priorities; of the theology of retribution at work in parts of South Africa that have little understanding of structural injustice and sees HIV/AIDS as a punishment; of a church that endorses an unhealthy and unjust status quo in Brazil and elsewhere; of creation groaning and suffering in the face of powerful people and profits; of ongoing discrimination against Dalits in India. May you revel in the diversity represented here, resonate with the range of issues and stories engaged with under the Five Marks and be strengthened as you engage in God's mission in your corner of the world – the world not only as we made it, scarred with compromise, but also the world that belongs to God and is alive with potential – 'charged with the grandeur of God'.

The second group of essays reflects on the context in which mission takes place and some of the issues that arise from these various contexts. As we look at this selection of essays we may be tempted to think, where is the thread, what is the motif that is holding this together? There is no thread nor motif. It is not neat and tidy. Perhaps this says something to us about the reality of mission in our world today. Mission is complex; it is multi-faceted; different concerns emerge from different places as we try to follow and present Jesus in our place. However, these different issues will touch us all as we allow new insights from different contexts to enter our perspectives and enlarge our borders.

And so we are confronted with the challenge of just whose religion is Christianity as we see it afresh. We are presented with the need for a larger intellectual framework as we must engage with living theology from the now many centres of Christianity around the world. Migration and its impact on the non-Western missionary movement, which diverges sharply from its Western predecessor, may be one of the consequences of our polycentric Christian world. We read of the church in the West struggling to engage with this new world of an increasingly confident Islam in a post-Christian West. Reading the Bible from an Asian perspective critiques and challenges our Western approach and goals in reading the Bible. The writer's Asian background offers new insights into how to approach and engage with a sacred text. The subject of worship is considered as vital for all of us as we engage in mission in a way that makes personal encounter with God come alive. This is brought into sharper focus as the contexts for these reflections are not only two highly secularised and post-religious cities in Japan but also the realm of the primal imagination, which immediately understands the transcendent as the normal Christian experience. Education as mission is presented as a new opportunity in our postcolonial world where Christian educational institutions can be alternative communities in their approach to and understanding of learning. The Five Marks are brought into conversation with Bevans and Schroeder's six constants of the Christian faith in an attempt to add depth and texture to them within the Anglican tradition. Mission doyen, Andrew Walls concludes with an overview of the context and some of the surprises of the last five hundred years of Christian mission, the Spirit blowing where it will. Now we do indeed live in an age of multi-centric Christian mission, which is a feature of this volume.

So we hope that this collection of essays will prove to be a *taonga* for you as you encounter the Five Marks – whether you are familiar with them or whether they are new to you – and as you mull over the second group of essays. I hope you may feel able to add this book, with all its imperfections and flaws, to your own collection of *taonga*. A tangible *taonga* as you hold it between your hands and an intangible *taonga* as it may spark new thoughts and visions; as it may offer other ways of finding and following Jesus in our daily rhythms of discipleship. *Taonga* are not perfect; they are treasures of this world – resonating with all the beauty and potential of creation, limited by the finite and the brokenness of this world; but perhaps even more precious as they hint of the possibilities and promises to come – in the new creation charged with the glory and the grandeur of God.

SECTION ONE:

The Five Marks of Mission

1. To Proclaim the Good News of the Kingdom (i)

Ken Gnanakan

Jesus commenced his ministry proclaiming, 'The kingdom of God is near. Repent and believe the good news!' (Mark 1:15). The good news of the Kingdom was declared and moreover he had a special anointing for this specific task – 'The Spirit of the Lord is on me, because he has anointed me to preach good news to the poor' (Luke 4:18). Two thousand years later this same good news continues to make its impact but calls for a renewed commitment from the church. The 'Five Marks of Mission' which were adopted by the General Synod of the Church of England in 1996 were a timely reminder emphasising this task – 'To proclaim the Good News of the Kingdom' set within a very holistic understanding of mission.

What is proclamation?

To begin our discussion, we should ask – What do we mean by proclaiming? As in English law even now, a proclamation in biblical times was a formal public announcement from royalty. There are several words used for 'proclaiming' in the Bible, but the basic meaning of the words always refers to the activity of the messenger conveying an important message which had been given to him either orally or in writing. The words are used in a variety of ways.

Luke's and Paul's use of the words range from merely informing to the more significant giving an important report (Acts 14:27; 15:4) or a command (Acts 17:30). There is also the sense of proclaiming or declaring in the sense we seek to discuss in this essay (Acts 4:2; 13:5; 26:20). Interestingly, John uses the words exclusively in a theological sense, for, as scholars think, John's is a realised eschatology in the present, in contrast to the proclamation of the age of salvation, the heralding of a coming event.

One thing is clear as we read the New Testament: proclamation did not acquire any particular form and hence we will need to draw from all the significantly varied perspectives that are presented. This is a good reminder to us in our world today as the church seeks to express itself in diverse, sometimes hostile contexts. There is no fixed format or tried and tested formula that must be prescribed for all contexts. We all proclaim Christ; but our methods and the application of the good news will vary.

Jesus Christ and the Kingdom are synonymous

Jesus proclaimed the good news throughout Galilee, calling upon people to repent and believe (Mark 1:15). There was a sense of urgency – the 'time has come' – and the Kingdom of God was central to Jesus' message. But apart from the urgency, the good news is that this kingdom is near – the Kingdom of God is near because Jesus is near. Here lies an important aspect of the proclamation of the good news – the inseparability of Jesus' person from the kingdom that he preached. The statement in Mark is not an isolated utterance. The aspect of inseparability of the Kingdom from the person of Jesus comes through even more clearly when we consider the claim – 'If I drive out demons by the finger of God, then the kingdom of God has come to you' (Luke 11:20). Jesus' power over Satan is a demonstration of the power of the Kingdom of God. The Kingdom of God is present wherever Jesus is present and exercises his authority.

Further, we note Jesus' reply to the Pharisee's question about the coming of the Kingdom of God – 'The kingdom of God is *within you*' (Luke 17:20ff.). The word is translated rather misleadingly as 'within you' but the actual reference is to the availability of the Kingdom near or amidst you, even among you. The precise meaning is – to be within your reach or even within your grasp. Rather than looking into the future for the Kingdom of God, Jesus points out that the Kingdom of God is present where he himself is present and exercising his influence.

The deep significance for mission of the kingdom in our world today is that God's Kingdom is established wherever the Lord Jesus Christ is present. And this begins with our proclamation. In other words, wherever God's people proclaim Jesus, the Kingdom is being ushered in and therefore demons shudder, satanic strongholds are pulled down, evil structures are challenged and men and women are liberated. God's power needs to be demonstrated through our proclamation.

However, this must not lead us to make triumphal claims or offer unrealistic promises as in various versions of the prosperity Gospel. Not all proclamation results in such triumphal encounters but we need to proclaim the message faithfully even amid increasing apathy and hostility, although we must be careful not to provoke people's antagonism with our insensitive forms of preaching.

The study of the parables of the Kingdom offers a varied perspective on our proclamation. We do not need to be thrusting the Gospel down people's throats whether they like it or not. We sow the seeds of the good news in various creative ways. These seeds of the Kingdom faithfully sowed now will grow into full realisation in the future. The 'mustard seed' and 'leaven' (Matthew 13) demonstrate that what is now insignificant or small will one day exercise an influence beyond comprehension. As we proclaim the Gospel all over the world we know there are some places where hardly any influence can be seen or felt but it is the seeds of the Kingdom we plant as we proclaim Jesus Christ and await greater things to be seen in God's time.

The future and the present

We must remind ourselves that Jesus spoke of the Kingdom as present as well as future. While this positively links sowing seeds through our proclamation now with the fulfilment of the Kingdom in the future, it also could be a perplexing aspect of the Kingdom. Jesus spoke of these distinct aspects separately, but frequently merged them together. We have noted the references to the Kingdom in the present, but Jesus clearly points to cataclysmic events in the future. We see this in the discourse on the last days in Matthew 24, Mark 13 and Luke 21. There are several other references to the future coming of the Kingdom. Matthew speaks of the Son of Man coming in his kingdom with glory (Matthew 16:27–28). Mark speaks of the Kingdom coming with power (Mark 9:1). In the Last Supper passage in Matthew 26:29 Jesus says he will not drink of the fruit of the vine until he drinks it in the Kingdom along with his disciples.

In recent decades, the extensive treatment of this subject by scholars such as Wolfhart Pannenberg assists us in seeing that the biblical emphasis is on the wholeness of history. The church in its proclamation today must accept history as a whole – the present ushering in the future as well as the power of this future giving significance to the present. The impact of the future influences the present, enabling the church to demonstrate signs and impacts of the Kingdom in our world today rather than being mesmerised with messages of distant dreams. Our mission is to call people to enter the Kingdom here and now but to await fulfilment in the future.

Importantly, in Jesus we already have the presence of the future. Rather than retreating to a purely futuristic understanding with no reference to the present, in Jesus Christ we are challenged to reconcile the two horizons creatively. In doing so, we underline both the knowable impact of the Kingdom today as well as the unknowable mystery to be fully revealed in God's tomorrow. Jesus' message was no other-worldly, utopian vision nor was it a totally present preoccupation. The two are interlinked integrally. And it is in this interdependence of present and future that we see the fullest meaning of the Kingdom and its relevance for our proclamation today.

What do we proclaim?

What did Jesus proclaim? Looking at Luke's record we note a powerful declaration – 'The Spirit of the Lord is on me, because he has anointed me to preach good news to the poor. He has sent me to proclaim freedom for the prisoners and recovery of sight for the blind, to release the oppressed, to proclaim the year of the Lord's favour' (Luke 4:18–19). The reference to Isaiah links Jesus and his ministry to the fulfilment of what the prophets had envisioned. It is clear that Jesus is taking on himself the role of 'the servant' for which he is being 'filled with the power of the Spirit'. This was just like the Old Testament prophets who were commissioned by God and spoke because the spirit of the Lord came upon them (Micah 3:8). Luke describes the birth of the early church similarly as it experiences the in-filling of the Holy Spirit at Pentecost.

But what is this good news that Jesus preached? There are very practical dimensions such as the blind would see and the oppressed would be liberated and these are clearly demonstrated in Jesus' earthly ministry that followed. Our proclamation is not merely for 'spiritual' solace but for practical impacts in the real world. Whether it was John Wesley and William Wilberforce's widespread social impacts in Britain or Pandita Ramabai's influence on downtrodden women in India, these are all expressions of the proclamation of the Gospel and not something that is contrary to or separate from a spiritual message. This is the kind of Gospel needing to be demonstrated in our world today.

The *Dalits* (literally the oppressed) in India, often called untouchables, or outcastes, await this kind of a liberating kingdom message. Although it is reported that millions are turning to Christianity and Islam, there are still millions who need liberation. Oppressed by Indian society and its caste system they are mostly poor farmers and landless labourers, scavengers, washer men etc. Although the Indian government is taking steps to alleviate their plight, discrimination against Dalits sadly continues in many rural areas. If the Gospel we proclaim has to do with deliverance of the oppressed, the church in India must preach this kind of a Gospel and bring about liberation of peoples suppressed by exploitation of various kinds.

Jesus Christ is also central for Paul. In the light of what we have considered earlier, our answer to the question of what the good news is that we proclaim, is – We proclaim Jesus (Colossians 1:28). Paul speaks of 'the preaching of Jesus Christ' (Romans 16:25). If Jesus and the Kingdom are synonymous, Jesus and the good news are equally so.

Here is powerful content to our Gospel message. In most of Asia the terms 'Christians' or 'Christianity' are increasingly taking on negative connotations. The church is a poor witness is some contexts; there is rising antagonism in other sectors. Although the church and Christians have become the brunt of attacks, there is a still a deep respect, and in fact reverence, for Jesus Christ. Some even openly or secretly worship Jesus! This is true whether in Hindu or in Islamic contexts and we should explore models of proclamation where Christ fits into local cultures rather than continue Western-style evangelistic methods that have alienated such people.

In summing up, let us consider some aspects of this good news we proclaim. First, the proclamation of the early church was the good news of the Kingdom. Not only did Jesus preach this message, he sent out his disciples with 'power and authority' to 'preach the kingdom of God' (Luke 9:1–2). Then seventy other disciples were sent out two by two (Luke 10:1) and they too were to proclaim 'The kingdom is near you.' These disciples are so privileged that they can now proclaim what even the prophets and the kings of old were not able to (Luke 10:24).

Secondly, the Apostles proclaimed Jesus as the one in whom the prophetic promises are fulfilled (Acts 3:18–26). More importantly, it is the resurrection that is now central to this message, as it is this pivotal event that has inaugurated the Kingdom of God. After the resurrection, the proclamation becomes the message of the Risen One, and in the resurrection narratives of all four gospels the disciples are witnesses to the resurrection. This is affirmed in the book of Acts as the replacement for Judas was also to be a witness. Obviously, the resurrection becomes a central part of the proclamation as this is the historic event that has ushered in the Kingdom here and now.

The Lord's Supper as proclamation

Historically we come from various streams of the church, with divergent views of the significance of the sacrament of the Lord's Supper. But there is one aspect that binds us all, and that is the fact that even this sacrament is an act of proclamation of the Gospel. At the table with his disciples, the Lord made a very penetrating statement – 'I tell you, I will not drink of this fruit of the vine from now on until that day when I drink it anew with you in my Father's kingdom' (Matthew 26:29). This important linking of the Kingdom in its eschatological dimension with our present is an important aspect of our proclamation.

After rebuking the church for disregarding the true meaning of the love feast, Paul reminded the Corinthian church, 'For the kingdom of God is not a matter of eating and drinking, but of righteousness, peace and joy in the Holy Spirit' (Romans 14:17). The Lord's Supper is in itself a celebration of the Kingdom and its values here and now, but even more, it is a proclamation of the Kingdom to come. 'For as often as you eat this bread and drink this cup, you proclaim the Lord's death until he comes' (1 Corinthians 11:26). The proclamation of the good news of the Kingdom to come is an integral part of the celebration of the first fruits of which we already taste.

Around the Lord's table, the future becomes the present. The experience is so overwhelming that the people of God are motivated into proclaiming the Gospel. The church has unfortunately got caught up in an institutional framework that has sanitised such celebrations into meaningless sacraments. The Lord's Supper binds the redeemed people of God in the joy of their Saviour's presence proclaiming the coming Kingdom. But rather than remaining in this bliss, they are thrust into the world to proclaim the message of the Kingdom.

Two models of proclamation

As we face our current context with increasing pressures of religious fundamentalism, it is time to review our practice of proclamation. Some tend to believe that it is only the confrontational kind of proclamation that is the true preaching of the Gospel, while others have seen the power of different creative presentations. Whatever the style we employ, there are some basic attitudinal problems we will need to eliminate. These are to do with the condemnation and arrogance we have often seen employed in such confrontations.

Peter in Acts 2 offers the kind of proclamation that the earliest Christians shared. The audience was Jewish. Israelites from many nations would have come to Jerusalem (Acts 2:5) at the time of Pentecost. The Spirit would be poured out on that day when the prophetic promises would be fulfilled in Jesus Christ. And now, says Peter, is the day when 'everyone who calls on the name of the Lord shall be saved' (Acts 2:21). Jesus has come in the fulfilment of the Old Testament prophecies. The prophets looked forward to the day when God would renew Israel, pour out his spirit and enable them to live in conformity to the covenant. Peter's proclamation is forthright, even daring in comparison to the frightened disciple he was prior to the resurrection. He presents a Jesus who came with power and performed signs and wonders. Jesus was crucified and God raised him from the dead. This same Jesus ascended to the right hand of the Father (v. 33). And God has made the crucified and risen Jesus both Lord and Christ (vv. 34–36). Peter puts forth his facts very plainly, even accusing the Jews for putting Jesus to death. His hearers, 'were cut to the heart' and said to Peter and to the other apostles, 'Brothers, what should we do?' Peter's reply is straightforward: 'Repent, and be baptised every one of you in the name of Jesus Christ' (v. 38). Peter warned and pleaded with them (v. 40) and about 3000 were added to their fellowship. This style of proclamation has continued and great numbers have responded. But we need to remember that this was not the only model of proclamation used in the Bible. In fact, this may not be the viable model in many places of the world today.

We must accept the need to change the manner and style of our communication. Asian and African evangelists deliver such confrontational messages as if they are in North America. Dressed like their American counterparts, they do not even consider the need to alter the language used. Aggressive 'crusades' are still conducted and warfare language liberally employed with no concern for the damage being done. There is arrogance reminiscent of the colonial days and people are reacting to such presentations.

In contrast to Peter's confrontation of the Jews, Paul in the Areopagean speech attempts to establish continuity between the Gospel and the worship of the Athenians. It is a very positive introduction – 'I perceive that in every way you are very religious' (Acts 17:22). He had definitely observed several things which brought him to this conclusion, chief among them being the altar to 'the unknown God'. The continuity that Paul establishes needs to be looked at for lessons for our proclamation today. Just like the 'faith' that Jesus was able to commend positively in the life of the Gentile centurion, Paul is able to commend the worship of the Athenians, even though this is to an unknown God.

Paul commends their sincere desire to worship the true God and not the material manifestations in the form of idols. This approach must be fostered in Asia where we meet many men and women with a sincere desire to worship the true God. Some deny idols, but even those trapped in idolatry display a longing for God. Traditionally, whether it was the missionaries who preached in Asia and Africa, or local evangelists in their own situations, there has been condemnation rather than commendation. Our attitude of presenting a radical discontinuity between one's present faith and the saving faith in Jesus Christ must be reviewed.

Sadly, preaching continues today in the condemnatory style that has offended many and even given rise to fundamentalist demonstrations against Christians. We have directed our message on sin against the religious practices of many sincere worshippers, taking a superior position as we look down condescendingly at the religions of our hearers. This has only built up barriers that hinder our proclamation today. There is an urgent need for seeing continuity between those to whom we present the Gospel and the Lord Jesus Christ to whom we want them to be led.

Paul has no problem accepting the Athenian sincerity and building on their conception, or lack of conception of God. One can see many such contact points in Asia and Africa on which a more positive proclamation of the Gospel could be built. Sincerity will not save them, we know. We must remember that this is only the starting point. Paul is not commending any of the known gods that they are worshipping, nor is he saying that their religion in itself is leading them to the true God. He is certainly willing to see within their religious attitudes an inherent desire to know the truth about God.

The Church and its proclamation

Right from the Reformation, proclamation has been crucial to the Church's being. Calvin, like Luther, was fighting against the institutionalised understanding of the Roman Church. Luther enumerated other marks of the true church, but went on to underline only the preaching of the word. The church is pure, Luther claimed, where the pure Gospel is preached, that the church does not make the word but it comes into being from the word. One can see the crucial role that proclamation played in Luther's understanding of the church.

Today, the Reformers' stress on proclamation will need to be fleshed out completely, considering what we have seen in the New Testament and the heavy stress on the accompanying demonstration of the kingdom. Certain sections of the church make an evangelistic proclamation and individual commitments to Christ part of every Sunday service, while others totally ignore such messages. The former aim at increasing the numbers in their church, and therefore there is only one purpose for their preaching. It is to put pressure on every member to go out and to preach to others who will come into their church. The latter see the church only as a gathering to observe the sacraments and little or no attention is paid to proclamation of the good news. The Gospel of the Kingdom must be considered anew so that our proclamation and our methods take on fresh significance.

While there is a need to renew our allegiance to proclaim the word faithfully, there is a greater need to flesh the message out in acts that express this kingdom. Proclamation is urgent, but demonstration is the priority. The world must hear the message of the Kingdom, but it will also want to see some concrete demonstration of this message. It is in this spelling out the Kingdom identity, in presenting the person of Jesus and not just the message of Jesus; in looking at Jesus and the way that his message was demonstrated with power and authority, that the church will be concretising the Kingdom of God through tangible expressions of the Kingdom of God.

Proclamation today

The Gospel – the *dunamis* of God – is dynamic and not static. It evolves into newer and newer forms in keeping with each local situation and according to the need of the hour. Historically, there was a time for a world-wide missionary movement which freely took the message of Jesus Christ all over the world. There were mass movements. There were also some remarkable individual conversions. The global Christian community is what it is today primarily because of the sacrificial commitment of thousands of men and women, 'missionaries' who even gave their lives for the proclamation of the Gospel. But the dynamic message grows as it addresses newer contexts in newer ways. The content remains the same; the outcomes are the same, but the delivery varies.

Men and women need to be confronted with the claims of Christ through an encounter with Christ himself. Error needs to be exposed and God's concern for bringing people into repentance must be passionately made known. But we must strive for the kind of proclamation needed in our context today. The early Christians confidently proclaimed the finality of God's revelation in Jesus Christ, despite all the prevailing philosophies and ideologies. Yet, they showed sensitivity in dealing with other sincere worshippers or God-fearing Gentiles. Without relaxing the claims of Christ, we need to see how best to proclaim the message afresh in our context. Our proclamation must be based on the uniqueness of the biblical revelation, standing on the full and final revelation of God in the Lord Jesus Christ, but related to our present world through the love of God demonstrated in Jesus.

The question will be asked: how can we communicate the Gospel of the Kingdom to a world that is alien to God's purpose? For the answer we look at Jesus himself, recognising the fact that he actualised the Kingdom in his life and ministry. Speaking with the authority of God, he reminded his hearers, 'The kingdom is near you.' We have seen that this meant nothing less than the fact that Jesus himself is the Kingdom. His nearness to us signifies the nearness of the Kingdom. When the church faithfully seeks to proclaim the message of its Lord and Master, and to live out this message in their own lives, then the presence of the Lord Jesus penetrates people all over the world.

We give to the world what we have. When the people of God are charged with the power of Jesus Christ, their words and their deeds are in consonance with the Kingdom. The message made flesh in the life of the Church gives to it the solid platform from which to proclaim the Gospel of the Kingdom.

It is in such terms that the Apostle John made proclamation very personal: '(We) proclaim to you the eternal life which was with the Father and was made manifest to us – that which we have seen and heard we proclaim to you, that you may have fellowship with us.' That which has been experienced personally is being shared so that others may enter this fellowship in the Kingdom (1 John 1:2f.).

1. To Proclaim the Good News of the Kingdom (ii)

D. Zac Niringiye[1]

One evening I was watching television and as I flipped through the channels, my attention was caught by what seemed to be some fiery preacher, with a massive audience. It looked like a well-mixed audience: multi-ethnic, young and old, male and female. He was preaching in English with a translation in *Luganda* (the language spoke by the majority of the people in central Uganda and understood widely beyond). There must have been many whose educational level did not enable them to understand English. Visibly his audience was charged by his preaching. They were clapping, standing, shaking and laughing. I watched the programme for a while and listened intently, asking myself what it was about his preaching that seemed to captivate his audience. He spoke about ordinary needs – physical health, work, adequate shelter and daily food – and he spoke about relationships – at work and in the home, singleness, marriage, and family. He passionately declared that God's word promised provision for all needs. It was there to be claimed. At the end he called for a response – 'for those who were ready to take God at his word and claim what he promised'. And they came to the front in large numbers.

As I pondered over the television preacher and his preaching, I could not deny that he was effective as a communicator. He was not boring at all: he was dramatic in his style and his preaching was spiced with much humour. He had his audience with him. He spoke a language they could understand. He spoke to their needs and circumstances. His preaching was good news to his hearers. The question that continued to linger in my mind was whether this was the good news of the Kingdom of God. Was it all seeking the honour of God or was it simply feeding the pleasures of the audience irrespective of the pleasure of God? Moreover, how was I to determine that what the preacher proclaimed was the good news of the Kingdom of God?

In considering the praxis of proclaiming the good news of the Kingdom of God, it is not enough just to consider the task of proclaiming. Although the theological-missiological reflection on the good news is beyond the scope of this paper, we cannot avoid reflecting on them because the two themes in this mark (the task of proclaiming and the subject of the proclamation – the good news of the Kingdom of God) are linked. We should not fall to the false dichotomy between theology and practice; between substance and form; between word and works; or between words and works. The nature of the good news of the Kingdom shapes the means and goals of proclamation. We learn this as we look at the story of Jesus and how he went about proclaiming the good news of the Kingdom of God. Following immediately after Jesus, we see the Apostles proclaiming the good news of the Kingdom of God – pointing to Jesus and his continuing work in them and through them, preaching repentance and forgiveness 'in his name to all nations, beginning at Jerusalem' (Luke 24:47). It is this standard that we should use – of Jesus and his first disciples, to examine contemporary praxis. It is the standard on which we should model any proclamation praxis.

Jesus' proclamation

All four narratives of Jesus' public life and ministry, Matthew, Mark, Luke and John, agree that Jesus' passion and mission were to proclaim the good news of the Kingdom of God and that he identified himself as the one embodying the Kingdom and its message. Matthew tells how in Capernaum 'Jesus *began* to preach, "Repent for the Kingdom of God is near"' (Matthew 4:17). Mark describes Jesus' ministry thus: 'Jesus went to Galilee proclaiming the good news of God. "The time has come. The Kingdom of God is near. Repent and believe the good news!"' (Mark 1:15). So when he began to teach and preach at thirty, the age at which tradition and custom allowed one to be a teacher, he had one message: the Kingdom of God. Matthew tells us that he 'went throughout Galilee, teaching in their synagogues, preaching the good news of the kingdom' (Matthew 4:23).

The challenge of understanding the Kingdom of God remains to this day, two thousand years after Jesus inaugurated it. Our understanding of the biblical vision of the Kingdom of God is clouded by notions of kingdoms in our various histories. For many in contemporary times, 'kingdom' evokes notions of something archaic, oppressive and often exercising brutal force. I recall the protest by a lady in a meeting over the use of the term Kingdom of God in explaining the mission of Jesus. Her quarrel was that kingdom conjures in her mind oppression and domination. In Uganda, when one speaks about a kingdom, the mental model for many is that of the ancient kingdom of *Buganda* (in central Uganda), whose vestiges still remain to this day – of a centralised, hierarchical and dominant structure of government. For, at the height of its dominance, prior to the advent of British colonists at the end of the nineteenth century, the kingdom of Buganda was the most powerful of all kingdoms in the region that later constituted Uganda. At the top, and indeed the centre of the kingdom was the *Kabaka* (king of Buganda), the most powerful person, considered as the symbol of social, political, economic and, to some extent, religious power. The whole land of Buganda belonged to him and all its inhabitants. No one in his kingdom was greater than him. He was given titles connoting the greatest of all men. He exercised total and, often, totalitarian power.

The problem with this model of kingdom is not about the absolute power vested in the king, but rather that such power is wielded by mortal and sinful men who use it to control and dominate others, and even sometimes enslave them. The language of kingdom therefore carries with it these connotations of domination and abuse of power. Such were the mental models that dominated the culture of Palestine at the time of Jesus' life on earth. The Roman kingdom had dominated them for years. For many, their imagination of the rule of the 'Lion of Judah' was one who would overthrow Rome and re-establish Jerusalem's dominance. The other problem that these models present is that they lay greater emphasis on the sphere and realm where the reign is exercised than on the nature of the reign itself. Jesus was aware that such were the notions of kingdom in the minds of his hearers as he announced the good news of the Kingdom of God.

The word translated 'kingdom' in the gospels is the Greek word *basileia*. When Jesus used the term *basileia*, the dominant meaning he poured into it was of the order of 'kingly rule' or 'sovereignty' or 'kingship'. It is less to do with the domain or community over which the rule of God is exercised. The expression 'Kingdom of God' is about God's sovereign and dynamic rule. It has to do with God's right to reign over all creation as her creator. It is Luke's record of the inauguration of Jesus' ministry that hints at the nature of the kingdom that Jesus was announcing. The setting in Luke is Jesus' home village of Nazareth in Galilee, in the local synagogue, where one Saturday morning,

> The scroll of the prophet Isaiah was handed to him. Unrolling it, he found the place where it is written:
>
> > 'The Spirit of the Lord is on me, because he has anointed me to preach good news to the poor. He has sent me to proclaim freedom for the prisoners and recovery of sight for the blind, to release the oppressed, to proclaim the year of the Lord's favour.'
>
> Then he rolled up the scroll, gave it back to the attendant and sat down. The eyes of everyone in the synagogue were fastened on him, and he began by saying to them, 'Today this scripture is fulfilled in your hearing.' (Luke 4: 17–19)

Thus the kingdom, of which Jesus spoke, was unlike that of Rome or Buganda. In reading the prophet Isaiah, Jesus was announcing that the time the prophets of old spoke about was being fulfilled in him. In him the fullness of time had come. In him God's reign was entering in human history visibly.

I recall one time when my wife and I were visiting the parish of Christ Church in Overland Park, Kansas. On a shopping visit to one of the malls in the area, together with the senior minister of the parish and his wife, we stopped at a fast food restaurant – the Backyard Burger – to pick up some lunch. The thing that caught our attention was the statement of the mission of the restaurant, captured in the strap line on the serviettes we were given with the lunch: 'it is all about you'. Then it clicked in my mind, that the simplest way to express what the

Kingdom of God is about is this: It is all about God! As Origen, one of the church fathers, observed, Jesus is the *autobasileia* – the Kingdom in person. In Jesus God's sovereignty is visible and re-established; he came to that which was his own (John 1:11), his world, to establish his will – purpose and rule – on 'earth as it is in heaven'. In him the rule, reign and dominion of God were present on earth in a new way. Indeed there is no way to know the Kingdom except by learning of the story of Jesus. His life and work in first-century Palestine demonstrated God's dynamic rule. His story defines the nature of how God rules and how such a rule creates a corresponding world and society. He came to the world to 'give them abundant life' (John 10:10) or as John expressed it elsewhere, 'eternal life'. 'This is eternal life that they may know you the one true God and Jesus Christ whom you have sent' (John 17:3). Eternal life, life in the Kingdom, is only possible in knowing God and Jesus Christ is he who embodies that reality.

Repentance was the first sign that a person or people submitted to the Kingdom of God. Jesus' miracles of healing, exorcisms and raising the dead, were signs and wonders authenticating him as the one bringing the good news of the Kingdom. They were also signs, pointing to the reality of the Kingdom as already present in their midst. Thus when the disciples of John confronted Jesus with the question as to whether he was the Messiah, his reply was that they should ponder the import of his miracles of healing and his preaching of the Gospel to the poor. There is another aspect to the miracles, especially the exorcisms: they were an assault on the evil powers that are opposed to the Kingdom of God. When he was accused by the teachers of the law from Jerusalem that he was possessed and was being used by Beelzebub, the prince of demons, he explained to them that the rule of God was active in deposing the powers of evil.

> How can Satan drive out Satan? If a kingdom is divided against itself, that kingdom cannot stand. If a house is divided against itself, that house cannot stand. And if Satan opposes himself and is divided, he cannot stand; his end has come. In fact, no one can enter a strong man's house and carry off his possessions unless he first ties up the strong man. Then he can rob his house. (Mark 3:23–27)

The exorcisms were simply a preliminary assault. The actual triumph over the powers would be accomplished in completely incapacitating them by tying the strong man – Satan, the prince of evil. Jesus was pointing to his death on the cross as the place for the final triumph over the powers.

The death on the cross was not the curse that he should avoid at all costs as Peter's rebuke of him seemed to imply, after declaring him 'the Christ, the Son of the Living God' (Matthew 16:16). According to Peter, the cross could not be the way of the Kingdom that God promised would be ushered in by the Messiah. But Jesus knew that 'the Son of Man [Christ] must suffer many things and be rejected by the elders, chief priests and teachers of the law, and that he must be killed and after three days rise again' (Mark 8:31). So Jesus sternly rebuked Peter, 'Get behind me, Satan!' he said, 'You do not have in mind the things of God, but the things of men' (Mark 8:33). Satan, the enemy of the Kingdom of God, was using

Peter. Jesus had to complete the work of binding the powers. The cross was the decisive battle. By his death on the cross, Jesus tied up the strong man, the evil one and all his powers. In his death he finished the work that it was his mission to perform. In this sense Jesus' death on the cross was not a detour or a hurdle on the way to the Kingdom, nor was it even the way to the Kingdom; it was the Kingdom come. It was the decisive event by which all the anti-God powers were defeated and the Kingdom of God fully inaugurated.

The resurrection was confirmation that the cross has accomplished the overthrow of the evil powers and the work of redemption. It is no wonder that after his resurrection, when he appeared to his disciples over a period of forty days, he continued with the message of the Kingdom of God (Acts 1:3). He also commanded his followers to announce to all nations repentance and forgiveness in his name 'in Jerusalem, and in all Judea and Samaria, and to the ends of the earth' (Acts 1:8) and promised them the Holy Spirit to be with them forever. His ascension and exaltation to the right hand of the Father was an attestation that the work of inaugurating the Kingdom was accomplished. So when the Holy Spirit came at Pentecost, it was the beginning of a new era, of the presence of Christ among his followers by his Spirit.

Authentic Gospel proclamation then must have at its centre the life and work of Jesus, in whom and through whom the Kingdom of God becomes a reality. Jesus is the good news of the Kingdom of God. This is what may account for the remarkable impact of the *JESUS* film – the two-hour docudrama about the life of Jesus based on the Gospel of Luke, which was released in 1979. Its power is in telling the story of Jesus plainly. According to the distributors of the film, on the JESUS Film Project website, www.jesusfilm.org, the film has been distributed and seen in every country of the world and translated into hundreds of languages since its initial release. It has had a remarkable impact on individuals and communities, leading to many turning to faith in Jesus. However, the down side for me is the over-emphasis by the JESUS Film Project on numbers of conversions, as though the result is dependent on the *JESUS* film strategy.

Authentic Gospel proclamation must also show the continuing life and work of Jesus by his Spirit through his disciples, then and today. The message of the Acts of the Apostles is that Jesus' life and work are not limited to the record in the gospels, but continue after his resurrection and ascension. There is a sense in which the *JESUS* film is incomplete, because it stops at the story as told by Luke and does not give snapshots of Jesus' life and work of making God's kingdom a reality by his Spirit through the last 20 centuries. St Luke opens his narrative of what we now know as the Acts of the Apostles thus: 'In my former book, Theophilus, I wrote about all that Jesus *began* to do and to teach until the day he was taken up to heaven, after giving instructions through the Holy Spirit to the apostles he had chosen' (Acts 1:1–2). Luke considers the account he is about to embark on as a continuation of what Jesus began to do and teach, as contained in the earlier account, that we now know as the Gospel of Luke. In other words the Acts of the Apostles are to be considered as Jesus continuing his work of announcing and making the Kingdom of God a reality, by the Holy Spirit.

I believe one of the reasons for the impact, all over the world, of the Alpha Course (an evangelism programme developed by a team at Holy Trinity Church, Brompton, an Anglican church in the centre of London), is its dual emphasis on the life and work of Jesus, then and today. It not only puts Jesus of Nazareth at the centre of the message, but it is also explicit in acknowledging the Holy Spirit as the primary actor today in the proclamation task. The topics dealt with in the ten-week programme, described on the Alpha Course website, http://alpha.org indicate this:

> Session 1 – Who is Jesus?
> Session 2 – Why did Jesus die?
> Session 3 – How can I be sure of my faith?
> Session 4 – How and why should I pray?
> Session 5 – How and why should I read the Bible?
> Session 6 – How does God guide us?

> On the day or weekend away – The main topic is the person and the works of the Holy Spirit.

> Session 7 – How can I resist evil?
> Session 8 – Does God heal today?
> Session 9 – How and why should we tell others?
> Session 10 – What about the church?

The emphasis here is that the methods and means of proclaiming the good news should focus on the story of Jesus as told in the gospels and also as lived out today by the enabling presence of the Holy Spirit.

The continuing life and work of Christ today, through communities of followers of Jesus, is by the Holy Spirit. It is deliberate not to refer to churches, because it is not the case that all churches are communities of followers of Jesus in whom the Spirit is at work. There are many churches in history and today who by their life, structure and organisation do not exemplify the life and work of Jesus among them. It is critical therefore that the methods and means employed to proclaim the Kingdom today manifest that it is not primarily a human endeavour, but a responsive act in obedience to the Holy Spirit. This is one of the lessons from the proclamation during the apostolic era, as recorded in the Acts of the Apostles. The apostles were simply Jesus' instruments. Their role is to let Christ work in them, by the Holy Spirit. It is instructive then to look at some examples of what the disciples did in obedience to the Holy Spirit, in proclaiming the good news of the Kingdom.

Peter and the nascent community of Jesus' disciples – Acts 2

The story begins with the coming of the Holy Spirit at Pentecost. Luke records that there were about 120 disciples of Jesus who had been meeting together, in prayer, waiting for the promise of the Holy Spirit in obedience to Jesus' instructions to stay in Jerusalem (Acts 1:4). Among them were the eleven apostles plus Matthias who had just been elected to replace Judas Iscariot, 'along with the women and Mary the mother of Jesus, and with his brothers' (Acts 1:14). They were all filled with the Holy Spirit.

Jerusalem was a hive of activity at the time, as it was full of pilgrims from all over, who had come to celebrate the Jewish feast of Pentecost – 'Parthians, Medes and Elamites; residents of Mesopotamia, Judea and Cappadocia, Pontus and Asia, Phrygia and Pamphylia, Egypt and the parts of Libya near Cyrene; visitors from Rome (both Jews and converts to Judaism); Cretans and Arabs' (Acts 2:9–11). They were puzzled and perplexed by what they saw and heard from the 120 Galileans. Peter took the opportunity, standing at the massive steps to the entrance of the Temple and explained what God had done and was doing in Jesus, whom God had manifested as both Lord and the Christ (Acts 2:36). Peter showed how all Jewish history found meaning and fulfilment in the person and work of Jesus of Nazareth. In a day when we are preoccupied with altar calls and numbers who respond, the amazing thing is that Peter did not demand a response. The hearers 'were cut to the heart and said to Peter and the other apostles, "Brothers, what shall we do?"' (Acts 2:37). Peter's message evoked awe and wonder at God and his work in Christ. He, like Jesus, stated that the appropriate response to God's work in Christ was repentance. Luke records that about 3,000 of them accepted the message and 'were added to their number that day' (Acts 2:41).

Gospel rallies or what are otherwise called crusades have been in vogue since the days of the Billy Graham evangelistic crusades that began in the 1950s. They seem to work best, as in the case of Peter's audience, when the listeners have had some nominal knowledge of the story of Christ. In a context where the church has become nominal, such Gospel rallies or revival meetings are opportunities that enable the people to consider the implications of the good news of the Kingdom in their lives, leading to repentance and renewal. This is in part the story of the East African Revival that broke out in the Church of Uganda (Anglican) in the 1920s, spreading to Rwanda and then to other Eastern African countries in the 1930s and 1940s. The context of the emergence of the East African Revival Movement in Uganda was a church that had grown, attracted a large nominal membership, become established and was increasingly becoming institutionalised. Preaching teams of revived ones travelled all over west and central Uganda holding revival meetings at church centres, calling people to repentance from moral laxity. Large numbers were drawn to these meetings. The public confessions of sins in those meetings mirror the public cry of Peter's audience: 'what shall we do to be saved?' And just like it happened in the Acts story, it happened in Uganda: a nominal church was transformed. The challenge today is that these Gospel rallies or crusades have turned into miracle-working fetes and prosperity-Gospel marketing ventures with hardly any calls to repentance.

Looking again at what we may call the Jerusalem revival meeting, it is instructive how the conversions were happening daily. Luke describes the life of the new community thus:

> They devoted themselves to the apostles' teaching and to the fellow-
> ship, to the breaking of bread and to prayer. Everyone was filled with
> awe, and many wonders and miraculous signs were done by the
> apostles. All the believers were together and had everything in com-
> mon. Selling their possessions and goods, they gave to anyone as he
> had need. Every day they continued to meet together in the temple
> courts. They broke bread in their homes and ate together with glad and
> sincere hearts, praising God and enjoying the favour of all the people.
> *And the Lord added to their number daily those who were being saved.*
>
> (Acts 2:42–47) [my emphasis]

Clearly the nature of community challenged the onlookers; hence the addition
to their number daily. The way they lived was instrumental in drawing others
in; their life together proclaimed the good news of the Kingdom of God; the
community itself was good news.

One of the significant lessons from this story is the place of Christian community in proclaiming the good news of the Kingdom. As one reads the story
and indeed the Acts of the Apostles, one gets the sense that proclamation of the
good news of Jesus was at the heart of being a Christian community. It is instructive that even in the case where only Peter addressed Jewish pilgrims, the text
says that 'Peter *stood up with* the eleven' (Acts 2:14). And the response is recorded
as addition to the community rather than just people turning to Jesus for their
salvation only. Proclamation should not be thought of simply as an individual's
task, seeking conversion of individuals – such as happens with mass evangelistic campaigns in stadiums where the 'super' evangelist does his thing.
Proclamation is a community task, transforming community. During the time I
worked among university and college students in the late 1970s through to the
1990s, I took an interest in finding out what was instrumental in the Christian
students' lives that drew them to Christ. Invariably, upwards of 75 per cent
would point to a relationship, either a family or peers that were pivotal in
drawing them to Christ. Relationships are central. Kingdom community is both
the means and goal of the proclamation of the good news of the Kingdom of
God.

The Alpha Course, that we referred to earlier, reflects how when community
is central to proclamation the impact is remarkable. The Alpha Course website,
http://alpha.org describes it as an opportunity for anyone to explore the
Christian faith in a relaxed setting over ten thought-provoking weekly sessions,
with a day or weekend away. At each weekly session people gather around a
meal, which gives people a chance to get to know one another, and hear a talk
on the fundamentals of the Christian faith, followed by a time where people are
free to listen, learn, discuss and discover together. It is not any wonder that its
use has transformed churches and individuals. Over 8 million people have now
attended an Alpha Course, running in tens of thousands of all type of churches,
including: Anglican, Roman Catholic, Baptist, Presbyterian, Methodist,
Salvation Army, Free Church, Pentecostal, Assemblies of God and House
Churches across the world, in over 80 countries. It is also run in different

contexts: prisons, universities or colleges, among young people and the armed forces. Churches in Kampala that have used the Alpha Course have grown numerically and in depth of discipleship.

Philip in Samaria and with the Ethiopian official – Acts 8

Philip provides an example of proclaiming the good news of the Kingdom of God in ways that impacted a whole city. He is also a great example of proclaiming the good news in a one-on-one encounter.

The story begins with the scattering of the believers – the 3,000 plus that were living in Jerusalem, fleeing the persecution masterminded by Saul (later called Paul), that broke out after the martyrdom of Stephen. Amazingly, instead of feeling sorry for themselves and mourning the persecution, 'those who had been scattered preached the word wherever they went' (Acts 8:4). Philip is then singled out as an example, because he is part of the fulfilment of what Jesus said would happen – that his apostles would proclaim the good news in Jerusalem, Judea, Samaria and to the ends of the earth (Acts 1:8). Philip went down to a city in Samaria and proclaimed the Christ there. Luke records that 'When the crowds heard Philip and saw the miraculous signs he did, they all paid close attention to what he said. With shrieks, evil spirits came out of many, and many para- lytics and cripples were healed. So there was great joy in that city' (Acts 8:6–8). The proclamation of Christ with words was accompanied with demonstrations of his power, with many signs and wonders. Many people believed and the impact was evident on the whole city. The work was authenticated by the arrival of Apostles Peter and John, who laid their hands on the Samaritan believers and they received the Holy Spirit.

The Samaritans were considered a marginal community to their Jewish neighbours in Judea. Philip preached the good news of the Kingdom of God among them with words and works. The demonstration of the power should not be considered secondary to the proclamation with words. The signs and won- ders were the reason for the impact on the whole city of Samaria. Words of good news of the Kingdom must be accompanied with works for the good news – pointing people to the power and presence of the Kingdom. This is especially significant among communities that may be on the margins. This has been the experience of many Christian communities, in times and contexts ravaged by poverty, HIV and AIDS, war and natural disasters – such as earthquakes, droughts and storms. At the height of the HIV/AIDS pandemic in Uganda, as a response to Jesus' command to reach out to 'the least of my brothers' (Matthew 25), churches developed programmes for HIV testing and counselling, for com- munity care and orphan support, removing the stigma from those infected and affected. Thus when the churches demonstrated the good news of the Kingdom of God in a context of HIV/AIDS in compassionate care and support towards those affected and infected, many people turned to faith in Jesus.

Philip's encounter with the Ethiopian official is from beginning to end the work of the Holy Spirit in an obedient person. Firstly, it is an 'angel of the Lord' who told Philip to take the road that he was travelling; and secondly, when he saw the chariot it was the Spirit who told him to go near the chariot. In each case, Philip discerned the prompting of the Holy Spirit and obeyed, not knowing what these actions would lead to. I am sure Philip could not believe himself when, on joining the chariot, he heard the official reading from the scroll of the prophet Isaiah concerning the Messiah. We are not given the flow of the conversation, but it must be that Philip asked the man who he was and where he was coming from. That is how we have so much biographical data recorded about him – a eunuch, a finance official in the palace of the queen and a proselyte, coming from a pilgrimage to Jerusalem. When the eunuch asked what the prophetic writings were about, 'Philip began with that very passage of scripture and told him the good news about Jesus' (Acts 8:35). The good news about Jesus must have included 'repentance and forgiveness in his name' (Luke 24:47), the acceptance of which was symbolised in the act of baptism, because when the eunuch saw water on the way, he made the connection and asked to be baptised. As in the case of the city of Samaria, the impact on the life of the eunuch is joy. He continued on his way rejoicing.

The proclamation of the Gospel among the Samaritans and Philip's encounter with the Ethiopian eunuch has much to teach us about the fact that the proclamation task is ultimately God's. Note that although Jesus had clearly instructed his Apostles that they were to be his witnesses beyond Jerusalem, it is only persecution that thrust them there. We see how God used persecution as an agency of spreading the good news of the presence of God's reign in Christ in Judea and Samaria. God uses the death of Stephen and the hostile, violent Saul! There are many contexts today where proclamation of the Kingdom of God will only progress through persecution and suffering. As we have seen, Philip's encounter with the Ethiopian eunuch was all organised by the Holy Spirit. One of the biggest challenges today is the over-dependence on methods, strategies, institutions and technologies for the proclamation of the Gospel. The challenge before us is to discern the voice of the Holy Spirit amidst the noises of our histories, cultures and lifestyles. The demons of our times are akin to the demon of which Jesus said that 'this kind can only come out by prayer and fasting' (Mark 9:29). There is an urgent need to rediscover prayer as part and parcel of the proclamation of the good news.

The story of Mildred Project, an outreach ministry of the Young Overcomers illustrates that the way the Holy Spirit works is not always predictable. Young Overcomers (YOMs) is a youth fellowship group of single adults under the auspices of the All Saints Cathedral, Kampala. Brian, one of the YOMs, narrates an incident when he was struggling to understand better God's purpose and work in and through his life. Then one day, a morning in June 2005, he happened to pass by Mildred on a street in Kampala, begging. Brian had spent the night before agonising in prayer, wanting 'to see God's face in light of what he was experiencing'. He felt the prompting to stop by and talk to Mildred. Instead of giving her the occasional pocket change he promised her that he would visit her own home (having discovered that she stayed in one of Kampala's slums known as Kyebando). It then dawned on him that the condition he was in enabled him to 'see' Christ in the eyes of the destitute. His effort to get his need addressed was a window through which God showed him the needs of this lady. He told the rest of the fellowship of this revelation and they joined him in developing a pilot project proposal to address not only the needs of Mildred but also those of her immediate neighbour as well.

Today, the YOMs are reaching destitute families, including Mildred's, through what they have called the Mildred Project. Their stated mission is to 'provide sustainable solutions to spiritual and material and social needs of the two families, which will enable them to experience Christ's love; find gainful employment for the family heads and cater for their basic needs and the education of their children'. Among other activities, they have bi-monthly fellowships with the families. As a result, Emmanuel, the head of the one of the families, and Bob Otim surrendered their lives to Christ and are now part of the nearest Church of Uganda Parish of Saint John's, Kamwokya, Church of Uganda.

Although the proclamation task is ultimately God's, we also see how Philip was faithful in doing his part: speaking plainly about Jesus, demonstrating the presence of the kingdom in signs and wonders in Samaria and listening attentively to the Ethiopian eunuch. Keturah, a colleague in the ministry in Kampala, tells how during an evangelistic mission emphasis week at All Saints Cathedral, Kampala in November 2006, listening and demonstrating the love of Jesus in tangible ways had an impact among the people in one of the slums of Kampala. One of the strategies was to team up with Christians from the slum communities and visit homes (door-to-door), preaching the love of Christ and demonstrating it through giving a few household items like soap and sugar. Just one story:

> Fredah, probably in her late 50s, was one of the missioners from All Saints Cathedral. She teamed up with two other Christians from the Kifumbira slum community. Their mission field was the people in this community. They picked up two bars of soap, two kilograms of sugar and set off. As they negotiated amongst themselves about which door to knock at, they saw a very old woman seated on her veranda. She looked miserable and lost in thought. Fredah suggested that they talk to this lady briefly about Jesus as they proceeded. The three agreed, they walked to her and said, 'Hello'. To their surprise, the old woman burst out and hurled several insults at them. She accused one of the locals, who came with the missioners from All Saints Cathedral, of hypocrisy, saying, 'Even you, you mean you have always been a Christian, and you never greet me just like everybody else? Are you greeting me now because you have seen visitors? Go away.' Then Fredah responded, in a very composed and caring manner: 'God loves you'. The old woman told Fredah to leave her alone and go away with her God. Fredah insisted on knowing how she was, 'leaving God aside'. The old woman was very angry and told Fredah to go away. Fredah felt she was not getting anywhere and decided to proceed to another house. Just before she left, she remembered she had carried the sugar and soap for whoever they preached to. She said, 'Well, we had

also brought some sugar and soap for you, so you could please have it as I go away.'

The old woman immediately picked the items, took them to her room for safe custody and asked Fredah to enter. Very uncertain of what was next, Fredah entered and sat. The old lady brought out photographs of her late children, in-laws and grandchildren and showed Fredah. She then asked Fredah to explain God's love, in the context of the old woman's circumstances. She went ahead to tell her of her loneliness, how nobody visits her, nobody greets her ... As she put her case to Fredah, Fredah just listened and looked at her. Her eyes turned red, and tears rolled down uncontrollably. At this point, Fredah could not take it anymore. She too broke down in tears. The two hugged and cried as the old woman continued to pour out everything. This brought her healing.

It was after this that they were able to greet and share a lot of personal information about each other. The old woman pledged to consider giving her life to Christ. The two have become great friends up to date.

Keturah reported that at the end of the week, 65 adults in the community had accepted to follow Jesus, including one of the leaders of the community – the chairman of the Community Council.

Paul in Athens – Acts 17:16–34

Paul's mission in Athens and his public proclamation at Mars Hill give us a model for proclamation among peoples and societies that have not yet had contact with any forms of Christianity, because Athens was such a place. On arrival in Athens Paul took time to know the city, its culture and peoples. He was struck and distressed by the levels of idolatry. He engaged in dialogue and debate with Jews and God-fearing Greeks in the synagogue and market places; and then in the public hall at Mars Hill, with the city's ruling council, her intellectuals and philosophers. Evidently Paul was persuaded that the Kingdom of God was good news for all, irrespective of religio-cultural history. There is no culture or peoples excluded from it because God is the God of all history. As a messenger of the good news, Paul's task was to make the connection between their stories with the larger story of God's revelation in Christ.

With the Jews and God-fearing Greeks, Paul sought to show that Jesus was the Christ – the good news of Jewish messianic expectation, attested to by his death and resurrection. Among those foreign to Jewish history, he showed how Christ is the clue to understanding God's purpose in their history. Paul clarified to his non-Jewish Athenian audience that God's purpose for all creation is fulfilled in Jesus, because in him was the unique, full and final revelation of the 'God who made the world and every thing in it ...' (Acts 17:24). He began his discourse not just with the gospel record, but with creation because it is the God of creation revealed in Christ. He even quoted from their writings to show that there was evidence in their own heritage that God's revelation and purposes were not foreign to them. Thus to both Jews and Greeks, and indeed any other peoples and nations of the world, Christ is the hope of redemption.

One of the most significant lessons from Paul's proclamation of the Gospel in Athens is the priority of listening to a people, their culture and life situation in the proclamation of the message of the Gospel. Listening and dialogue are rooted in the conviction that every culture, era or society has within it something equivalent to 'the unknown God' of the Athenians, which ought to be the starting point of the proclamation. The God of the Kingdom that is good news to all the peoples and cultures of the world is the God of all history. Every culture and epoch in history has within it signs, pointing to his presence among them. But there is more to listening and dialogue: since the good news is about the Kingdom of the God of creation, proclamation is rooted in the conviction that every culture has within it the capacity not only to receive the good news but to be a transmitter. Listening and dialogue has to do with learning the language of that culture and context in order to proclaim the message in its idiom. This is the basis for the priority of translation in proclamation. In this sense all authentic Gospel proclamation must entail dialogue and translation. This ought to serve as a corrective to many approaches that do not take seriously the listening and dialogue process. It is in listening to a people's story that we are able to make a connection with the story of Christ; and in listening a new language is learned in which the message is proclaimed. This puts a premium on the urgency of translation for the cultures and peoples who to date may not have the Bible in their everyday language.

It is important that the language and methods used in proclaiming the good news are relevant to the particular context. Although we live in a globalised world, there is a uniqueness to the various cultures and societies. Urbanised Africa is different from the rural; post-communist societies are different from post-Christian societies; and then there are the vast regions of the world where other major religions of the world, such as Islam, Hinduism and Buddhism hold their sway. Today many societies that may claim to be Christian are simply nominally so and have not yet really heard and seen the good news of the Kingdom of God. We should not assume that a method that God has used in one context will work in a different context. The mistake is made when evangelism programmes that have worked effectively in North America and Europe are transferred wholesale to Africa, Asia and Latin America.

Conclusion

The task of proclaiming the good news of the Kingdom of God is one of the cardinal purposes of any Christian community. Jesus spelt this out clearly in his parting words to his followers, as recorded in the gospels. The apostles echoed it in their letters. Apostle Peter's words to the believers scattered all over the Roman world then and to us today are worth quoting here:

> But you are a chosen people, a royal priesthood, a holy nation, a people belonging to God, *that you may declare* the praises of him who called you

out of darkness into his wonderful light. Once you were not a people, but now you are the people of God; once you had not received mercy, but now you have received mercy. (1 Peter 2:9–10) (*my italics*)

Proclaiming the good news of the Kingdom should not be treated as an add-on to the business of being a Christian or the church or even be limited to one of the departments of the church, as is often the case. Proclamation of the good news is the church's *raison d'être*.

In this sense, the proclamation of the good news of the Kingdom of God is human. It is an act of communicating the life and story of Jesus, as recorded in the gospels (which locates the beginnings of the story in creation) and present in the lives of his followers then and today. The story is mediated through human words and works, articulating and demonstrating the Jesus work of reconciliation and forgiveness. We have the responsibility of obedience, engaging in listening to cultures and contexts in order to discern his presence. Dialogue is part of this listening process. Listening and dialogue are dynamic processes that should enable us to be constantly translating and incarnating the story among different peoples, in different contexts.

However, the primary actor on whom the results ultimately depend is the Holy Spirit because it is the Holy Spirit that convicts 'the world of guilt in regard to sin and righteousness and judgment' (John 16:8), and leads people to repentance, forgiveness, and the reconciliation of all things to God in Christ. It is the Holy Spirit who transforms lives and communities for the Kingdom of God. It is especially important to emphasise this in this era when we are tempted to substitute the Holy Spirit with human ingenuity, strategies and technology. It is he who will finish the task. Ultimately, it is all about God.

2. To Teach, Baptise, and Nurture New Believers (i)

Emmanuel Egbunu

> Then Jesus came to them and said, 'All authority in heaven and on earth has been given to me. Therefore go and make disciples of all nations, baptising them in the name of the Father and of the Son and of the Holy Spirit, and teaching them to obey everything I have commanded you. And surely I am with you always, to the very end of the age.' (Matthew 28:18–20)

'The Great Commission' as the passage above is often called, conceived discipleship to be the end product and natural outcome of global evangelisation. And the medium of this lifelong transformation of converts is teaching – not by human wisdom or knowledge, but rather 'teaching them to obey everything I have commanded you'. The divine priority given to teaching makes discipleship imperative for all who respond to the proclamation of the Gospel. The authority behind what is taught is not merely human, but divine. And in this regard, Paul the apostle declared to the erring Galatian Christians, 'I want you to know, brothers, that the gospel I preached is not something that man made up ... I received it by revelation from Jesus Christ' (Galatians 1:11–12).

Of all the possibilities of transformation that one may experience, the most fulfilling is to be transformed into the likeness of Christ as we gaze on him in growing intimacy through prayer, the word and obedience. We have no higher calling than to become like Christ. It is by far the most fulfilling achievement both for us and before God.

⌐Christianity that is devoid of clear biblical convictions which produce godly character will find little use both to the Lord and to the needy world.⌐When young converts are not steadily nurtured (sometimes exclusively), they become like abandoned babies. The neglect of thorough follow-up to conserve the fruits of evangelism has been the major factor for the prevalence of untaught Christians whose ideas of Christianity are a travesty of biblical discipleship.

Among the puzzling realities of the phenomenal growth of Christianity in the developing world is the apparent credibility gap between the widespread profession of faith by a great number of adherents, and the disproportionate lack of evidence of positive change in society and the environment. This fact alone has been the arsenal for all sorts of castigations, as well as the justification for such responses as Ethiopianism,[1] Liberation Theology, Black Theology, and similar ideologies which attempt to provide answers to inescapable questions. As Andrew Walls rightly points out, 'Theology in the third world will be, as theology at all creative times has always been, about *doing* things, about things that deeply affect the lives of numbers of people.'[2] One must concede that the mission agencies and their churches have wrestled with these issues within the context of ever-increasing socio-economic challenges which call for an intelligent and relevant interface between Christianity and these felt needs.

To be sure, Christianity has made many tall claims to have answers to our biggest questions, and those who are well informed cannot deny that the Holy Bible and Christian history are replete with instances of credible divine and human interventions down the ages. However, the efforts being made by the church, and the expectations of the watching world appear to have a considerable gap yet. For this reason, stories of Christian expansion in the developing world have often been greeted with the taunt that it might be one mile long, but only an inch deep!

Human need always cries out for remedy, and whatever falls short of that is considered irrelevant to the situation – whatever else it is. This undergirds the conflicts and consensus in the encounter of Christianity (introduced by foreign missionaries) with the native worldview. As was the case with the Jewish crowds that followed Jesus because he had fed them with bread (John 6:26), responses to new movements like the Christian faith are contingent upon its interface with felt needs in the immediate situation.

That the search for tangible remedies, rather than merely theoretical answers, has been the *raison d'être* for response to the Christian faith is neither peculiar to the developing world situation nor is it at all unreasonable. Indeed it is the point when the Christian manifesto is scrutinised by the suspicious native; the point when the first 'taste of the pudding' is analysed before the subsequent stages of submission and a more sustained identification with the new faith.

Deducing from the case of the Jewish crowds that went after the Lord Jesus because he had miraculously fed them with bread, it is not possible to relate meaningfully with Christ's further statement, 'Do not work for food that spoils, but for food that endures to eternal life, which the Son of Man will give you' (John 6:27) until we have been left with unfulfilled longings after the first encounter with the new faith. Christianity that provides answers to questions not being asked, rather than providing solutions to the daily tyranny of crushing needs and tantalising hopes, will remain a half-measure with multitudes of patronising, but half-hearted adherents who, in the time of crisis, will always resort elsewhere for 'realistic' answers. The situation might not be too far from the somewhat embarrassing scenario presented by Ayandele about those early days of Christian encounter, when he said,

> ... one must wonder whether Christians could justifiably claim that they have conquered paganism ... Indeed, for those who care to in-

vestigate ... scratch the African pastor and you would discover that he has greater faith in the charms and amulets he wears surreptitiously and in the 'witch-doctor' to whom he pays nocturnal visits than in the Holy Bible and Jesus Christ; scratch the Christian medical doctor and you would discover that he pays greater attention to the diviner and the psychical fears instilled by his village milieu than his scalpel and the white man's tablets; scratch the prominent layman politician and you discover that his public bold face and animal courage are against the background of his endless grovelling before masters of supernatural forces in traditional society.[3]

The ideals of Henry Venn's 'Native Pastorate', which had recommended the dismantling of the missionary scaffolding and the eventual euthanasia of the mission, have been rightly celebrated over the decades. Upholding those ideals, Bishop Samuel Ajayi Crowther had recommended to the personnel of the Mission during the conference of 1867 to 'respect the customs, the laws, the traditions, of your hearers'. Wise as this counsel was, it inadvertently became the weapon of self-destruction in some of the communities which enjoyed the facilities offered by the missionaries while holding to their customs as their core values. Some of those who were considered converts were, in a number of cases, sympathisers, job-seekers, or opportunists who used the missionary facilities as the stairway for the realisation of their 'greater' ambitions. The mission could therefore not really count on her converts to make a solid impact on the society.

On the other hand, to cater for the growing number of the 'mixed bag' of converts in Nigeria, churches were also established in several towns and villages along the banks of the Niger, the Delta states, the Niger and Benue Confluence and in the interior villages. While the converts enjoyed the benefits of Western education and medical facilities they also had to learn the liturgy of the Church of England, the hymns, and the ceremonies such as Baptism, Confirmation, The Lord's Supper, Holy Matrimony, and the other services of the Prayer Book.

With the apparent success of the educational and medical arms, there was no reason to suppose the liturgy was not the divinely approved medium of worship and expression of faith, regardless of the cultural trappings that were inherent. Even though translations of the Bible, the liturgy and the hymns were being undertaken during this period, the scenario was unmistakably that of intellectual Christianity. There was much to learn about this new faith (and civilised English ways) and there was much to unlearn about their culture, traditions and pagan past. They became converts to a new faith and new culture; and strangers in their own homes within the higher call to pilgrimage in the Christian life. They became native strangers who lost confidence in their culture and yet lacked sufficient grasp of the new way of life for a spontaneous, natural and intelligent response.

Furthermore, the new convert's soul became stifled in the attempt to conform to the cultural patterns of this new-found faith in which he was to express his new joys in a foreign language and concepts that often did not have much corresponding affinity. Given this scenario, the illiterate who was genuinely converted felt incapacitated by his inability to read or write, and so had to memorise whole hymns and creeds and prayers to be able to participate in the services of this new faith. This subtle contrast between intellectual Christianity[4] (which consigns it often to mere ceremonials) and a relevant, vibrant and authentic expression of a living faith has been the bane of missionary Christianity in the developing world. A cursory look at the names and doctrines of some of our independent African churches as well as the new generation denominations emerging everywhere tells the story only too loudly.

The process of evangelisation and conversion has metamorphosed considerably since the days of foreign missions when there were often captive audiences enthralled by the white man's education and medical facilities. Emerging congregations have become more probing in their response to faith within the context of underdevelopment for which the agents of colonisation (and foreign missionaries were often lumped with this group) are held culpable. The converts go through the motions of the Christian religious expressions almost flawlessly, but find their consciences wrestling with intimidating contradictions about the demands of Christianity and the challenges of underdevelopment.

New wine in old wineskins

The gestation period required to defuse the suspicion and threat that the native feels towards the 'invader' – be it the Christian missionary, the colonial master, uncensored media culture, and indeed any other ideology – appears to be often underestimated by the invading party, notwithstanding the engagement with social anthropology. Ignorance (or disregard) of these suspicions and threats that are always real to the native, makes the points of encounter more tumultuous than necessary. While the invading party believes it has something precious to offer, it is natural for the indigenous party to feel it also has something precious to protect. Those who embrace these new teachings and ways of Christianity by becoming converts are therefore seen as renegades by their fellow natives. The African convert's dilemma has not always been lost to a number of discerning Christians even from the West:

> Most Africans, when they had access to the Bible, were not interested in criticisms of its accuracy. They were fascinated to find how similar was the biblical world to their own, with purifying sacrifices, instructive dreams, important ancestors, the family with a large and extended membership, many wives for patriarchs and kings, disasters through curses, healing through spiritual power, dancing in joyful worship (did not King David 'dance before the Lord'?) and many miracles after prayer. If the missionaries told them that such African traditions had been superstition or at least not civilized, they could point to the Bible which they were told was the final authority ...[5]

This matter about the Bible being the final authority is the keystone of the protest by the leadership of the Global South against the revisionist agenda of the West in the wake of the sexuality debate. Against accusations of hatred for homosexuals, Archbishop Akinola has consistently insisted that love for God requires that we stick with the historic faith once delivered to the saints, and the teaching of the Bible as binding on all without subjecting it to the changing opinions of men and women. I believe that our pastoral responsibility cannot excuse rebellion in the name of cultural peculiarities.

The above situation notwithstanding, there were also genuine conversions in those early days of encounter with Christianity which inspired bold and un-compromising witness by even people down the social strata like one Joshua Hart, a slave in Bonny (the delta region of Nigeria) who had become a convert and, as a result of his Christian conviction, refused to partake in sacrifices to the dead. He said, '"If my master requires me to do any work for him, however hard, I will try my best to do it. If he even requires me to carry the world itself on my head, I will try if I can do it. But if he requires me to partake of things sacrificed to gods, I will never do it.'[6] He was later martyred by being thrown into the river and pierced with spears when he would not renounce his faith under any persuasion or threat.

Baptism

At the point of conversion, the lifelong journey of discipleship begins with baptism as the initiatory rite. Baptism which is a sacrament given in the context of conversion includes, as already noted, 'teaching them to obey everything I have commanded you' (Matthew 28:20). It is a sacrament in which the new convert steps out of his old life to identify with the death and resurrection of Christ (Romans 6:3–5). The pattern of the early church of the apostolic period is instructive here:

> Those who accepted his message were baptised, and about three thou-
> sand were added to their number that day. They devoted themselves to
> the apostles' teaching and to the fellowship, to the breaking of bread
> and to prayer. (Acts 2:41–42)

With the ultimate goal of discipleship being Christlikeness, the great challenge for the convert is this: how should he integrate his new Christian identity with his native (not necessarily ungodly) idiosyncrasies without losing either? He lives in this state of constant ambivalence until, by the living and enduring word of God, as well as the faithful labour of a missionary, evangelist, or pastor, the Word that became flesh and made his dwelling among us, is formed in his life (John 1:14; Galatians 4:19). This is a lifelong process of growing intimacy with Christ.

Despite widely varied traditions and doctrinal positions, baptism remains the unifying initiatory rite for all Christians and, as such, its essential significance should be taught clearly to new converts. The Lambeth Report (1988) reflecting on 'Baptism and Ministry' reaffirmed, 'We believe that our baptism, resting as it does on the work of the risen Christ, is both the call and the empowering of all ministry in the Church: and that the theological expression of that ministry is seen in the liturgical rites of initiation contained in the various Prayer Books of the Anglican Communion.'[7]

Rick Warren, in his famous book, *The Purpose-Driven Life*, upholds the fundamental significance of baptism: 'Your baptism declares your faith, shares Christ's burial and resurrection, symbolizes your death to your old life, and announces your new life in Christ. It is also a celebration of your new life in Christ ... being included in God's family is the highest honor and the greatest privilege you will ever receive. Nothing else comes close.'[8]

Discipleship

At the centre of Christian discipleship is the need to relate to the Bible as the authoritative revelation of God in all matters of life, salvation, and godliness. The new convert must be taught to know that, over and above the wisest opinions and traditions of men, the Holy Bible is the unshakeable foundation for faith. Even the variables of the hermeneutical spiral and the shifting sands of postmodernity must never become an excuse to denigrate the word of God to the level of human philosophy and opinions. For new converts, these Scripture passages are very important foundations for spiritual nurture and growth:

> Deuteronomy 8:3: He humbled you, causing you to hunger and then feeding you with manna, which neither you nor your fathers had known, to teach you that man does not live on bread alone but on every word that comes from the mouth of the LORD.

Given the increasingly disproportionate emphasis by new generation churches on material acquisition, ephemeral luxuries and physical well-being as incontrovertible indices of divine favour, new converts need a foundation for faith that rests on the nourishing potential of the word of God over and above everything else that provides mere physical satisfaction. In a setting where wealth is often acquired by corrupt means, and many are poor, such lopsided emphasis on the so-called 'health and wealth' Gospel is misleading and sometimes difficult to resist, resulting in shallow Christian lives. It should be taught that becoming Christians can also include hunger and other humiliating experiences and converts need not be ashamed when that becomes their lot. In his hour of temptation, Christ found inspiration from this passage.

> Psalm 119:9–11: How can a young man keep his way pure? By living according to your word. I seek you with all my heart; do not let me stray from your commands. I have hidden your word in my heart that I might not sin against you.

The greatest temptation a young convert faces is in the area of the thought life. The word of God dwelling richly in our hearts is the effective antidote against the unending barrage of impure thoughts.

2 Timothy 3:16: All Scripture is God-breathed and is useful for teaching, rebuking, correcting and training in righteousness ...

Whatever the Bible says is a sin cannot become other than that on the authority of anyone else. It is an objective and reliable guide to godliness.

Closely related to the knowledge of the Scripture is the need to develop a strong prayer life. In more affluent societies, prayer tends to be reduced to mere formality rather than the challenging exercise of faith that it is for those in settings where their very survival depends more on prayer than political will and infrastructure or a welfare system.

Mass evangelism and community discipleship

The communal nature of the African society finds more kinship with the centres of early Christian expansion before the individualistic Western style of Christianity developed. Andrew Walls, endorsing K. S. Latourette's view about the first mark of Christian experience writes, 'the first sign of the expansion of the influence of Christ is the presence of a community of people who willingly bear his name, an "Israel" that maintains his worship ... The influence of Jesus not only produces group response; it works by means of groups, and is expressed in groups. The influence of Jesus ... operates in terms of social reactions.'[9] When this principle is ignored, then the tragedy of the lone convert is inevitable.

More contemporary approaches include Evangelism-in-depth of Nicaragua in the 1960s, and the New Life For All in Nigeria of the 1970s. Mass evangelism has recorded much success through the use of films like the Jesus Film of the Campus Crusade, gifted public preachers and miracle workers in public squares and stadiums. Other strategies include revival programmes in churches. The big challenge after such great harvest of souls is the follow-up and discipleship: how will the Bible verse given to the new converts – 'Therefore, if anyone is in Christ, he is a new creation; the old has gone, the new has come!' (2 Corinthians 5:17) be worked out in daily living where their situation has not changed? How does this affect the work ethics of the converted civil servant and professional? Or the converted petty trader and the accomplished businessman, the farmer, the civil servant, the politician, the policeman, the magistrate or judge, the husband, the housewife, the preacher himself, the contractor, the unemployed, the local militia or freedom fighter (who has no confidence in the security and judicial structures and so takes the law into his hands), and the student?

Women and youth

The women, youth, and artisans are not always in the minority as is sometimes assumed – if anything, they form three-quarters of our worshipping communities. In not a few instances, when they are left in ignorance, they have been the victims of the snare by some other groups of dubious identity as far as the Christian faith is concerned. They form the highly mobile group, which, if well nurtured, can become the major exponents of the faith. Further, our worship life can be enriched as the women and youth especially are given opportunities to use their musical gifts, or are engaged as Bible Study teachers. In a study about the exodus of our youth, Bishop Olusina Fape notes that a way to turn the situation around is to organise special seminars and retreat programmes to bring them together more regularly to discuss issues of common interest. He identifies such issues as, 'choice of life partners, sex before marriage, coping with unbelieving parents, career choice, how to succeed academically, living a victorious life'.[10] He believes this will convince them that the Church is concerned about their future.

Catechizing

While catechisms are patterned after denominational standards to present the essentials of the Christian faith such as the Decalogue, the Creeds, and the Lord's Prayer, the nurture of new converts was never taken lightly by the Church Fathers. Be it the Catechetical School of Alexandria (the first theological school in Christian History), or Luther's Short Catechism, or even the Shorter Catechism produced by the Westminster Assembly (1648), the formation of Christian understanding and character received uncompromising priority. In our time therefore, effective teaching to nurture new converts must necessarily include a number of important concerns which may be mentioned below:

A robust Christology

The Lord Jesus had asked his disciples, 'Who do people say the Son of Man is?' (Matthew 16:13). An accurate understanding of the person and mission of Christ as revealed in the Holy Bible is the bedrock of Christian discipleship. Acknowledging the revelation granted to Peter that he was the Christ, the Lord went on to say, 'And I tell you that you are Peter, and on this rock I will build my church, and the gates of Hades will not overcome it' (Matthew 16:18). The deity of Christ as well as the reason for his incarnation as revealed in prophecy and the gospels is to be clearly taught to new believers as a solid foundation for faith. The centrality of the cross in our salvation, sanctification, and future hope should be taught to make us bow when we read about the passion, sing about it, and commemorate the Lord's Supper and Good Friday. The havoc done by the heresies in the early centuries of the church (mostly centred around the person of Christ) should warn us about the centrality of the doctrine of Christ to our faith. People need to wonder afresh and ask, *Who is this?* Then they might be better able to understand the next important question about why he came.

Inculturation

It has come as a rude shock to many African church leaders that the Western curriculum of our seminaries needs to be revised to address the burning issues in our experience. What would Christ do if he were in our setting? For quite a long time that curriculum was patterned after Western priorities without discernment or question. So we turned out ministers who did not know where the people were itching! With a relevant training curriculum for Bible teachers through Theological Education by Extension (TEE), seminars and workshops or preaching conferences, much can be accomplished towards equipping them to minister more relevantly. In this regard, Andrew Walls points out, 'The indigenizing principle ensures that each community recognizes in Scripture that God is speaking to its own situation.'[11] When all categories of our public preachers are exposed to hermeneutical principles, then the message of the Bible is not left to the allegorical ingenuity of the preacher without due regard for the time-tested principles of biblical exposition.

The nurture of young converts

With a good Sunday School programme for children and adults, as well as well-trained teachers, the nurturing of young converts is guaranteed. This is the most natural, non-threatening learning situation which is interactive for both young and old, whether in the church or house group setting. The benefits of such groups cannot be overemphasised. Indeed, this has been a strategy employed with great success in the new generation churches where a newcomer is identified, befriended, and immediately assigned to small groups that are best suited to the visitor's neighbourhood and level of Christian understanding. Where confirmation classes are given the right attention by focusing on Christian beginnings, Christian beliefs, and Christian behaviour, the problem of 'overgrown babies' (cf. Hebrews 5:12) is minimised. This is followed by teachings about basic Christian doctrines, the means of grace and the sacraments. A number of new generation churches have found this to be a most effective way of nurturing new believers, especially where evening services are no longer practicable in urban settings with chaotic traffic and criminal tendencies towards the close of day.

Devotional materials

The use of good devotional notes for personal and family meditation in a natural setting where the intimidating presence of the 'expert' and their complicated pretensions give way to simple faith is an important avenue for growth. This is because it brings the Bible into the private and family life situations rather than consigning it to certain compartments of life such as public worship situations only. This also removes the danger of people who are unable to relate the Bible to their regular challenges and so see no contradiction between their Christian claims on Sunday and the business or office situation in the week.

Social concern

The teaching of the Bible on social concerns, politics, and development issues will make the teaching about God attractive. In Nigeria for example, the advent of Christianity was a direct consequence of the anti-slavery campaign by the British in which Samuel Ajayi Crowther, who became the first black bishop in contemporary mission history, was rescued. Ironically, even though some foreign missionaries did a lot to correct social ills, like infanticide, and murder of twins (Mary Slessor is the unforgettable heroine here) they did not truly encourage active participation in secular politics since it was seen by some mission agencies as a dirty game that was too risky for the heavenly minded convert. It should be made clear that Christians are called upon to be part of making positive change in society. Preparing politicians and businessmen at all levels with Christian convictions and biblical ethics remains one of the most effective ways of securing social and moral transformation in society.

Related to this is the need to share resources for the benefit of the less privileged. Christ's teaching in Matthew 25:31ff. makes the point quite pungently about the need to make necessary sacrifices for the relief of others. Surely the social problems all around us require a more positive response from a Church that is not economically handicapped and morally bankrupt to deal with the greed that ignites war situations and the refugee challenges that abound.

Clarifying the nature of the supernatural

The difference between magic, occultism, and genuine miracles is one which always needs to be properly taught to believers coming out of a background of traditional religion. This is because the impression is often conveyed by new generation churches, with their breathtaking testimonies of miracles, that the mission churches have been unable to provide credible alternatives to the void that is often created when a new believer turns his back on the traditional religious practices. Such previous religious engagements were fraught with the vivid reality of shrines and the regular interface with the spirit world and the occult: witchcraft, magic, necromancy – which they had regarded as the key to mysteries, warding off evil, acquiring spiritual power, and the cure of sicknesses.

The Christian Gospel, however, introduces the power of God for salvation (Romans 1:16), for adoption (John 1:12–13), for witness (Acts 1:8), and for miracles through the manifold gifts of the Holy Spirit (1 Corinthians 12; Ephesians 4:7–11). We must not be evasive on issues of the supernatural, as has been the embarrassing posture. The Bible has much to teach about angels as well as demons; blessings and curses; spiritual warfare and victory; and the reality of faith to enjoy the miracles of God. Commenting on the response of Africans to Christian faith and the Bible, Ogbu Kalu draws a contrast between the attitude of the foreign missionaries on the one hand, and on the other, the points of appeal to the native convert: 'the missionaries read the Bible through the lenses of the Protestant emphasis on Word over Spirit and the Enlightenment de-sacralization of the universe. The Africans, on the other hand, read the Bible through their own traditionally "charismatic" worldview: they knew there were spirits in the sky, the water, the land, and the ancestral worlds. Only, now, they proclaimed the power of Jesus over these other powers.'[12]

Leadership development

Leadership development among native converts has been a sore point in much missionary endeavour. Even with all the three-self principles enunciated by Henry Venn, there seemed to be a reluctance to affirm the budding leadership potential of native converts. Philip Jenkins points out that, 'For any missionary venture, the ordination of native clergy must be the acid test of commitment to moving beyond an imperial context, to leaving the veranda.'[13] Indeed, the tragic end of Bishop Samuel Ajayi Crowther is directly related to this crisis of confidence. An excellent treatment of this subject has been provided by Roland Allen, who observes that the training of the first converts sets the pattern for the future:

> If the first converts are taught to depend upon the missionary, if all the work, evangelistic, educational, social is concentrated in his hands, the infant community learns to rest passively upon the man from whom they receive their first insight into the Gospel. Their faith having no sphere for its growth and development lies dormant. A tradition rapidly grows up that nothing can be done without the authority and guidance of the missionary, the people wait for him to move, and, the longer they do so, the more incapable they become of any independent action ... In allowing them, or encouraging them, to do this, the missionary not only checks the spiritual growth of his converts and teaches them to rely upon a wrong source of strength; he actually robs them of the strength which they naturally possess and would naturally use.[14]

This is crucial to the process of multiplication through discipleship as set forth by Paul in his letter to Timothy, 'And the things you have heard me say in the presence of many witnesses entrust to reliable men who will also be qualified to teach others' (2 Timothy 2:2). The priesthood of all believers, which encourages participation by the layperson, must be taught, to encourage greater involvement in the evangelistic and disciple-making process.

Conclusion

The legacies of this encounter have left a sweet and sour aftertaste which compels a cry for an evaluation of the conversion process: its blessings, its ambiguities, and its tragedies with the hope that we can attempt a separation of the wheat from the chaff and a process of rehabilitation. This is not new, as Kwame Bediako points out:

> The phase of Christian history which offers the most instructive parallels to the modern African context is the beginning of Hellenistic Christianity in the early Roman Empire. With Christianity virtually

transposed from its original Jewish matrix and fast becoming a pre-dominantly Gentile phenomenon, it was from the circles of Gentile Christian thought that a significant body of Christian literature emerged, in which the problem of Christian identity and the nature of continuity with the pre-Christian tradition began to be faced in earnest.[15]

There is a need to understand the social setting of the native convert – how his past (the superstitions, taboos, social hierarchy, and respect for authority, etc), affects his present worldview. Then we must ask how the great truths of our Christianity, its liturgy and hymns can be enjoyed without alienating the simple village believer who also has a vibrancy about the religious experience in a way that is second nature to him, using his own lyrics, instruments, attire, and dance patterns.[16]

2. To Teach, Baptise, and Nurture New Believers (ii)

Ande Titre

Introduction

Masiya, teremuka mbio, teremuka. This song, sung in Swahili by desperate Congolese Christians, is a call for Jesus to precipitate, very soon, his coming in order to alleviate their pain by establishing his complete reign. The urgency of this call is expressed by the verb *teremuka*, come down, instead of *kuja*, come.

The situation in Congo is marked by much suffering: conflict, oppression, poverty and many other circumstances which bring death rather than life. But God sent his people to participate in the mission of God in such a context. Mission is God's way of loving and serving the world. The aim of God's mission is the transformation of life, not only of individuals but also of the whole society, even the created order. All mission is done in a particular context so, although there is a fundamental unity to the good news, it is shaped by the great diversity of places, times, and cultures in which we live, proclaim, and embody it.[1]

This article comes out of my experience, based on my Episcopal ministry in the Province of the Anglican Church of Congo. There is an assumption that the barbarous socio-political situation has hindered the focus on God's mission in Congo. Although the church leaders have lost direction in mission, they are still teaching, baptising, and nurturing the new believers. It is like a driver who has lost their direction, but is still driving fast to reach the terminal. The concern of this article is to find how to rediscover our direction and how to make baptising, teaching, and nurturing one of the primary frameworks for the *Missio Dei* in the Congolese context. I'll begin with a brief overview of the socio-political situation, move to the outworking of the 'second mark' in the Anglican church of Congo, and end with what the Diocese of Aru intends to do.

The Congolese socio-political context

The Congo, as a country, is a 'creation' from independent ethnic groups, by Leopold II, the King of Belgium. The people of Congo come from several different major African ethnic structures in Africa. There are more than two hundred ethnic groups; most are Bantu, the rest are Sudanese, Nilotic, and pygmy. This cultural diversity is exciting, but also challenging for God's mission.

The political system during the colonial and post-colonial era was built on the principle *dominer pour servir* which meant that ultimately domination would lead to the welfare of the Congolese. It aimed to assemble people in ethnic groups that could easily be controlled and manipulated. Meanwhile, it also kept the principle of 'divide and rule'. It caused a lack of true unity among the tribes. As result of this system, violence, anarchy, misery, raping women, spread of HIV/AIDS, lootings, corruption, shameful exploitation not only of the poor, but also of national resources, the greed of the rich, and lack of respect for each human being are increasing. Tyrannical regimes have misused their power to reduce the lives of people to meaninglessness. The question is: How is this possible in a Christian country such as Congo? Unfortunately, the Protestant churches, including the Anglican Church, have adopted the policy of accommodation to the Congolese socio-political turmoil, with a serious impact on the role of the church as an instrument of God's mission.

Spiritual deficiency

In the Province of the Anglican Church of Congo, as in many other churches, Christians truly experience the wonder of worshipping in large congregations with vibrant music and dance, although they serve in conditions of hardship and crushing poverty. New 'charismatic' prayer groups are mushrooming, with an emphasis on healing and miracles. It gives hope for the future of the church in Congo. However, this wonder is like a decorated tomb with bones inside because of the superficiality in the ministry of teaching, baptising, and nurturing. Growth is often measured by the number of the Christians, new parishes, or dioceses. It is numerical and geographical growth. It is more about belonging, often for social reasons, rather than being a community seeking to build their faith and grow in their knowledge in Christ. Immediately after my consecration as Bishop of Aru Diocese, I was surprised by the fact that the main spiritual activity for building the faith of the believers was the worship and sermon on Sundays. Christians meet during the week for development work and social events. Numerical and geographical growth should be accompanied by deepened commitment, spiritual maturity, more courageous discipleship, and faithfulness in worship, service, and witness.[2]

Teaching ministry

The historic succession in the episcopate is a sign of communion with the apostolic church through time and space. Bishops are commissioned to build the unity of God's holy, universal, and apostolic people, and so set them free to engage with the world around them. The historic succession keeps the catholic scope of the church. Bishops are to keep the unity of the local church, but also the universal church. As the 1998 Lambeth conference put it, 'while we are firm in our commitment to the local congregation, that does not make us congregational'.[3]

Bishops vow to guard the apostolic faith. As witnesses to the 'faith once delivered to the saints' bishops are expected to be more than guardians intent on preserving orthodoxy; they are looked upon to be teachers who are able to bring the Scriptures and the creeds of the church to life in the present day. In this sense, during the consecration service, the bishops of the province of the Anglican Church of Congo (PEAC) vow to 'spread the Gospel, and explain the teaching of the apostles to keep unity, peace and order in the church of Christ'.[4] The bishops of PEAC ordain and send ministers. In licensing clergy and lay workers, the bishops signify that those whom they license are faithful ministers of the word. Unfortunately, they are not often well equipped theologically and practically for this ministry and mission. It consequently results in a superficial faith in the face of many challenges like those below:

- Lack of an appropriate theological education. Theological and Bible schools do not have sufficient infrastructure and curricula for contextual training for mission and ministerial formation. The training centres are simply seen as 'passports' for the ministry instead of a workshop which shapes for mission and ministry. Ministerial philosophy is not clearly formulated. There is also a lack of appropriate theological literacy and the teachers are not motivated because they are not well paid. These inadequately trained ministers, some-times bishops themselves, face the challenge of relating theological and biblical understandings to practical situations in preaching, pastoral care, and ethics, and of refreshing theology and practice.
- Bishops often fail to understand their ministry and its functions of teacher, encourager, team-leader, pastor, and disciplinarian and so act inappropri-ately. For instance, many bishops are still using the 'African Chief' model of leadership in countries where democracy is the cutting edge, and where the ministry of all believers is promoted.
- Lack of a critical mind. The whole teaching method in Congo, both in churches and in the state education system, does not encourage reflection and ques-tioning. It is often an exercise in rote learning, which can then be repeated back to examiners on examination day. The system does not develop a critical mind.
- Around 70 per cent of the church members have a low level of education. Catechists have essentially a primary school education while priests generally complete secondary school. Most church leaders are from this group. The consequence is that they often struggle to make sense of all God has given and revealed in the Bible and supremely, in our Lord Jesus Christ. They lack capacity to combine theological understanding with a lively memory of the Christian inheritance to interpret new facts and fresh experi-ences. It has also resulted in an inadequate engagement with contemporary thinking, culture, and society when the teaching ministry is to bring the Scriptures to life in the present day. Of course as teachers, the leaders should

show interest in the questions and concerns of their contemporaries. This needs true wisdom in prayer and spiritual discipline to discern the new insights for faith arising from this interaction of the Christian tradition with new ways of thinking.

This has led to a purposeless preaching which obscured truth, hindered joyous Christian living, destroyed dedication and initiative and the committed service of Christians for Christ. If, for the apostles, the important themes of preaching were the death of Christ, the power of his resurrection, the testimony of Scriptures, and the forgiveness of sins, then for the Congolese the themes in general seem to be respect for authority, offerings (money), description of heaven, and ethical issues such as drinking, smoking, and immorality. It is more about hell and condemnation. Of course these are biblical themes, but too much concentration on them gives a negative view of the world created by God.

Moreover, it must be underlined that teaching is a formal order from God. It is not simply a privilege, but also a commitment to ensure and safeguard the well-being of the people of God. It is to teach the truth as revealed in the Scriptures, to rebuke the false teaching spread in the world and in the church, to reproach bad behaviour and attitudes, and to learn to live according to the will of God.

Baptising ministry

The Lambeth conferences have insisted on the foundation of the church in the sacrament of baptism and accompanying baptismal faith: 'all who believe in our Lord Jesus Christ and have been baptised in the name of the Holy Trinity are incorporated into the Body of Christ and are members of the church'.[5]

It means that baptism brings believers into membership of the body of the church. Our foundational unity with each other and with all our fellow Christians is rooted in our baptism in Christ. As the primary sacrament which marks us as Christians, baptism is the common bond for all Christians across the world. Baptism is the basis for communion: 'By one spirit we were all baptised into one Body'. This gives 'ecclesiological significance to baptism as the instrument of our incorporation into Christ's messianic office as our Prophet, Priest and King; an incorporation which qualifies us to carry out prophetic, priestly and royal functions in the church'.[6] It is a communion between Christians in a hierarchical, corporate, and communal basis, with involvement both of laity and clergy in church government. Paul Avis, considering the expansion of the Anglican Church in the context of its ecumenical discussion, the ordination of women, and the issue of sexuality, appealed to a 'communion-through-baptism' model of church based on the Anglican tradition: 'our communion as Christians in the church is founded on our initiation in Christ by baptism on confession of the fundamental baptismal faith. It holds Christ, the Christians, and the church together.'[7]

In the PEAC, baptism is considered as the primary sacrament which marks us as Christians. However, baptism is more seen as a sign of belonging, the condition of membership and eternal salvation. To be baptised is to avoid eternal condemnation and to gain eternal happiness.

'Communion-through-baptism' as proposed by Paul Avis, has been less effective in the Congolese society where ethnicity, violence, and division are common. The frequent violence and bloody clashes between ethnic groups are committed by those who were baptised and are church 'members'. Most of the political leaders who have caused much suffering to civilians were baptised in the church and backed by church political theology. The blood of family and tribe in Africa is thicker than the waters of baptism. At the core of an African's priorities and allegiances, blood relationship is more important than the church as family, even for an African who has become a Christian. Bishop Albert Obiefuna of Awka, Nigeria, had noticed the same problem with the non-effectiveness of 'baptism' during his intervention in the tragic civil war in Rwanda: 'when it comes to the church, it is not the Christian concept of the church as a family that prevails but rather the adage that "blood is thicker than water"'.[8]

However, as extolled in our new diocese of Aru in Congo, baptism is not only about belonging and membership of the church, but it is also about communion. The bishop and other church leaders should be aware that the current religious and socio-political realities call for a deep and true conversion by the power of the Holy Spirit.

Nurturing new believers

In the Great Commission Jesus commanded us to make disciples: 'Go and make disciples of all nations … teaching them to obey everything I have commanded you' (Matthew 28:19–20). In order to make disciples today, the church must invest time and effort in a long and careful process of nurturing. Belonging must be followed by teaching, worship, and behaving in conformity with Christian ethics and doctrine. The church must provide ongoing accompaniment during the disciple's journey.

The church in Congo has attempted to create opportunities for 'growth' into unity through face-to-face encounters that bring diverse parishes and other communities together. Conferences and seminars are planned for Christians by the departments of Christian education. Theological Education by Extension also provides an opportunity for nurturing the Christians in some parishes. But again the lack of appropriate materials and well-trained facilitators is a big challenge. Furthermore, each parish does encourage holiness and spiritual transformation through worship. Unfortunately, it is not often linked to the outworking of the worshipper's vocation in society. The prayer groups are mushrooming, but they need to be biblically based and appreciative of the church tradition from which they have arisen, as they often become divided.

Unfortunately, much effort in the church in Congo has been put into the domestication of the Christians. Church teaching has been influenced by the political emphasis on the 'blind obedience to authority'. Obedience to authority is inculcated within African cultures. Authority is conveyed from the top down. One standing above the recipient in the hierarchy of leaders is superior and this gives him the right to be obeyed by his subjects. Moreover, unquestioning submission to the leader's authority is reinterpreted as a constitutional recommendation within the PEAC. The provincial secretary himself is on record as saying, 'respect of hierarchy, order and discipline are fundamental in the Anglican Church of Congo for the growth of the church'.[9]

Furthermore, the concept of 'fatherhood' fits well into the structures of submission. The holder of the hierarchically superior office becomes 'father' in relation to his 'sons' who hold subordinate positions. As in the political tradition, fatherhood embodies the principle of unity of command, and reinforces unity of viewpoint and action. Authority is one and indivisible. At each level, the Christian family is unified under the leadership of its 'father'. However, this principle of fatherhood does not allow women to have authority, even among the Bakongo where motherhood is supposed to be valued.

Nurturing has thus been reduced to domestication of the structures of our society for the sake of the maintenance of the church. The Congolese dioceses do not offer enough support and encouragement to the Christians in their congregations, but instead they are seen as demanding and draining of resources. The parishes have become the 'milch cow' providing for the needs of the diocesan centres.

Building a mature community

In order to build a mature community, the diocese of Aru intends to have:

Scripture-formed Christians

Jesus' prayer for his disciples was: 'Sanctify them in the truth; your word is truth' (John 17:17). This means that the Christians need to be saturated in the word if they are to live holy lives. John Wesley offered a good example of how to be a Bible Christian. He was *homo unius libri* (a man of one book). The Bible was his constant 'yardstick'. Wesley once said, 'My ground is the Bible, Yea, I am a Bible bigot. I follow it in all things, both great and small.'[10]

The new Anglican diocese of Aru in Congo encourages Christians to depend on the Bible and to use it as the primary source of authority as well as to practise it in personal life and ministry.

The Diocese of Aru believes that the eternally true word of God gives us a sense that we are following a reliable path that has a proven track record of bringing success to those who have taken it. This gives us courage to go through the tough times believing that God would honour his word.[11]

At the grassroots level, organised small groups meet regularly for Bible study. This provides a good time for sharing and praying. They learn the Bible and develop skills in applying the truths of Scriptures to the theological and practical challenges they face. Seminars and workshops organised by the diocese help us to build the capacity of our priests, catechists, and other leaders to be aware of how to interpret new facts and fresh experiences. They are also helped to integrate their Christian tradition with new ways of thinking so they discern the new insights for their faith. It is a Bible-based interaction, taking into account other subjects such as psychology, anthropology, philosophy, sociology and linking to those social and developmental activities as previously mentioned in this work. Thus the bishops and other leaders must be anchored to the word of God that gives freshness and relevance in mission.

Theologically empowered Christians

From the 'parrot' model of learning based on memorisation, we have moved to a participatory and reflective model of learning. We have transformed our Bible School into a Theological Institute which enables us to develop creativity, participation, and a critical mind. It is a liberating education which, as in Paulo Freire's words, enables education to become 'the practice of freedom as opposed to education as the practice of domination'.[12] It aims to create men and women who are discoverers. The members of the church are equipped not only in theological colleges and Bible Schools, but also through seminars and conferences, where they question the status quo in the church and make a critical assessment of the situation.

Education has thus become a dialogue between human beings: to speak is not the privilege of a few persons, but the right of everyone. We have also made continuing theological education a high priority for our clergy and lay leaders, so they teach and empower the baptised to read the signs of the times and become interpreters and prophets for a bewildered people.

A community of knowledge

Considering the enthusiastic response of the people to the Gospel, we have decided to equip individuals and groups for discipleship. We expend much effort on empowering the laity, women as well as men, youth and older people. The bishop, the 'Rabbi', trains the trainers and oversees the training in the whole diocese. Our aim is to enable the community to become a community of knowledge. The principle is that the trainers equipped by the bishop are not to keep to themselves what they have heard. The vision is to guarantee active spiritual maturity in an ongoing way. We need to have Christians capable of living a model Christian life and of being witnesses for Christ.

This training is done locally by our priests and diocesan staff within the departments of Christian Education and the Theological Education by Extension. Booklets in the local languages are produced locally and provided to equip all the people of God for mission and ministry. Therefore this 'non-academic' training enables them to become mature in Christ through spiritual formation. They are helped through practical exercises to develop a willingness to listen and observe, so that they may come to an intelligent understanding of the signs of God in their lives and in the community.

Laurenti Magesa suggested that 'clan' was a good model of the church in Africa for it adheres to important theological principles and time-honoured mechanisms of subsidiarity, solidarity, participation, and socialisation in church life and practice; and he argued that it mandates the practices of democracy in a church faithful to its calling to bring about and witness to the fullness of life in the world.[13] The institution of the clan in Africa may be said to be the best expression of Jesus' commitment to egalitarian social relations, and its spirituality consists in participation sharing, which is the central principle for human existence, the mark of true humanity. This principle provides a person with the right to be listened to and respected as a member of the community.

However, although clan has been described as the basis of the African experience of unity, harmony, and solidarity, it was a closed social unit where non-members of the clan were excluded. The overriding concern of the clan unit was the protection of the whole unit's integrity and economic welfare in the most satisfactory way possible. When it became necessary to co-operate with other clans, it was because there was a common objective to be achieved or a common danger to be averted. The community of knowledge is not built on the clan principles, which reinforce clanism, tribalism, selfishness, and greediness, but a Scripture-formed community universally oriented, 'washing each other's feet'.

Inculturation

The Aru diocese recognises that the local context is very important if the Gospel is to be incarnated in the heart of God's people. Jesus must speak to people in their current context so that Christians can 'feel at home'. The diocese promotes local values such as solidarity, harmony, unity, participation, and sharing through its teaching and its way of living. Natural family values such as love for others, openness, and acceptance help to build a Christian sense of mission that finds its proper context in service. This local context is valued in order to contribute to the world-wide Christian family.

However, the diocese is careful in its teaching to consider the warning against a mere preservation of cultural heritage. As Theresa Okure, a Nigerian theologian formulated it: 'It is not to preserve cultural heritage, but to proclaim the Gospel of Jesus Christ in a way which makes sense to our people, and transforms our life and our culture.'[14] As the experience of blood relationships has proved exclusivist, and the use of 'family' and 'fatherhood' has led to *utii* theology (Swahili word used by Kenyan theologians to mean blind obedience to the leaders), we carefully select African categories in shaping the understanding of the biblical message.

Political awareness

Christians in Congo were taught to be apolitical, based on a spirituality of separation, not transformation. It is very individualistic in its concentration on personal sin and the spiritual journey to heaven, rather than communal in concern for righteousness and social and political justice.

The diocese of Aru understands that our world cannot be abandoned to the devil. It teaches that the church exists to proclaim Jesus Christ as Lord and Saviour and it enters into the saving activity of God as it engages holistically with the cares of life. Christ preached, but also healed people; he challenged the order of his day and he touched the lives of the unprivileged. So, through our teaching, we make the Christians feel that God cares for the things which vitally affect their daily lives. Social and political actions are integral to our Christian mission. The diocese of Aru emphasises that nurturing is to make the believers become a kind of task force to act for the transformation of world structures so that God's kingdom is a present gift here and now. The baptised are thus encouraged to have prophetic voices and courageous stances.

Conclusion

We have received from God the ministry of reconciliation and work as ambassadors in the name of Christ. The ministry of teaching, baptising, and nurturing the new believers must contribute to the ministry of reconciliation which is of great importance in a region such as central Africa where there is division between nations, ethnic groups, and Christian denominations. 'The important thing for our church is', as Archbishop Janani Luwum said, 'to be alive and to preach a message which is relevant and helpful to the present generation based on the Bible and not on man's aspiration.'[15]

3. To Respond to Human Need by Loving Service (i)

Melba Maggay

Introduction

For the past three decades, there has been a recovery of the holistic nature of the Gospel among the churches. This was framed in various ways by significant gatherings held in various contexts and time settings. The Lausanne movement which started in 1974 marched under the banner of 'the whole gospel for the whole person for the whole world'. In Malaysia in 1987, concerned activists, evangelicals, and charismatics formulated their understanding of holistic mission as 'word, works and wonders'. In 2001 at Oxford, 140 leaders of organisations working among the poor from 50 countries formed themselves into what is now known as the Micah Network and, under the immediate shadow of the 9/11 bombings, came up with a declaration on 'integral mission'.

Today, faith-based social initiatives among communities of the poor have mushroomed, particularly in the Majority World. The pressure is on to develop fresh ways of understanding the biblical undergirding of such initiatives. Massive global poverty is making traditional ways of 'doing missions' obsolete, and has caused a crisis for theologies and prevailing paradigms of social engagement.

In the following, we revisit a major biblical theme which has always put together what historically has been rent asunder: the command to 'love God and neighbour'. In the process we explore the landscape of biblical teachings on what it means to serve the poor and the needy among us.

'To love God is to love the neighbour'

It may startle some to know that the greatest commandment, according to Jesus, is not the 'Great Commission' but the mandate to 'Love God and neighbour' (Matthew 22:34–40). Many of our enterprises as communities of evangelical faith are centred on 'evangelism', narrowly understood as proclaiming salvation for the hereafter and getting people to come to our side and believe what we believe. Yet Jesus' understanding of what it means to truly obey God has little to do with getting people to assent to our creeds or other such propositions. To follow God is to love him with passion, and, similarly, to love our neighbour with the same care and total attention that we shower on ourselves.

This was Jesus' reply to the lawyer who wanted to 'test' him, representing a gang of Pharisees conspiring to entrap him in his talk. The question had for its context the rabbinical understanding of the Law. The rabbis counted 613 distinct commandments in the Law, of which 248 were positive precepts and 365 were prohibitions. They classified these as either 'light' or 'heavy', according to the seriousness of the subject. Hence the query, 'Which of these is the greatest commandment?'

The new thing about Jesus' answer was that he puts Deuteronomy 6:5 in the same breath as Leviticus 19:18 and gives them equal weight. The Deuteronomy quotation was not a novelty, for it was the kind of thing that a rabbi would commend as an excellent reply. 'Love the Lord your God with all your heart and with all your soul and with all your strength' forms the second part of the *Shema*, the Jewish profession of faith, which begins with 'Hear, O Israel, the Lord our God, the Lord is one.'

Quite unusually, Jesus then proceeds to say that 'the second is like it: "Love your neighbour as yourself." All the Law and the Prophets hang on these two commandments.' The Leviticus text, says Jesus, is 'like' the first one. As such, he puts it on the same level, making it equally 'heavy'. The two commands, says Jesus, are like pegs on which all the teachings of the Law and the Prophets hang. They sum up what the Lord requires. On this, the Jerusalem Bible Commentary notes that the effective partnering of these two commandments to become one has no parallel in Jewish literature.

To love God then is to love our neighbour, and to love our neighbour is to love God. What does this mean?

Turning from idols of our time

First, to love God, it seems to me, is to turn from the idols of our time and bring our lives and central structures – like family and governance – under his lordship. It means naming the powers that rule our lives, our cultures, and our life systems, and dethroning them. For churches in the West, it may mean not just turning away from materialism, but confronting the forces that make the rest of the world poor. For those of us in the Two-Thirds World, it may mean breaking free, not just from the stranglehold of nature and ancestral spirits, but hierarchies, despotic authorities, and systems that keep people poor and oppressed and without rights.

On an individual level, it means that we see to it that all we do really proceeds from the love of God. Often, there is a great deal of stress and anxiety in those who care for the needy among us. It may be that our lifeline to God has dried up, and we have ceased to drink deeply of the only well that sustains life, health, and passion. It may be that we have 'hewn out cisterns for yourselves, broken cisterns that can hold no water' as Jeremiah puts it. Like Israel, we trust in the jars of clay that our hands have fashioned, only to discover, in the heat and drought of summer, that the water has seeped through the cracks, lapped dry by the parched ground. It is in the nature of idols that they fail us when we most need them.

One sign that our hearts are going astray is when the daily battle against the evils of poverty and injustice begins to erode our own inner spirit. We lose confidence in the quiet efficacy of the kingdom to change our societies. Our idealism quickly turns into cynicism, and the experience of failure drives us to show some success in the difficult work that we do. Sooner or later, it is this drivenness, and not the call and love of God, that fuels the things we do. Now and again, we need to ask, 'where does the power come from?' If it is not from God, it is coming from some other source, some powerful idol that has begun to grip our soul.

Secondly, loving God and loving our neighbour is a single, not a sequential act. It is not that when we love God, we shall, in the next instance, love others also. Jesus makes the two commandments virtually one, such that there is no sense in which we can love God without at the same time loving our neighbour.

Scripture elsewhere illustrates how this works. Matthew 25:40 tells us that the poor, in a very real yet mysterious sense, are 'proxies for Christ', to borrow the phrase of the Jesuit, Aloysius Pieris. Part of the mystery of the incarnate God is that he has so identified with those on the margins that their hunger, nakedness, and strangeness have become his. What we do with the poor, we do with Jesus.

James picks up this theme strongly by refusing the division between word and deed, faith and works, or, in contemporary language, religion and social action. 'Religion that God our Father accepts as pure and faultless is this: to look after orphans and widows in their distress and to keep oneself from being polluted by the world' (James 1:27). In this, James echoes the Old Testament concern for 'the poor, the widow, the orphan and the sojourner', those who are swept to the margins and are rendered vulnerable because of scarce resources, outright lack of means for survival, or not having the right ethnicity or nationality. True religion always has social and moral consequences.

Conversely, it seems to me that we cannot truly love our neighbour without, at the same time, loving God. There is no force on earth, besides the grace of God, that can deliver us from the insatiable appetite for profit, or the many subtle ways by which we use 'the greater good for the greater number' to camouflage our interests and eliminate competition or opposition. Biblical pessimism about human nature tells us that no amount of social engineering can neutralise the acquisitive instinct and will to power, or reorder the sinful bent towards selfishness and greed.

Also, failed communist experiments have shown us that without subjection to God, our social projects either send people to 'killing fields' or that vast labyrinth of despair called the 'Gulag archipelago'. The Russian novelist Fyodor Dostoyevsky, writing in the nineteenth century, predicted with a great deal of prescience that 'with the downfall of the altar of God, we are left only with the superman or the anthill'. What he meant by this is that apart from the high and humbling view that we are made in the image of a great God, we lose a sense of proportion about ourselves. We either elevate ourselves to the status of a super-man to whom 'everything is permitted', as the character, Raskolnikov in *Crime and Punishment* puts it, or we get reduced to an army of automatons who have value only in so far as we are part of a grand collective. We then play god and treat others who get in our way as insects to be exterminated.

Thirdly, to love God is to love beyond boundaries, or our sense of *sakop* (group alliance), be it race or notions of what constitutes purity or 'uncleanness'. This is the pointed message of the parable of the Good Samaritan in Luke's version of the stor. (Luke 10:25–37). Here, the 'expert in the law' was taken aback by Jesus' backhanded charge that he put to practice what he well knows to be the way to life. He evaded having to apply to himself the meaning of loving God and neighbour. Instead, he engaged Jesus in an abstract discussion of a technical detail: 'And who is my neighbour?' Jesus refused to get drawn into the finer points of this theoretical question. Instead he told the story of how a member of a despised race – the Samaritans – proved to be more of a 'neighbour' to someone in need than the religious leaders of his day. Both the priest and the Levite 'passed by on the other side', perhaps to avoid having to touch what looked like a dead body. Apparently, fear of ritual contamination took prior importance to helping the man, in contrast to the Samaritan who was simply moved to pity and took all the trouble and expense needed to take care of him. Jesus then asked, 'Which of these three do you think was a neighbour to the man who fell into the hands of robbers?' Thus he shifted the issue from 'who has the right to be called my neighbour?' to 'who has actively served as neighbour?' To Jesus, it is not important who or what kind of people should get help – they could be morally unsavoury characters like prostitutes, traitors like tax collectors, or Gentiles like the widow at Zarephath. The more relevant question is, 'who is prepared to be a neighbour to anyone in need?' Jesus shows up false religion here and radically breaks down fences, refusing barriers of race, religious scruples, and pieties in the face of someone's need for compassion.

Serving the poor: some issues

In responding to the needy, the church has tended to put emphasis either on social compassion or social construction. The pendulum tends to swing between purely personal involvement or structural engagement, depending on such factors as whether the church is in a minority or majority situation, theologically tending to withdraw because pessimistic about the world or confidently engaged because the kingdom is now at work in the world.

Historically, the Jews were told to create a society where, because of the memory of their own slavery, the poor, the weak, and the stranger are to be treated with special care. There were gleaning and harvest laws meant to provide for landless poor like Ruth and Naomi (Exodus 23:10–11; Leviticus 19:9–10; Ruth 2). There were legal safeguards against taking advantage of those who are especially vulnerable, like the widow and orphan and the alien in their midst (Exodus 22:21–24). Their internal economy forbids lending to the needy with interest. The poor debtor must be treated with courtesy, and his collateral, like the cloak that he uses against the cold, must be returned by sunset (Exodus 22:25–27; Deuteronomy 24:10–13). These are but some of the host of legislation designed to 'remember the poor'. In both the Old and New Testament, there is strong concern that Israel should put them at the centre of their vision. (See, for instance, Deuteronomy 14:28–29; 15:7; 24:14–15; Psalm 41:1; Proverbs 19:17; Matthew 19:21; Galatians 2:10.)

The Early Church built on Judaism's legacy of institutionalised charity. They pooled their resources together, enrolled widows into some kind of feeding programme, and in general functioned as a social safety net for those who were especially needing help among them (Acts 2:44–45; 5:1–11; 6:1–7).

Missionary movements, like the modern ones that rose from the evangelical awakenings of the eighteenth century onwards, likewise built schools and hospitals in their wake, doing various works of mercy in far-flung places alongside evangelisation. The impact of such work can be seen in the likes of Nelson Mandela, who in the 1998 World Assembly of the World Council of Churches in Harare paid tribute to such efforts. As a boy he was too poor, he said. If not for the mission schools, he could not have gone to school. Such institutions of social compassion are important in themselves and have their own value and integrity. They are not to be treated as mere means to an end, like evangelism or some such enterprise.

At the same time, it is important to grasp that mere social development can run into a bottomless pit. Development experiences in Africa and other places show that incessant political conflicts, tribal wars, bad governance and other such systemic ills result in unsettled demographics and perpetual instability. Painstaking development gains in grassroots communities can get easily wiped out by political disasters.

People of faith have shown themselves to be fairly good in the concrete delivery of social services. The presence of a volunteer force, dedicated staff, and relatively high standards of professional and ethical commitment are today enabling many faith-based organisations to win the trust and respect of donor communities. There is need, however, to address the larger context of poverty and injustice. Besides relief and development, we need to engage in politics, recompose power elites, restructure social arrangements, and engage in advocacy on behalf of those who cannot speak for themselves (Proverbs 31:8–9).

There is the idea among us that evangelism is, in itself, a response to the need for social transformation. Changing individuals will automatically mean change in societies. This is not always true. Often, there are larger, much more complex forces at work that keep people in bondage to poverty in many societies. We are not just battling against flesh and blood, but against 'the rulers, against the authorities, against the powers of this dark world and against the spiritual forces of evil in the heavenly realms' (Ephesians 6:12).

My own sense about Paul's language here is not only that there are spiritual forces behind much of the degradation of our societies. There are subhuman 'powers' and 'principalities' that need to be confronted, life systems and structures that entrench the demonic, causing the defeat of well-meaning efforts and crushing the individuals that dare to transform them. Previous studies, like that of Walter Wink,[1] have dealt in depth with the theological meaning of these 'powers'. For our present purpose, it is enough that the passage gives us a handle on why sociologically, human institutions tend to develop internal contradictions and end up becoming the very opposite of what they set out to be.

The reality of 'principalities and powers', of complex social forces that perpetuate oppression and inequality, compels us also to deal with the structural causes of poverty. Subjective change in inner attitudes towards social status, wealth creation, and wealth sharing needs to be accompanied by objective changes in economic and social relations.

In ancient Israel, this was supposed to happen through a periodic rearrangement of structures like the sabbath laws, particularly the Jubilee Year. On the fiftieth year the slaves are to be released, the debts cancelled, and ancestral lands redeemed and returned to the original owners (Leviticus 25). Those who suffer economic reversals within the 50-year cycle are to be given a new start, freed from generational servitude and indebtedness and to be once again in possession of their patrimony and economic means. It is unfortunate that even in Israel this law was never really implemented, such that by Isaiah's time, we see extreme poverty and concentration of wealth: 'Woe to you who add house to house and join field to field, till no space is left and you live alone in the land' (Isaiah 5:8).

Can we end poverty? Travelling through Europe, I noticed banners emblazoned in churches, 'Make poverty history'. This is the tagline of the Micah Challenge, a global campaign with a two-fold aim: a) to deepen the engagement of Christians with the poor and b) to hold governments accountable to fulfil their public promise to halve poverty levels in their countries by 2015. As someone living in a corner of the world where poverty looks like a never-ending wrong, I thought this was a bit too optimistic. It struck me, though, that such confidence is perhaps peculiar to Europe, and may spring from a history of having substantially reduced poverty, or at least, enough to make the poor invisible.

Scripture, it seems to me, is both optimistic and realistic about ending poverty. In the early years of Israel, when the nation was yet in its incipient form, Moses declared that 'there should be no poor among you ... if only you fully obey the Lord your God and are careful to follow all these commands I am giving you today' (Deuteronomy 15:4–5). Israel was to be a showcase of a nation who, because carefully obedient to the laws of loving God and neighbour, is able to eliminate at least absolute poverty. To the extent that other societies are similarly sensitive to God's demands for justice and equity, there should be no absolute destitution among them. At the same time, the passage tells us that 'There will always be poor people in the land'. This strand of thinking finds reinforcement in Jesus' famous remark that 'The poor you will always have with you, but you will not always have me' (see Matthew 26:11; Mark 14:7). Certainly, by some stroke of misfortune or a complex of reasons, some people will inevitably fall through the cracks. But far from encouraging fatalism, this fact is supposed to rouse people to compassion: 'Therefore I command you to be open-handed toward your brothers and toward the poor and needy in the land' (Deuteronomy 15:11). By such generosity, coupled with structural safety nets, those who are poor and marginalised should only be a fraction of the population in a normal society.

Conclusion

Since loving God and loving our neighbour is a single act, what we do with the poor among us is a test of what we are as a society and as a people of God. We are told that the giving of a cup of water can be a sacred act, on a par with more obviously spiritual tasks like the casting out of demons. Such gestures of compassion, if done in Jesus' name, will by no means lose their reward, he says (Mark 9:38–41).

This linking together of love of God and love of neighbour is what gives sacramental value and eternal significance to our small gestures of compassion. It is what makes work such as that of Mother Teresa's among the sick and the dying in the streets of Calcutta a compelling sign of the presence of Christ. As she disclaimed once in an interview: 'We are not social workers,' she said, correcting mistaken notions that this is all being done for merely humanitarian reasons. No, she said, ' … we do this for the love of Jesus.'

Ultimately, it is the love of God and neighbour that will make any work endure.

3. To Respond to Human Need by Loving Service (ii)

Haami Chapman

What do you want? Where do you live? Come and see? (John 1:35–39)

Introduction

In October of 1971 Thelma and I married. Like any young couple we were excited about our love for each other and our dream of a future together. Among our many expectations we had a deep conviction that Jesus had called us to follow him. Like the disciples of John the Baptist (John 1:35–39), Jesus was calling us to 'come and see'. It was an invitation to join him in the 'places where he chose to live', to sit with him, to see what he saw, to hear what he heard, to feel what he felt, to laugh with him and weep with him, to celebrate the things that he celebrated. We had no idea as to where this would take us. We had simply said 'Yes Lord, we will'.

Mixed cultures, a mixed history

I have both a Māori and Pakeha heritage. Māori are the indigenous people of *Aotearoa* (the Māori name for New Zealand) and are of Polynesian descent. Pakeha was the name given to the British/European settlers who came after James Cook's voyage in 1768. Thelma was born in England to Irish parents.

Through a series of migrations from the Pacific region, Māori settled in the uninhabited islands of New Zealand around AD 800. Colonisation of *Aotearoa* by the British began in the early 1800s, soon after the arrival of missionaries and the signing of the Treaty of Waitangi in 1840 – a covenant intended to guarantee the rights of Māori. It was at this time that two great people groups, Māori and Pakeha, each with knowledge, skills, wisdom, and courage, honed over hundreds of years, began to forge a future together. As the writer Paul noted, it is God who determines the 'seasons and places of our habitation' (Acts 17:26).

Though many benefits came from colonisation, the overall cost to Māori was very high. Massive land loss through the imposition of British Land Law as well as land confiscation through land wars left many Māori disenfranchised. In the early 1950s Māori 'urban drift' – migration to the cities in search of work – exposed and exacerbated issues of racism.

The pace of change demanded of Māori and the devaluing of cultural norms – the 'glue' that had held our society together and was now deemed irrelevant, evil, or law breaking – were destroying us as a people. This set us on a trajectory or pathway that would see many families dysfunctional, self-destructing and with three generations dependent on the state welfare system. Alcohol and drug abuse usually accompanied this pathway. Children became the greatest casualty. According to UNICEF, New Zealand has the third highest level of child abuse per capita in 27 countries of the OECD.[1] After 140 years of seeking a future together the good, the bad, and the ugly was showing itself on our streets and especially in the *whanau* (family).

A large Māori protest movement would eventually form, demanding an end to discrimination and Eurocentrism. The movement would insist on the recognition of Māori culture and the honouring of the Treaty of Waitangi, a covenant which had been generally ignored. A new way was emerging into which Thelma and I were being called.

A journey in indigenous theology

It is important at this point to share the theological and cultural context of this journey. What we – Thelma and I – were about to embark on would take us back in to the very core of the Māori indigenous and cultural context, challenging many of our entrenched theological assumptions. Here we would discover God's presence – found not in the programmes, projects, and resources so abundantly available through the variety of Christian initiatives we were involved in – but in the beauty, the brokenness, the history, and everyday lives of our people.

We discovered we were not introducing or 'bringing God' to our community. Long before we arrived God was there. He was there reflected in the memory of pre-European revelations to Māori through creation and conscience – a partial revelation and marred by sin, to be sure, but a revelation nonetheless. It only awaited the full disclosure that would be found in Christ, made known through his Word. We would also discover that God was not dualistic, separating 'the spiritual from the natural and scientific'. Instead, in Scripture and the understanding and traditions of our people we found God to be holistic, involved in every aspect of our lives. He was there in all the moments of our days, in our homes and families, our successes and failures, our good days and bad days.

More than this, we also discovered that life's problems had a purpose. They drove us to his presence where there was nothing he could not heal. Furthermore, we discovered that healing itself had a purpose, driving us to rediscover the God-given beauty that exists within every individual, family, and community.

The cross had dealt with our failure, we came to understand, enabling us to envisage, design, and create a new future. We discovered God's unconditional love.

The following four stories capture some of our journey:

Story 1. You've just turned me away!

I had worked late that day and arrived home around seven in the evening. I was keen to get home to Thelma as she was very close to having our first child and the days were long for her. Sitting on the front veranda stairs was a stranger, a gentleman who, as I later gathered, had heard me share the good news about Jesus in the prison where he was serving his sentence. As part of an evangelistic team that regularly visited at the institution, I had often said that if anyone needed help when they got out of prison, all they needed to do was just give us a call. So he did!

He had arrived earlier that afternoon and was happy just to wait for me to get home. Thelma had prepared dinner so we ate and talked late into the night. I listened as he shared his life's story – a tale of crime, violence, and abuse. His was the life of both victim and perpetrator where violence, especially against women, had become the coping mechanism and focal point of anger and pain. The result was long stretches of incarceration in our institutions and prisons.

By midnight it was obvious he had nowhere to go. I had to leave home early in the morning for work and, after hearing his colourful story, there was no way I could let him stay. It was bad enough he had just spent much of the afternoon at our home alone with Thelma. So I did what any normal husband would do. I rang a friend of mine who flatted with other young men and arranged for him to spend the night there. He was very grateful, having enjoyed the evening, the meal, the opportunity to talk and to share his heart and his story. A few minutes later my friend arrived to pick him up and we said our farewells.

As they drove away the Lord spoke these words deep within my spirit, 'You've just turned me away.'

We discovered a wonderful truth that night. Jesus had come to visit us in the wounds and brokenness of this stranger's life. When Jesus spoke to me that night his words were not words of judgement or condemnation but words of sadness. Someone he loved so dearly, someone in need of a place to stay for the night, had just been turned away. On our knees and with tears of guilt and shame Thelma and I asked the Lord to forgive us for our blindness. We promised we would never turn him away again and, every now and then, he comes and visits for a while!

Story 2. Can I have some lace curtains please?

It was now 1978. With two sons to care for and two years of theological college behind us, we were living in a suburb called Porirua, a place whose reputation said, 'You don't want to live here or bring your kids up here.' But we were happy there, believing we had heard Jesus calling us to this place, serving along-side a local community church that had a vision for what we called 'real mission'. Our catch cry was 'Put Jesus back out on the streets again.'

We hadn't been in the new setting long when I received a call for help. Responding enthusiastically to assist a lady in need, I discovered all she wanted was for me to rescue her dog that had got stuck under her house! It wasn't Jesus on the street as we had imagined.

Not long after that, the kind of encounter we were looking for happened in the person of a lonely, hurting, young woman who had sought help from the newly opened Community Law Office staffed by myself and lawyers from our church. We were excited because the circumstances of this young lady validated our existence. She was only sixteen or seventeen, her baby just a few weeks old. It seemed that she was still a child herself. And she was Māori.

This was the real stuff of ministry! We were here to make a difference with the love of God.

Thelma and I sat with the young lady on the floor of her one-bedroom state house. No furniture, no beds – just a grubby mattress and a couple of blankets on the floor with the bare minimum of kitchen utensils. That was it. She had come to the city as part of the Māori urban drift under government-funded apprenticeship programmes for rural Māori youth. Now here she was with no job, no friends, too ashamed to go home and with a baby to care for.

We were here to help and from my perspective it was obvious what she needed: furniture, bedding, extra things for the baby, food in the cupboard etc, etc. But when Thelma asked what she needed all she said with tears in her eyes was 'Can I have some lace curtains please?' I was about to respond with some stern advice on what her priorities should be when Thelma's touch on my arm and a certain look that I've become so familiar with over the years indicated to me to keep my mouth shut.

Lovingly, Thelma walked with this young lady through her situation and came eventually to the reasons why she wanted lace curtains. Her flat was down a slight embankment and above her was the footpath and roadway. Everyone who drove or walked by looked directly into her windows. Almost every room was open to the public's gaze. From her perspective (not mine), curtains provided privacy and the bit of lace, a little dignity.

Years would go by before I would come to realise that people actually know best about their circumstances. We who are the trained and educated assume our educational qualifications make us the experts and therefore solvers of people's problems. But I've discovered problems have a purpose. They drive us to his presence – and there's nothing that his presence cannot heal.

We bought Jesus some privacy and dignity that day and threw in some household furniture, food, and other stuff just for the fun of it!

Story 3. How dare you bring this monster into our community!

For weeks TV news channels, radio talk-back shows and newspapers ran the story of the Parnell Panther – an accused rapist, women basher, bank robber, and thug. 'Lock him up and throw away the key', was the only solution most social commentators, editors, police, and political representatives could come up with.

Mark had served his time and even though many did not want him back out on the streets they had to let him go. After six months of parole in his home community in the far north of New Zealand I sat with him in Auckland and listened to his heart. I had learned a few things by now and understood a little of what, 'from out of the heart the mouth speaks', could mean. Mark's was a heart that from its earliest moments as a child had known much rejection, abuse, and violence, a heart that had been wounded and broken many times. In consequence, over the years, Mark's heart had developed coping mechanisms destructive to both himself and society.

Obvious in our conversation was that Mark was looking for a job. The not so obvious was that he was looking for a place to belong. His c.v. was short: 'I hate pigs (police) and I do dope but I'll always be up front and straight with you.' I offered him an opportunity to come walk with me in my journey – not to work for me but to serve alongside of me, my wife Thelma, and our family.

Porirua days were long past now but memories of encounters with Jesus had helped to mould and shape our thinking, our theology and practice. We had come to the conclusion that the most powerful place to influence people with the love of God was our family home.

By now our son Hamiora was 19, John was 17, Hannah, our daughter, was 13 and Luke, our youngest son, was 11. We were helping to run an International Christian Leadership Training Centre situated on a very beautiful property in a fairly wealthy suburb of Auckland city. Alongside our co-directors, we created an environment where people from all walks of life and from many parts of the world could come. Our prayer was that by searching the Scriptures and experiencing God's unconditional love they could discover him, and in the light of that awareness and experience choose to follow him. It was into this environment that the 'so-called' Parnell Panther would come.

The first day I took Mark home he refused to come into the house to meet Thelma or to eat at our table. She was female and white. Mark's hatred for anything that resembled or represented the system and the people – white New Zealanders – that he had fought against for so long ran very deep. With quiet humility, Thelma prepared a meal for Mark and me to eat together outside. Two months later he decided to move in with us.

On moving day we arranged for Mark to catch a bus from the other side of the city where he was staying, to a local bus stop five minutes from our home. There, our son Hamiora would meet him to bring him to our home. Within a few minutes of leaving to meet Mark, our son was back – but not with Mark! A huge confrontation involving several police officers and detectives was taking place at the bus stop. By the time I got there, further police reinforcements had arrived. A detective driving by had recognised Mark waiting at the bus stop and assumed the worst. I tried to persuade the senior officer that Mark was with me and, in fact, was moving into our home. But they arrested him anyway on some charge or other and took him away. They released him later that day.

Within an hour of returning home I was receiving irate phone calls from neighbours. 'How dare you bring this monster into our community,' was the message I received from one caller, followed by some very colourful language. No amount of explanation could satisfy the concerns, the fear, and the phobia that spread throughout the community. It seems the first port of call for the senior officer I had talked to was the head of Neighbourhood Watch.

Who would believe that in a very special way, in the midst of this man's wounds and brokenness and all the ugliness of his history, Jesus had come to visit?

That was some years ago now. It was not always easy because wounds can take a while to heal, often a lot of muck has to come out – and that takes time. But grace is a wonderful thing. It gives us time to heal. We got a lot of flak over the years, from both Christian and non-Christian community members. Some felt it was totally irresponsible of me to expose our family, especially Thelma and Hannah, to such risks as Mark and the world he had come from posed. But we were under no illusions as to the potential danger. When Jesus called us to follow him there were no guarantees that all would go well, no assurance that everything would be fine, no promise of security or comfort – only a promise, that if we would follow him and join him in what he was doing, we would discover truth, and the truth would set us free.

We still journey together with Mark today, walking and working together in our community. Now, he does in his home, with his beautiful wife and family, what we did with him. It's a simple ministry of an open door, an open cupboard and an open fridge, welcoming Jesus when he visits, usually in the wounds and brokenness of someone's life. And yes, after Mark, many others did follow. But those are other stories!

Story 4. A leader's cry for help – 'We want to change but we don't know how, can you help us?'

A New Zealand judge, on sentencing two young brothers some years ago, called them 'nothing but a pack of mongrels'. Their reputation had earned them the label. The name stuck and soon, behind prison bars, a gang called the 'Mongrel Mob' was born. In the 1970s and years to follow they would cut a pathway of violence and destruction from the top of the North Island to the bottom of the South. They would become the most feared gang this country had ever known. People asked, 'How could any individual or group of people do such horrific things – how could they even live like this?'

In Roy's case the driving force was simply a heart consumed with blame and anger masking a deep heartfelt need to belong. When he was eight years old he had been taken from his family and made a state ward all because he stole a bicycle. For Roy this ultimately meant being moved several times between institutions and foster homes, never seeing his parents, thinking they no longer loved him. At age eleven he discovered it was the state, 'the system', that had kept his parents from him. This 'system' he learned to hate and thus mapped the pathway for his life.

Roy was told by well-meaning adults that 'unless he changed' he would graduate from foster care, to borstals (youth detention), from borstals to prison, and then from prison to maximum prison. He did just that and in the borstals and prisons found a way to meet his heartfelt need to belong – he joined the Mongrel Mob. They became his family and together with them he waged war against the system and all it stood for. Eventually he would form the chapter of the Mob known as 'Notorious', becoming the leader of one of the most violent and abusive gang chapters in this country's history.

Leadership can be a strange thing. It comes in many different forms and through many different circumstances. When Mark (remember Mark from our previous story) introduced Roy to me he had just been released from prison. After years of being in and out of prison, fighting the system at every turn, and after years of not seeing his children grow up, a new purpose lay on his heart. Mark's story had given him new hope – and a new challenge. Could he lead his chapter into a different future? 'We want to change,' he said, 'but we don't know how. Can you help?'

That was 1997. The following ten years would unveil an incredible story. No longer would the Auckland chapter of Notorious focus on crime. Instead they would focus on loving their families and especially their kids!

Though the pathway to transformation for Roy and the rest of the chapter would be difficult, the reason why would be simple – unconditional love. We began to journey with this community, walking together through a variety of self-evaluation processes and capacity–building initiatives. Our first task was to restore the memory of what had worked in the past. Most of them were Māori and deep in their cultural history they discovered values and beliefs long forgotten, and there they also discovered the presence of God. With this new-found awareness they began to leverage a new future off the best of what they had found in their past – and to envisage a future that put their children and their families first.

Large gatherings of some 200 plus members of the Mob met regularly at our family centre but most meetings with the core leadership were held in our home. We talked, we shared meals, we planned, we evaluated. We laughed together and we wept together. We buried their dead.

Out of the 35 or so key leaders we first met with, only two have returned to prison in ten years. In strict economic terms, that is a saving of close to 25 million dollars to the New Zealand tax-payer. But of far greater importance to Roy and the Notorious community is that they have begun to rediscover what love could look like. Expressions of affection toward their wives and children, gestures never seen before in their community, are now common. What they envisaged is becoming a reality.

Alienation from both ethnic society and general society is being reversed as Mob members participate more and more in the local community and in nationwide events. A company they formed is creating and providing work opportunities for their members. What's more, a *60 Minutes* documentary in 2006, highlighting their story, has had a huge impact on the country. It gave people hope. Judges that once locked them up now congratulated them for their efforts. Alienated family members have been reconciled. Equally significantly, rival gang members, once sworn enemies, now want to know how they can achieve the same.

Roy's story – the story of the Notorious chapter of the Mongrel Mob – is an example of community transformation being driven from within. They are a special group of men and women wanting more than anything to have a better future for their children and themselves. They are a community taking responsibility for their own circumstances and future.

So often in Christian ministry people from such circumstances as the Notorious chapter of the Mongrel Mob have been encouraged to remove themselves from family and friends as a pre-requisite to faith. We chose to encourage them to stay where they were simply because of the influence they have and can continue to have among their own community. More importantly, there was the need for them to discover that Jesus comes to walk in their world, just the way they are. That he came not to 'change' their lives but to 'exchange' his life for theirs.

Final thoughts

Many of the people with whom we work have been deemed the most violent and abusive in our country. Some have been rapists, killers, and bank robbers – men and women incarcerated for many years, reminded continuously by government, the media, the public, the church, and even themselves they are the country's worst.

Much of their struggle has been rooted in the home. And, tragically within Māori and Pakeha communities, home has come to be one of the most violent places of life. More hostility occurs in the context of the family home than anywhere else. But, and this is the good news, the family home can also be the most caring place, the place where God's loving intentions can best be discovered.

In our ministry we had to make a choice – focus on the problems or the possibilities? Should we focus first on Genesis 3 with the ugliness and failure of sin or should we focus on Genesis 1 – God's intention of 'unconditional love with life in all its fullness'? We focused on Genesis 1 and what we focused on became our reality!

We determined to restore the memory of what has worked within our indigenous Māori communities, to contextualise these God-given indigenous cultural values and beliefs into our modern world. We decided to celebrate being Māori, confident that God was with us and that we could trust what he was doing in each other's lives. We knew that *aroha* (unconditional love), *manaakitanga* (honouring and respect), *awhinatia* (caring and supporting), and *kaitiakitanga* (guardianship) were values that worked – and that they worked especially in the context of *whanau* (family and extended family).

Over time we came to the conclusion that the institutional church had had very little influence on the community with which we were involved and, sadly, was the last place to take them. Instead, as with Jesus, the first place to take them was home. Our home, therefore, became the primary place of ministry. There people would discover God's unconditional love, becoming empowered to take control of their own circumstances and destiny. In time, church life would follow.

We have been privileged to walk with the least, the lost and the last of our communities these many years and we honour them and their courage. They are rediscovering what love could look like, especially love for their children, their spouses and families. And, as they experience more and more the meaning of unconditional love they are beginning to discover that Jesus Christ is the source of it all.

So these are stories not so much about us, but about him – descriptions of little encounters that we have seen and been a part of over the past 35 years. Hopefully they will also convey the tremendous privilege and honour it's been to simply follow him and, in so doing, be ourselves unconditionally loved along the way.

4. To Seek to Transform Unjust Structures of Society (i)

Valdir Raul Steuernagel

Set your hearts on his Kingdom first, and on God's saving justice, and all these other things will be given you as well.

(Matthew 6:33, NJB)

Social transformation likes company: the marks of mission walk arm in arm

As the years go by we keep discovering how much we need others and how much our reality of life is interconnected. In fact, it is rarely so that we understand things better or even correctly if we look at them alone, as if life could exist by itself. A paragraph, even a paragraph in life, will be better understood if we look at the context in which it was or is written or even lived out. Context, therefore, is essential in the definition of significance and meaning.

As we follow the making of this book we see the 'five marks of mission' outlined and specifically developed. Much has already been said about these marks, their integration, and their specificity. Therefore, when it comes to the fourth mark, we need to affirm integration again. The affirmation that we seek social transformation must be seen in the context of mission, and never projected as a 'lone ranger'. The mission of the church must be holistic, focusing on the *shalom*[1] God provides for his human creation as well as for his whole creation. A *shalom* that is whole, affecting and embracing all of human life and all human beings. A *shalom* that reaches out to feelings, intuitions, thoughts, and actions. Reaches out to singing, crying, laughing, and hoping. Reaches out to food and hunger, water and thirst, fatigue and sleep. To nakedness and clothes, sickness and health, hopelessness and seeds of hope. It's *shalom* for everyone, to be experienced everywhere. It's the gift of *shalom* given by the God of love to all and everyone.

God's *shalom* is not an individual gift, it's a community gift. It relates to more than just one person, one community, one clan, one language, one place. Individual and collective, personal and community are not categories and life experiences that God would keep separately. They are integrated in God himself and it is impossible to look at one of them without focusing on the other. You cannot possibly address one without considering all of them. God is all-embracing, very inclusive and extremely good in loving each one in the same way he loves all.

Let's bring the five marks of mission back to our memory in order to stress their integration. The first two go well together and affirm that the message of the Gospel must be lived out. It must be announced, embraced, nurtured, and lived out in community:

- To proclaim the Good News of the Kingdom.
- To teach, baptise, and nurture new believers.

These two marks tell us that the Christian faith presents us with an interpretative content, whereby we can see who we are, where we come from, and what we are here for. The Christian faith formats our understanding of life, gives us a perception of reality and a way to look at the world and into the future. As such, the Christian faith is not a theory but a life-sharing story that connects us to our life origins and purpose as well as to the other, and the community of others. The Christian faith must be lived out and shared; otherwise, it cannot be understood and embraced. It must be nurtured, or else it will not grow into all the tissues of our lives and of our relations. It needs to show its reality and significance by being lived out in a community that is called to be no less than a sign of who God is and what he wants. A sign of God's Kingdom.

The third mark of mission makes a beautiful transition between the *kerygma*, the *diakonia* and the craving for justice:

- To respond to human need by loving service.

It is service of love expressed as an act of compassion. It is compassion motivated by the story and model of the Gospel as lived out by Jesus Christ. It is his compassion becoming an expression of the first fruits of God's desired justice for people, communities, and societies. It is service as an expression of thirst for justice, even becoming an announcement of the justice of the Kingdom.

A serving attitude is the Christian way of entering into the remaining two marks of mission. One is a search for transformation which denounces unjust structures and announces God's justice into our systems and structures. The other one is the recognition of his creation and of the integrity of this creation, which is not a mere object of exploitation but is a sacred offer for us to have life with quality. It was created by him and must be managed for him. They are:

- To seek to transform unjust structures of society.
- To strive to safeguard the integrity of creation and renew the life of the earth.

Justice as a mark of mission: are we there yet?

While we need to affirm the five marks of mission and look at them in their integration we also affirm each of those marks in their specificity. Therefore, we affirm justice as a fundamental expression of God's search for transformation, as a mark of mission and the need to integrate it into our portfolio of mission.

To define the specificities and the frontiers of mission is one of those challenges that are always with us. We tend to play safe and feel more secure with more narrow and defined frames. By nature, we tend to be conservative and walk on secure paths, and by ideology we are exclusivist. We tend to define in order to justify our own ways. We try to protect our zone of affirmation and comfort. We tend to define in order to affirm ourselves and criticise others.

With the understanding and practice of mission it is not different. The environment where I come from has been struggling with this very question and practice: how to understand mission and build up a practice which balances a clear missionary intentionality with a consistent inclusiveness. Looking at my own journey I must confess that I have not been exactly consistent, be it in theological or ministerial ways. I see myself moving between a narrower and a broader understanding of mission, and struggling to keep the specificity of mission, while at the same time affirming its inclusiveness. My two benchmarks are the expressions given by Stephen Neill, when he says that 'if everything is mission, nothing is mission',[2] affirming the specificity of mission, and by John Stott, when he says that mission is 'everything the church is sent into the world to do',[3] affirming the breadth of mission. I today affirm those two trends and want to understand the mission of the church as intentional as possible and as broad as possible in order that Christ is recognised and affirmed, for life to be promoted, for community to be developed, and for justice to flow in God's river as a sign of God's eternal obsession with *shalom*.

In the past and in my environment, the struggle was between evangelism and social concern, in a discussion that consumed far too much time and energy. We were unable to look into the eyes of the Scriptures and we did not listen enough to the cry of a suffering world, both of which needs go together.

At that very time, mission, and specifically cross-cultural mission, was seen as mission from the 'First' to the 'Third World', to use old concepts. Mission from the rich to the poor, from the empire to the victims and dependents of that empire. From more 'sophisticated' cultures to more 'primitive' cultures. Mission was an initiative of the West, while the Southern people and nations were mere receivers.

Today the agenda has changed. The initiative in mission has moved largely to the South, if not always in numbers and statistics, then in passion and adrenaline. Europe struggles with its own ecclesial crises and survival and does not have many resources, much willingness or even authority to be involved in mission. The strength of mission is still a reality in the USA, even if wearing less of a mission agency clothing and more of a mega-church clothing, which calls for direct field involvement and which brings alive legitimate fears of cultural and economic imperial attitudes. However, that the church is alive, is growing and becoming cross-culturally aware in significant parts of the South is a new and joyful fact. But, just to be aware of mission – particularly cross-cultural mission – does not automatically mean that we can be confident about the emergence of a more comprehensive and substantive mission agenda – as if such an agenda was born into the tissue of a growing Southern church.

The agenda today is certainly much more indigenous and has become, also in the South, more cultural and cross-cultural. It could also be said that there is more ideological awareness in the mission agenda today, if a market agenda is to be considered ideological. A 'sellable Gospel' is on the market today and has many consumers, feeding a growing evangelical-charismatic-Pentecostal church. Its impact in society, as an agent of transformation for justice, however, is not easily identifiable in so many poor and exploited places of our Southern societies. A poor society, in the Southern hemisphere, still needs to know a God who wants more than individual prosperity, and to discover that he is commit-ted to transformation, that he loves a sort of justice that carries the smell and taste of God's incarnation in Jesus Christ. A smell and a taste that should arrive in the life of the poor, and witness them discovering a God who plants in their hearts a seed of hope that goes deep into the tissues of their family and commu-nities. The Southern church, frankly speaking, seems to know little about a God of justice and the building of a discipleship community committed to it. A mission community committed to justice is still a challenge for many and in many places.

The path of transforming discipleship: revisiting the call of the disciples

The gospels are quite consistent with the fact that Jesus called a group of people to be his disciples; people who would walk closely with him during his years of ministry and continue to follow him after his death and resurrection. By consis-tently naming those disciples, the synoptic gospels allow us to know that things get quite personal and intense when Jesus calls.[4] When reading the explicit and different synoptic 'call passages' we see and affirm the need to see them as a whole, in an integrating manner.

The Gospel of Mark reads:

> He went up to the mountain and called to him those he wanted, and they came to him. And he appointed twelve, whom he also named apostles, to be with him, and to be sent out to proclaim the message, and to have authority to cast out demons. (Mark 3:13–15)

Matthew says:

> Then Jesus summoned his twelve disciples and gave them authority over unclean spirits, to cast them out, and to cure every disease and every sickness. (Matthew 10:1)[5]

The different dimensions in Jesus' call relate to meaningful and foundational aspects of our lives: the inward and the outward, the verbal and the relational, the healing and the liberating, the touching and the restoring, the announcing and the denouncing. In his call we see the importance and the place of words as well as the basic need for signs. We see the reality of pain and the experience of liberation and of wholeness. Presence, company, announcement of hope and intervention for liberation are essential aspects of discipleship and should become constitutive dimensions of the mission life of the church, as modelled by Jesus.

The disciples are called to:

- **Be with Jesus**, building relationships and nourishing a sense of belonging. Disciples are called to give and to receive. To do and to be. They are called to be with Jesus and this is a life experience to be learned from Mary, who 'sat at the Lord's feet and listened to what he was saying'. She chose the best part and this will not be taken from her (Luke 10:42). To be with Jesus, nurturing his presence, feeding company with him and cultivating his intimacy, are essential expressions of the mission of the church.

- **Go and preach the Gospel of God's Kingdom**. The words of the message of the Gospel must be spelled out in order for us to know, understand, and respond to it. To know comes so very normally through listening. The message of the Gospel must be shared; it will not be known unless it is shared. Word has to become a reality in the mission of the church, and the name of such a word is Jesus. If Jesus is not announced, and if he is not at the centre of our mission, our mission is not a Christian mission. The Gospel needs to be proclaimed, understood, embraced, and confessed.

- **Heal the sick!** Wellness and wholeness are a real necessity and a real possibility. The Christian faith, being incarnational, is seen at its best when in contact with people at their most acute perception of life and reality. Today as yesterday, this happens, very often, when one faces need, pain, and suffering. Significant time and energy of Jesus' ministry was spent in contact with people expressing different levels of pain, needs, and abandonment. Wherever he went he was surrounded by people in need, and to them he gave special attention and time. By touching people and proclaiming them into wellness he made the face of mission very clear: recognise the world's reality of pain, enter into it, and get engaged with it in such a way that people would be called to, and could experience presence, love, touch, healing, restoration, and celebration. It is not little, but the demands of life are not little either. It is not much – it is only as much as is the need of restoration, of wholeness and integration. And, it is absolutely real. It is a life experience that becomes a sign of the arrival of God's Kingdom. It is the announcement of the possibility and necessity of transformation.

- **Drive out the demons!** This is to experience liberation and an affirmation of identity. It is amazing to see how complex the reality of life is and what a mixture of things there is in our own lives. This can look very rational today, very emotional tomorrow. It can sound objective in the morning and completely illogical in the afternoon. It may feel free as a bird in a stage of our life and absolutely oppressive at another time. Science, logic, and knowledge are very abundant in our environment, but so are angels and demons – be it in our inner life or in our cultural, social, or economic patterns, be it in our local communities or be it at big political and economic levels. The Gospel always arrives discerning reality, denouncing an enslaving idolatry and oppressive injustice, identifying with the poor and the suffering, and intervening for liberation, wholeness, and peace, even at the cost of a thousand pigs. The Gospel brings with itself the experience of liberation and peace: 'They came to Jesus and saw the demoniac sitting there, clothed and in his right mind, the very man who had had the legion' (Mark 5:15).

Other passages could certainly be selected when addressing the subject of transformation and justice from a Gospel perspective. This one, however, is a typical mission text, one that deals with the sending reality of those who are called to belong to and walk with Jesus. It looks at the way Jesus called and tasked his disciples, setting a model for the church to understand and practise mission.

In the school of mission to which I belong it has always been said that we are called by Jesus in order to be sent out, by him, into the world. Our mandate was to preach the Gospel, call people to conversion and then establish a local church. Much of the Protestant-Evangelical modern missionary enterprise embraced and affirmed such a tradition, as also witnessed in Latin America, my home place.

Although it has been rewarding to embrace this tradition, it has also been good to discover other aspects of the very mission of God, in whose footsteps we search to understand the mission of the church. One is the discovery and rediscovery of a loving God who cannot be captured by any tradition and is absolutely committed to pursue 'his own loves'. A God committed to express his inclusive love, in a special way, to those who suffer life more than enjoy life, as so well expressed by the abused child, the abandoned mother, and the lonely refugee.[6] This embrace of God is an absolute expression of who he is, and of the way he reaches out to the other, particularly the suffering other; it signals his eagerness for a transformation that carries the flavour of his Kingdom.

A second discovery has taken me to the world around me, asking me to look at and encounter a world of poverty, oppression, and injustice. Walking in this direction means facing the challenge of looking at the surroundings as Jesus did: to touch people as he did and transform people as he wanted to: 'the blind receive sight, the lame walk, those who have leprosy are cured, the deaf hear, the dead are raised, and the good news is preached to the poor' (Luke 7:22).

A third aspect has led me to better discover the very presence of God. To see that Andrew, Philip, Thaddaeus, and others were called by Jesus to be with him was of key importance in this journey of discovery. To enjoy his presence, to build a relational trust with him – his priority list – ought to come on our list too. Since my tradition is very action-oriented and proclamation-driven, it is challenging and enriching to be invited into a spirituality of presence. A spirituality of listening and of chewing. Of silence and of smile. Of few words and of much eye contact. Of embarrassment and of profound encounter with the heart of God.

It is exceptionally good to go back to the call passages of Jesus and see them coming together in:

mission

- A spirituality of presence aiming for relational trust.
- A journey of proclamation aiming for integration in the Kingdom community.
- An intervention for restoration, aiming for *shalom* in life.
- An experience of liberation, aiming for identity and affirmation of personhood.

As those dimensions come together, we witness to the emerging picture of what mission is all about and of how much the aim for transformation is a substantial dimension of it.

The mission of the church, as it has often been said, has to be expressed in LIFE, WORD, DEED, and SIGN. LIFE, because in the Christian faith there is no truth that walks outside of a body. As such, an incarnational faith needs to be lived out. WORD, because a real life experience gains special meaning when expressed in words of understanding and of significance. DEED, because they touch fundamental dimensions of our lives and express God's desire for wholeness. This is very often seen in the restoring of a sick body: 'Be well,' Jesus said, announcing the possibility of a new life reality. And SIGN, because in a world of suffering, oppression, and enslavement, the message of the Gospel represents the possibility of liberation, restoration, and the building of a community that knows to whom the power and the glory belong.

Transforming justice becomes so much of a reality in the world of mission because it is so much a part of what God desires for us and of what Jesus lived out in his time and modelled for us to live out in our times. Human and social transformation is a result of mission and becomes a reality in the discipleship journey. It is transformation towards a new way of life and model of society, as an experience, as a value, and as a gift to be shared with others. It is an integral part and outcome of the mission life of the church.

> The mission of the church has a profound commitment to transforming justice. As such, it expresses well the nature of God and affirms his incarnation.

The sound of justice in the transformation journey: listening to the pain of suffering

The book *Mountains Beyond Mountains*[7] describes Paul Farmer's journey of incarnation in the reality of Haiti. Dr Farmer is a Harvard graduate medical doctor, but it is in Haiti where he immersed his life and developed his human, social, and political work. There are moments and expressions in the book which are worthy to embrace: 'But WLs',[8] he says 'think all the world's problems can be fixed without any cost to themselves. We don't believe that. There's a lot to be said for sacrifice, remorse, even pity. It's what separates us from roaches.'[9] Or, he debates the argument that 'medicine addresses only the symptoms of poverty', or that 'good works without revolution only prolonged the status quo', generating 'dependency'. The reality, however, was that 'the poor were suffering. They were "dying like smelt"' and Paul Farmer believed in sending resources 'down "the steep gradient of inequality", so as to provide services to the desperately poor – directly, now'. They called it 'pragmatic solidarity' and said: 'A goofy term perhaps, but the great thing about it was that, if you really practised it, you didn't have to define it, you could simply point at what had been accomplished.'[10]

Transforming justice, from a biblical perspective, is incarnational. It is beautifully and profoundly incarnational. It touches the very heart, feelings, and wounds of those who are the victims of injustice. It is not only concretely immersed into reality but it is painfully connected to those who suffer injustice.

Justice is neither an aseptic programme nor an abstract promise. It is never an ideological discourse. Justice is concrete because it acknowledges and suffers the pain of its absence. The announcement and promise of justice is an encounter with injustice. It is denunciation of that sort of injustice that produces oppression, exploitation, suffering, and idolatry. Justice is announced and promised as an act of identification with the victims of that very injustice and idolatry and the announcement of a new reality that generates a movement of change and a dream of honey and milk. It does this by using the language of promise addressed to those who were once experiencing slavery.

In Latin American theology, especially in the so-called Liberation Theology, the Exodus passage, which deals with the slavery of God's people and their experience of liberation, became paradigmatic for a continent that has experienced oppression, exploitation, and violence for so long. It became a paradigm for the recognition and denunciation of injustice, and a paradigm of hope as well. It inspired a new possibility. Let me call attention to some dimensions of that experience:

> Then the Lord said: 'I have observed the misery of my people who are in Egypt; I have heard their cry on account of their taskmasters. Indeed, I know their sufferings, and I have come down to deliver them from the Egyptians, and to bring them up out of that land to a good and broad land, a land flowing with milk and honey, to the country of the Canaanites, the Hittites, the Amorites, the Perizzites, the Hivites, and the Jebusites. The cry of the Israelites has come to me; I have also seen how the Egyptians oppress them. So come, I will send you to Pharaoh to bring my people, the Israelites, out of Egypt.'
>
> But Moses said to God,'Who am I that I should go to Pharaoh, and bring the Israelites out of Egypt?'
>
> He said: 'I will be with you; and this shall be the sign for you that it

is I who sent you: when you have brought the people out of Egypt, you shall worship God on this mountain.' (Exodus 3:7–12)

The encounter with this paradigmatic text means encountering a God who cares, and whose expression of care is deep and radical. This is a God who *sees*, *listens*, and *comes down*. This is an incarnational God, whose loving nature makes him a God of justice.

To discover a God who cares and identifies himself with those who suffer oppression and injustice was a liberating experience to many Christians in Latin America. They had been told, so very often, that God was represented by the church. Yet, they had seen the church walking hand in hand with those who produced, for so long, that very injustice. By being taken to encounter the God of Moses, they saw a God who identified with them and committed himself to them in order for them to experience justice, which to them was experienced as liberation.

God lives out an identification for liberation. Going back to the Exodus passage we see that God lives out identification for liberation as an experience of justice. To landless people, living in slavery, he promised land: a land 'good and spacious', a land where they would see their children playing, a place where those children's mothers would not be concerned about the next bottle of milk for their little ones, where there would be plenty of honey to cure or even prevent their coughing. The vision that God gave them was connected to their daily needs. It was a vision that put them on liberating feet.

To people who were enslaved by an exploitative regime he promised a trusting walk into liberation. A liberation which would invite them to have the courage to go and to experience the opening of the waters, the guiding cloud during the day and the fresh manna every morning. Like most liberation journeys, theirs would not be an easy one. But the watching of the sunset at the end of the day, without having to work into the night at demanding jobs, was an unavoidable experience to feed their journey.

To people spread out in a slavery regime, he would promise to make them into a community, a people with identity. From now on they would have a name and not be a mere number. From now on they would not answer when someone called them simply 'you'; instead, they would identify themselves as being part of 'the people of the promise'. A promise to be fulfilled by their God, and they would become God's people.

While justice is not abstractly perceived, it is not romantic either. The justice journey is very realistic and tries to deal with our own reluctance and with a conflictive experience of reality. Moses had to face his own unbelief and suspicion as well as face Pharaoh and the whole package of the Egyptian exploitative system. Besides, in the journey of liberation the unbelief was there again and the people embraced it as much as their belief. They had also to face the fact that they were not going to an empty land. They must conquer an occupied land, which makes us ask the question of justice from the other side of the story. Even God seems to provide only what seems to be 'selective justice', which never stops short of being puzzling.

In the Exodus passage, God shows us the way and points to his own mission journey – a journey in which he 'comes down' because he listens well and cares deeply. A journey in which he shows on whose side he is and how committed he is to bring to reality a transformation path which takes the people from the experience of injustice to justice.

The main point is to affirm that in our missionary journey we need to listen, especially to those who are crying, who are suffering, and who are lonely. We must respond to their cry and go to those places where God is already present. Places of the orphan, the widow, and the stranger, in the prophetic language of the Old Testament, or the abused children, the single mothers, and the refugees, in the language of today. In such places the mission of the church needs to identify and embrace the path of liberation. In this path the powers of injustice are confronted and people walk into the experience of liberation, which is simultaneously an experience of God's guidance and providence.

> God turns toward the very places from which humans tend to turn away.
>
> (D. Bonhoeffer)

Falling in love with the God of justice!

It happened not long ago. Spending a day in a monastery with a friend, my eyes found a saying hanging on a wall. It was beautiful and I wanted to copy it in order not to forget it. It sounded fresh and invited me 'to do justice and to love kindness, and to walk humbly with God'. Surely and to my embarrassment I had not recognised a word coming from Micah. It was a classic, after all:

> He has told you, O mortal, what is good; and what does the Lord require of you but to do justice and to love kindness and to walk humbly with your God? (Micah 6:8)

Besides the fact that with age it is common to start forgetting things, I had to recognise that I was forgetting what I did not want to remember. As a survivor of the revolutionary dreams of yesterday I did not know, so very often, what to do with the word justice. As a witness of a new emerging day called 'neo liberalism' with their altar called 'free market', I became confused, especially when seeing so many churches bringing that altar into their worship places, repackaging the Gospel in order to adapt it to this new day and this new *cultus*. I did not know what to do with myself and my 'out of fashion' theology of the Kingdom of God, my own silence with what the 'Lord requires of you', and my own journey into the avenues of the *bourgeois*.

I might be using too many colours to describe a simple encounter with a momentously forgotten Bible passage. However, it became to me a moment of conversion and a parable of what should not be done: to 'forget' what is central and essential. The Lord loves justice and wants that justice to arrive and change the life of the oppressed, exploited, and abandoned one. There is a stream of living water that runs through Scripture and says continuously and clearly that:

- God is a God of justice, and loves it.
- Justice is not a mere concept but a relational reality that can be best seen in the life of the poor and the oppressed, witnessing their liberation. It is transforming justice.
- God's people will experience God's justice and are called to be an agent of that justice in this world.
- While the Old Testament speaks of justice quite often and very clearly, the New Testament does not repeat it with the same intensity, but endorses it in such a way that the new community of God has to be seen as a community of justice.

To us I say: The Word of the Lord and the cries of the people join in calling us to do more than count our blessings, more than shape our inwardness, more than reform our thoughts. They call us to struggle for a new society in the hope and expectation that the goal of our struggle will ultimately be granted us.[11]

The Southern church and the window of justice: is this an open avenue of mission?

From one of my trips to Bolivia, I still remember the title of a sermon heard in Santa Cruz de la Sierra. I was there for a pastors' conference and the evening was dedicated to open worship in one of the local churches. This is common there, and members from different churches are expected to come. They will come; you can count on it.

It was Wednesday and the worship ought to be special, since many pastors were around. I do not remember much of that evening service, but the title of the sermon still resounds within me: 'This is God's hour for Latin America'. While I never forgot that evening, I never really knew how best to look at such an emotional, affirmative expression. In fact, I was never able to overcome my mixed feelings about it.

That evening, the expression came out with force and excitement, as it happens very often in Latin America today. It's good to be at a place and to be part of a generation that sees the church (in this case, the Evangelical Church) exploding, in number and in ministries. In the number and sizes of church buildings and in the diversification and multiplication of their activities; in witness as well as in active participation in society. Today, there are more Evangelical Christians in churches and at the working place than yesterday. They are there in schools as well as hospitals; in the soccer field and in the world of arts. In publishing and at the Congress. Therefore, I listen to the title of that sermon and I say, 'Yes – that's it!'

But I also hear the sound of that statement with a sense of fear, challenge, and responsibility. Fear, because that statement lives at the frontier of arrogance – and arrogance is a killer of the same opportunity affirmed by that celebration. I must recognise that we Latin Americans get easily excited with events that make us happy. Yet all of us know that excitement tends to provoke feelings, expressions, and commitments that might not be sufficiently grounded in Scripture, in experience, and in daily life questions and answers. We need fear to make us sober. To make us reverent. To make us 'normal'.

We must be responsible before the open doors the Lord is giving us as well as to the many people coming to some of our many churches. In other words, we need to be responsible to the Gospel, to the community, and to our newcomers. For us to do that, we need to go beyond numerical growth, and do much more in solidly grounding our growth. This means many things: discipling our new Christians; mentoring our Christian leadership; developing a sound and con-textual theology; stressing a relational and service-oriented community; calling to and captivating our young generation; improving and deepening our evange-listic commitment and activities; strongly engaging in the discernment and proactive involvement in new and growing mission frontiers; consistently engaging in cross-cultural mission; making a transforming impact in society; and always praying *Maranatha*.

Each one of those 'grounding tasks' would require some careful grounding itself, and there are several ways in which we could address and evaluate those different dimensions. A very important one connects to our mission responsibil-ity within society – in social and economic terms. Our expression of connected-ness to a God of justice, who always calls for unjust structures within society to be transformed into structures that generate opportunity for life and life to be lived out in its fullness.

Let me be specific by talking about my own country, Brazil. The Evangelical Church, to which I am connected, has been historically a small and a minority church. It is a church that, throughout its history, has experienced small yet continuous growth. Its contribution to society, somehow, has outgrown its size, earning trust and credibility within our society. In more recent decades the church has become bigger and bigger as its influence has also grown. Today the Evangelical Church in Brazil, which is mostly charismatic and Pentecostal, is no longer a hidden minority as we have gained visibility and become a fact in society. In other words, the Evangelical Church today is seen and asked for. As a consequence of such growth we need to ask what sort of impact this very growing church is having on society.

A recent study of the Center for Public Policies of Fundação Getúlio Vargas, entitled *Economics of Religion in Brazil*, came up with recent trends concerning the religious landscape of Brazil. While the decreasing numbers of the Roman Catholic Church have stabilised, the Evangelical Church keeps growing and went from being 16.2 per cent of the population in 2000 to being 17.9 per cent of it in 2003. The study also indicated that this growth happened basically at the peripheries of the big urban agglomerations.[12] These are places where the state is mostly absent and the formal economy is barely existent. It is in those places that the Evangelical churches establish a network of survival and belonging for the disinherited of society. That is where the churches become so very often a symbol of God's caring love and a micro expression of some justice in a very cruel and unjust society. It is at that level that the presence of God's hour in this place of the world can be seen and embraced. It is the Gospel becoming an expression of grace, hope, and comfort to people living at the very outskirts of society.

The significant challenge relates to the movement at the macro level, whose need is undoubtedly there, and for the church to live according to its size and to capitalise on its influence and on the nature of the call of the Gospel. While the economic situation in Brazil has stabilised and is gradually flourishing the churches are keeping their micro-emphasis, which is necessary and important but not enough. In fact, when it comes to the macro level this segment of the church is performing badly. This can be seen at three levels. First, it is seen at the political level. With the church's growth, the need and the temptation to engage politically have become very real, and today 'Evangelicals' are identified as a group even at the National Congress. Our presence there could barely be worse. At that level those evangelicals are mostly playing according to the old Brazilian political 'clientele' model: the church members vote in their church's candidate as indicated by the senior leadership of that very church. Once elected, the goal is to get as many government benefits as possible for their respective groups. Some corruption schemes were recently uncovered and the names of Evangelical political representatives were unfortunately there.

The second aspect is one of a theological nature. By preaching a theology of prosperity, which is individualist and inspires competition, the earlier network of support is broken. *Economics of Religion in Brazil* established a comparison with the traditional Protestantism as interpreted by Max Weber and says that the 'emergent religious movements released the private accumulation of capital through the church'. It goes on to affirm that the 'more expressive link between the entrepreneur spirit and the religious organizations would be one of the marks of the new religious expressions in Brazil and Latin America today'.[13] In other words, the theology of prosperity might generate entrepreneurship and access to some wealth, but it generates neither community nor social awareness and commitment to justice, which are essential components of the Gospel of Jesus Christ.

The third aspect relates to a non-incarnational perception of reality while dealing with a spiritualised sense of reality. Life reality is demonised and dealt with at a non-historical level. Therefore, at the same church event demons are exorcised, prosperity is announced to 'everyone who believes', and a large amount of offerings are taken, with the announcement that God will only give to those who give.

Therefore, the same church that offers an embrace, dignity, and a network of support to the most outcast people of society is unable to transform such a network into a vehicle of search for justice, and to engage in that journey for justice. The church embraces and simultaneously exploits. It brings people out of misery but does not take them to a level of community and justice awareness. It helps the family to come together but does not help them to discover community. They support the poor but exalt only those who have experienced 'real prosperity' as a sign of their faith.

The little and forgotten town called Dr Ulysses is a small example of what I am trying to say. While 80 per cent of the town of 6000 people are Evangelicals,[14] it also has one of the lowest HDI (0.627), and is one of the poorest places of the well-to-do state called Paraná.[15]

Therefore, we need to construct a syllogism whose result is far from encouraging. If the church is growing at the rate it is, while the unjust structures of society are almost the same,[16] we need to ask: What kind of Gospel are we preaching, and what sort of church are we establishing? In other words, we are a non-challenging part of our unhealthy and unjust status quo. Social transformation is not happening while the church is growing. Furthermore, it is sad to say that it is not looking like this will happen tomorrow. The seeds we are planting will not provide a transforming harvest. The Gospel we preach does not have the flavour of justice. On the contrary, we are feeding an unjust social structure by preaching a Gospel of prosperity, embracing a dualist practice of spiritual warfare, practising cultural ethical standards, and promoting aesthetic values, which in Brazil are always sensual and rhetorical and are seldom an expression of a legitimate desire for a just society.

If this is the hour of God for Latin America we need to experience a conversion that calls for changes to the unjust patterns of society. Isn't this part of the mission of the church? Isn't this what the disciples were also called for? Isn't this what we, as members of God's church, need to do wherever we go and by whatever we do, as an expression of God's mission in the world of today?

> He went up the mountain and called to him those whom he wanted, and they came to him. And he appointed twelve, whom he also named apostles, to be with him, and to be sent out to proclaim the message, and to have authority to cast out demons. (Mark 3:13–15)

Prayer

> It helps, now and then, to step back and take a long view.
>
> The Kingdom is not only beyond our efforts,
> it is even beyond our vision.
> We accomplish in our lifetime only a tiny fraction
> of the magnificent enterprise that is God's work.
> Nothing we do is complete, which is a way of saying
> that the kingdom always lies beyond us.
> No statement says all that could be said.
> No prayer fully expresses our faith,
> no confession brings perfection.
> No pastoral visit brings wholeness,
> no programme accomplishes the church's mission.
> No set of goals and objectives includes everything.
>
> This is what we are about.
> We plant the seeds that one day will grow.
> We water seeds already planted,
> knowing that they hold future promise.

We lay foundations that will need further development.
We provide yeast that produces far beyond our capabilities.

We cannot do everything,
and there is a sense of liberation
in realising that. This enables us to do something,
and to do it very well. It may be incomplete,
but it is a beginning, a step along the way,
an opportunity for the Lord's grace to enter and do the rest.

We may never see the end results, but that is the difference
between the master builder and the worker.

We are workers, not master builders; ministers, not messiahs.
We are prophets of a future not our own.

(Prayer of Oscar Arnulfo Romero, 1917–80)

4. To Seek to Transform Unjust Structures of Society (ii)

Bev Haddad

Ministry in the HIV and AIDS South African context: palliative or transformative?

A journey into working with the poor

South Africa's history of racial oppression is well documented.[1] As a child of Lebanese immigrants, I grew up in a society that defined your identity by the colour of your skin. My maternal grandfather had secured our place in the society by ensuring our legal status as 'white', but he could not protect me from the social discrimination that I experienced in my daily life. For most of my childhood I accepted my privileged position in society and adopted the racist values of my family. It was only as a university student that I began to deal with identity issues and recognise my complicity in the system of *apartheid*. Ten years later, during the mid-1980s, I came face to face with what it meant *practically* to work with the poor and marginalised in our country.

Employed as a lay parish worker in a large, affluent, 'white' parish in the suburbs of Cape Town, we were called upon by the Western Cape Council of Churches[2] to offer our church hall as a temporary shelter for 'illegal urban migrants' whose homes (mostly constructed out of wood and plastic) had been destroyed by the South African authorities in an attempt to force families to return to the rural areas. It was the month of July, the coldest and wettest month of the year. Women and children arrived in our pristine environment with only the clothes they were wearing. Cold, hungry, sick, and despondent the group of about thirty huddled in a corner of the hall. It became my task to mount a relief and welfare programme over the next three months until the housing issue had been resolved with the relevant authorities. Those three months changed my life.

I came to understand more deeply that the poor were poor because social structures worked against certain groups of people in a systemic and unjust way. More importantly, I began to question why my faith, up until then, had not taken seriously what it meant to work for justice in a practical way and so bring about social transformation. At precisely this time, the *Kairos Document*[3] was published by a group of (mostly) Black theologians calling for the church 'to read the signs of the time'. The *Kairos* theologians mounted a scathing attack on the church's complicity with *apartheid*. They identified three types of theology: state, church, and prophetic and in doing so argued that for too long the church had supported the unjust status quo. The church, they declared, needed to embrace a prophetic theological stance that openly condemned racial injustice and took an option for the poor.

The following year, while pursuing theological studies, I devoured the work of Black South African theologians such as Itumeleng Mosala and Buti Tlhagale,[4] and Allen Boesak.[5] I probed the arguments of those in the Black consciousness movement such as Steve Biko[6] and began to read the work of liberation theologians such as José Bonino[7] and Gustavo Guiterriez.[8] It struck me anew, that to be involved in the work of social transformation meant fighting against injustice whatever the cost. Perhaps more significantly, the work of liberation theologians forced me to rethink whom I regarded as my main interlocutors and dialogue partners in my theological reflection.[9] Was it the poor? If so, what role did marginalised women play in my faith and practice? Ultimately, what kind of theologian and minister of God's liberating life did I seek to become? These and many more questions became clearer as I embarked on doctoral studies and worked as an assistant priest in a Zulu-speaking congregation in Vulindlela, a semi-rural community on the outskirts of Pietermaritzburg, KwaZulu-Natal in 1996. I continued in this position for three years, and returned to work in the area as a researcher and trainer in 2004.

During the early years of my work in this community, it was important to deal with issues of identity and subjectivity in relation to those I worked with. Giyatri Spivak[10] has argued that one of the tasks of the intellectual who works with those who are 'other' than herself is to 'unlearn one's privilege as one's loss'. This 'means working back critically through one's history, prejudices, and learned, but now seemingly instinctual, responses'.[11] If this 'unlearning' does not take place, there is a closing down of creative possibilities, of other options, and of other knowledges. Herein lies the loss. Through this process of 'unlearning' my privilege, I came to understand that my collaborative efforts needed to effect social transformation within *myself* and not just within those I worked with. Given my Lebanese ancestry and complex racial identity within the South African context, I came to realise that I had to make choices in constituting my identity. It was then that I chose to actively seek to be constituted by those who are 'other' than myself through collaborative work. I have thus consciously chosen to name myself as an activist-intellectual out of a commitment to *practical work* across the racial, cultural, and class divide. I am an activist-intellectual by choice, and I am also a woman-priest by vocation.

A key aspect of this collaborative work within the Vulindlela community has been the use of the contextual Bible study methodology. This method is premised on the understanding that both formally trained readers of the Bible and those readers who do not have this academic training have resources to offer one another. This approach embraces a number of commitments which all assume the central role that the Bible plays in the lives of poor and marginalised communities.[12] These include, among others, a commitment to read the Bible *critically* from the particular perspective of the poor and marginalised, as well as a commitment to read the Bible *communally* and *collaboratively*. Doing contextual Bible studies together with members of the community became the basis of all my social transformative work in Vulindlela. Initially, this was in work with a group of semi-literate churchwomen, and much later in work with both male and female church leaders.

HIV and AIDS: the new challenge

Before liberation in South Africa, my commitment to liberating praxis involved the struggle against *apartheid*. As pointed out earlier, the *Kairos* theologians declared that a *kairos* moment had been reached during the mid-1980s. The church was urged to regain a prophetic voice, resist the status quo, and challenge the prevailing state theology that justified *apartheid*. Twenty years later there is a new *kairos* moment. It is a moment when more than ever there needs to be a commitment to action that brings liberation and life to millions of people in South Africa and the rest of Africa.[13]

The HIV and AIDS epidemic is claiming the lives of people in our communities and congregations every day. It is estimated that 5.5 million people are living with the virus.[14] Research carried out in 2005 has shown that incidence rates continue to rise sharply with young women in the 15–24 year age group accounting for 90 per cent of new infections.[15] The same study has also shown that women in the 20–29 year age group are six times more likely to be infected than men of the same age. Mortality rates have increased by 79 per cent between 1997 and 2004, with a large proportion of these deaths attributed to the AIDS epidemic.[16]

In my early years of work in Vulindlela with women, getting anyone to openly acknowledge that HIV and AIDS existed, let alone that it was the 'sickness' that was killing their young people, was not an easy task. During the 1990s, people generally did not refer to HIV or AIDS directly. Rather, they referred to it as 'this thing' (*intoyakhe*) or named it as a more acceptable illness such as TB, chest pains, or pneumonia. Many declared that the family had been bewitched through evil spirits (*amagobhongo umeqo*).[17]

Working with Vulindlela women using the contextual Bible study method, the first opportunity to discuss HIV and AIDS opened up unexpectedly in 1998 while discussing Mark 5:21–43. This text includes a story of a woman who has been haemorrhaging for twelve years and touches Jesus' garment in order to be healed. At the end of the close reading of the text, I asked how the story might be the same for women today. One group member immediately responded, '*Ingculazi*' (AIDS). This response was unexpected because of the deep secrecy and silence surrounding AIDS in the community. Probing her further she replied, 'AIDS is comparable to this because it is incurable. The doctors fail to cure it, it eats you till you die.' A second member continued, 'It's just that in these days if you happen to be bleeding it is assumed that you have AIDS because the haemorrhage also was incurable, a person would die without it being cured.' The discussion continued as to how the woman with the haemor-rhage might be like a woman with AIDS. It was acknowledged that in both instances 'bad' blood ran through the veins of the women, suggesting the deeply personal and intimate nature of their illnesses. The Vulindlela women implied that because this was so, they had no one but God to turn to. This declaration led to the suggestion that in situations of 'blood diseases', it is the 'power of God' that also runs in their veins which enables them to have life in the face of these diseases that bring death. In smaller groups, they were then given the task of drawing a picture that showed the relationship between the 'bleeding woman' and HIV and AIDS. The first group clearly depicted a woman being infected by her partner through him having sex with many other women. The second group drew human figures running away from an infected woman, indicating the stigma and discrimination that was (and remains) prevalent in the community. It was only much later, in 2004, when I returned to work in Vulindlela as a researcher and trainer that I was able to address these issues of women's vulnerability to HIV infection as well as the deep-seated HIV stigma and discrimination that existed.

While teaching theology at the School of Religion and Theology, University of KwaZulu-Natal for the past four years, I became increasingly interested in understanding the response and role of the church in the HIV and AIDS epi-demic. During this period, the church was being recognised as a strategic player in curbing its spread in Africa.[18] Yet the church in South Africa had been slow to confront the crisis of HIV and AIDS. It was only when deaths of young people became so numerous that it was impossible to deny that a disease of epidemic proportions was at work, that small initiatives began. These largely took the form of palliative home-based care for those who had developed full-blown AIDS. Some prevention messages began to filter through to congregations, but these tended to be moralistic and judgmental. Stigma and discrimination deep-ened and increasingly those who were HIV positive stopped going to church. One woman declared, 'Church groups always come when we are dying or even already gone. But when we are trying to live with HIV, when we really need them most, Christians are nowhere to be seen.'[19] During an HIV positive sup-port group meeting, one participant stated, 'I would rather come to this Bible study than go to church.'[20]

From palliative care to social transformation

David Korten has argued that engagement in social transformative work in com-munities can be analysed along a continuum of what he terms 'generations of practice'.[21] The first generation of practice is that which responds to crisis situa-tions in the form of welfare and relief. Here, the external agent, be it the church or non-governmental organisation (NGO), plays the role of initiator. Second generation practice refers to what he terms 'community development'. It takes the form of local development projects carried out in communities to meet particular needs such as poverty, unemployment, or lack of food security. Here, the external agent plays a facilitative role, engaging with community members in setting up the project. Korten, recognising the limitations of these forms of engagement, has argued that for our work in communities to be truly trans-formative, there needs to be work at the level of changing policy and procedures (what he terms third generation practice), and at the level of mobilising movements of people for social change (fourth generation practice).

It became clear to me, that while the church was engaged in welfare and relief practice, there were complex structural issues pertaining to the epidemic, such as unequal access to anti-retroviral treatment, that needed to be addressed. The church was, and still is to a large extent, silent on this matter. Treatment issues are complex and require the church to intervene at the level of policies and procedures that are affecting those who are HIV positive and poor. It also requires that we join hands with existing social movements such as the Treatment Action Campaign,[22] to ensure equal and fair access to treatment for all those who need it. But even more worrying was the seeming impotence of church leaders to curb the epidemic by their words and actions. HIV incidence continued to increase in Vulindlela and the rest of South Africa. At clergy meet-ings, I would listen to them sharing their burdens about the increasing number of funerals they were leading each weekend. In 2004, I returned to work with church leaders of all denominations in Vulindlela in order to try and understand the epidemic from their perspective and to act as a catalyst for a greater and more meaningful response to the epidemic. At the first meeting, with about fifteen persons present, one leader summed up their mood by declaring, '*Kufana nokuthi sihlala kwabafileyo*' (It is like we are living among the dead).

So began my HIV and AIDS work with male and female church leaders over a two-year period. After a series of group discussions and individual interviews, together with staff of the *Ujamaa* Centre for Research and Community Development,[23] we pioneered a training programme that was conducted over ten weekly sessions. These trainings were held a number of times with same-sex groups and attempted to address a number of issues related to the HIV and AIDS epidemic in a contextual and culturally sensitive way.

If the training was to have any impact, it needed to begin by addressing 'policy' matters pertaining to stigma and discrimination. From my perspective, what was preached from the pulpit became 'policy' to the hearers. I became concerned by the increasing evidence that suggested that clergy did not believe the epidemic was a punishment from God, and yet continued to preach that people who were HIV positive were sexually promiscuous.[24] Clearly, leaders were in a dilemma; pastorally they would not condemn people, but when pushed to preach prevention, they were extremely condemnatory. This con-tradiction, I came to realise, had much to do with their limited and uncritical theological training. Gerald West has argued that the dominant theology within the church is a theology of retribution that argues that prosperity is a blessing from God and a sign that one has lived a good and moral life. As West points out, this kind of theology has little understanding of structural injustice and has tended to be propagated by those who benefit from systemic privilege.[25] It has devastating effects on those living with HIV and has also rendered the Vulindlela church leaders impotent. They have no way of explaining what God is doing in the world, and because of a lack of theological resources to deal with the magnitude of the crisis, they resort to what they know. Namely, if bad things happen to people, they must have done something wrong. Yet, they want to reach out to young people and their families. Their moralistic preaching far from being simply their judgement on sexual behaviour, it could be argued, is rather their desperate attempt to stem the ever-rising tide of death. So, a large aspect of the training programme attempted to develop *'positive theology'*.[26]

Linked to developing a theological framework that begins with the experiences of those who are HIV positive, is the need to encourage culturally and contextually relevant HIV prevention messages. Culturally, questions of gender subordination and patriarchy needed to be addressed. In the South African context, women's subordinate position means that they cannot negotiate safe sexual practices within their relationships. Startling statistics are emerging that show that married women are considered most vulnerable to infection because they cannot insist on condom use.[27] Issues of masculinity and the role men play in the spread of the virus were addressed directly in training with male leaders. In the training sessions with women leaders, space was created for them to share their experiences of sexual subordination and to discuss possible ways of dealing with the risks in their relationships.

The training programmes were well received and they have undoubtedly contributed to more open and frank discussion on the HIV and AIDS epidemic within church groups and from the pulpits on Sundays. However, there is still much transformative work to be done to ensure that the poor do not continue to be victims of the epidemic.

Organising movements for social change: ongoing future work

⌐As suggested earlier, for our work in communities to be truly transformative we need not just to tackle the immediate needs of people, but also to address unjust laws and policies.⌐This, as David Korten has pointed out, requires the mobilising of masses of people into a social movement to lobby and effect change. During the *apartheid* era, the South African church joined other groups within civil society to form social movements to resist racial discrimination entrenched in the laws and policies of the country. A good example of this was the 'Standing for Truth Campaign' during the late 1980s. The church was at the forefront of this campaign that involved masses of people of all races participating in acts of civil disobedience. This social movement was a small part of a much larger agenda that eventually brought down the system of *apartheid*, but it played a role and enabled the church to be an agent of social transformation.

The church has been slow to act in a similar way in addressing laws and policies that continue to make the poor vulnerable to succumbing to AIDS and eventual death. It is not incidental that the epidemic has largely touched poor communities in South Africa. Poverty is a key factor in the spread of the HIV virus. Poverty has also meant that anti-retroviral (ARV) treatment has not been affordable to the majority of infected South Africans. This time it has not been the church at the forefront of the social movement lobbying for universal access to this treatment through a sustained roll-out programme of ARVs in public health clinics across the country. It has been a movement of largely HIV positive people, the Treatment Action Campaign, who themselves have organised for change. The voice of the church is seldom heard on this matter while the poor continue to die.

The church in Vulindlela and elsewhere has an enormous opportunity to organise, mobilise, and lobby the government to continue ensuring that lives are not lost to the epidemic. As was the case during *apartheid*, we have the capacity to effect change, provided there is political and theological will, and the strategic use of our human and material resources. As suggested earlier, the church is seen as a key role player in the epidemic by the rest of civil society and yet its silence is deafening. The time has come to shake off the lethargy resulting from inappropriate theologies that keep us trapped in our moralistic impasse and to choose to embrace theologies that bring liberation and life to those who need it most at this time in our country's history. The South African church, including myself and others, needs to return to our social activist tradition. Congregations such as Vulindlela need to become hotbeds of social activism as they participate in local, national, and international campaigns to ensure that all who need treatment, including pregnant mothers, receive it.

This of course is not enough. The poor of South Africa and the rest of Africa will continue to become victims of the epidemic unless the structural causes of poverty are tackled. Herein lies the challenge, not just for the South African church but for the global church at large. Our God who is the giver of life calls us to share the material resources of the world so that even in the midst of the HIV and AIDS epidemic, all might experience well-being through access to basic human needs such as land, housing, and food security. In our globalised twenty-first-century world, this dream is even more elusive than ever for the majority of the population. So the call comes to us all. The work of social transformation is far from over and we each have a part to play in continuing to believe that we can make a difference to the lives of others. Belief, however, is not enough. Now is the time to act.

5. To Strive to Safeguard the Integrity of Creation and Sustain and Renew the Life of the Earth (i)

Calvin B. DeWitt

Creation is a symphony of material and life cycles empowered by earth's star the sun, whose energy drives global circulations of air and water – flows shaped by unequal heating and varied topography of land above and below the sea. Solar energy captured by green plants fuels molecule-to-molecule and organism-to-organism transfers, helping to weave earth's integrative biogeographic and trophic fabric that interlaces all life. Its creatures produce and consume, multiply and diminish, develop and decompose, each with peculiar roles in sustaining biospheric integrity. This is creation's economic fabric – Creation's Economy. As we human creatures are part of this fabric we are also its stewards – stewards of this symphonic gift, stewards with divine appointments to safeguard the integrity of creation and sustain and renew the life of the earth. Unfolding in the canon of Scripture, vindicated in Christ's resurrection, and celebrated in the Holy Eucharist, this economy is the comprehensive contemporary context of Christian mission.

'To strive to safeguard the integrity of creation and sustain and renew the life of the earth' – the fifth mark of mission – has been part and parcel of the human task since Adam. With its beginnings in Eden, this mark was affirmed by God's covenant with every living creature (Genesis 9), was vindicated through the sacrificial service of the Son of Adam, Jesus Christ (1 Corinthians 15), and incorporated in the Great Commission. God's love, expressed in the inexpressible gift of the Son of Man, brings hope for the whole creation – equipping people everywhere to serve and to safeguard the garden of God.

Living in the garden of God

Each of us inhabits a place on the earth – town or country, hill or plain, north or south. The place I inhabit, on the crest of a low drumlin shaped by continental

glaciation, looks out over a sodden jewel-in-the-landscape, blessed with creatures that emerge and return each spring to pulse annually across the great
marsh. I have devoted my life to safeguarding the integrity of God's creation.
Moreover, as I became aware of the immensity of creation's degradation and
destruction, I extended my care to include ecological restoration and renewal.
With my wife and neighbours, I get my hands dirty and feet wet to restore and
renew wetlands, prairies, woodlands, farms, and gardens to joyful beauty and
praise to their Maker.

> O sing unto the Lord a new song: sing unto the Lord, all the whole
> earth. Sing unto the Lord, and praise his Name: be telling of his
> salvation from day to day ... Let the heavens rejoice, and let the earth
> be glad ... Let the field be joyful, and all that is in it: then shall all the
> trees of the wood rejoice before the Lord. For he cometh ... to judge the
> earth: and with righteousness to judge the world, and the people with
> his truth. (Psalm 96, *Book of Common Prayer*, 1662)

The *oikoumene* of God

God's creation sings anew every morning in multi-part harmony. Creation's
Economy is an economy of divine faithfulness and steadfast love (Lamentations
3:22–23), declaring God's glory (Psalm 19:1), and manifesting God's divinity and
everlasting power (Romans 1:20). Writing of economy (*oikoumene*), in 1791, the
Swedish biologist Carl Linnaeus wrote:

> By the Oeconomy of Nature we understand the all-wise disposition of
> the Creator in relation to natural things, by which they are fitted to
> produce general ends, and reciprocal uses. All things contained in the
> compass of the universe declare, as it were, with one accord the infinite
> wisdom of the Creator.[1]

Eastern Orthodoxy reflects this perspective when it defines theology as: 'the
rational fruit of the study and examination of the whole work of Divine
Oeconomy, from the creation of the world until the last times ... realized by the
Church within history and time'.[2] Applying this to the local level, Calvin writes,
'Let him who possesses a field, so partake of its yearly fruits, that he may not
suffer the ground to be injured by his negligence ... Let him so feed on its fruits,
that he neither dissipates it by luxury, nor permits it to be marred or ruined by
neglect. Moreover, that this economy, and this diligence, with respect to those
good things which God has given us to enjoy, may flourish among us; let everyone regard himself as the steward of God in all things which he possesses.[3]

Creation's Economy contrasts markedly with our human economy. Poet and
artist, William Blake visualises these two economies as wheels – a small one as
human economy and a large as Creation's Economy.

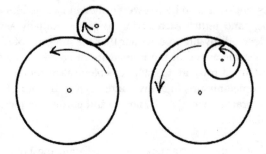

Fig. 1. Visual representation of Blake's two wheels. On the left illustration is the human economy (the smaller wheel) operating outside Creation's Economy (the larger wheel); on the right is the human economy operating within the larger Economy of Creation.

This is the way he expressed it:

> I turn my eyes to the schools and universities of Europe.
> And there behold the Loom of Locke, whose Woof rages dire,
> Wash'd by the Water-wheels of Newton: black the cloth
> In heavy wreaths folds over every nation: cruel works
> Of many Wheels I view, wheel without wheel, with cogs tyrannic
> Moving by compulsion each other, not as those in Eden, which,
> Wheel within wheel, in freedom revolve in harmony and peace.[4]

The wheel of Eden – the economy of which Adam and Eve were appointed stewards – was a wheel moving harmoniously within a wheel; Eden's economy cycled in harmony with God's creation. When it operates outside of Creation's Economy, degradation results.

Degradation of the life of the earth

God's commission to Adam to safeguard Eden suffered from his deciding 'to know good and evil'. Re-conception of the divine economy from all-embracing wheel and great teacher into 'natural resources' – begun in Adam – is now pervasive. The human economy has been translocated from 'wheel within wheel' to 'wheel without wheel'. Even its once-stewards and guardian-overseers are re-conceived as human 'resources'.[5] The result is that these two wheels now turn in opposite directions, with immense degrading consequences. Degradations of creation – beginning locally, extending regionally, and reaching globally – manifest an arrogation of Creation's Economy – a failure of people to be responsible stewards of God's gift.

Many of these degradations can be quickly identified – pollution of air, land,

and water, loss of farmland to erosion and salinisation, deforestation and habitat destruction, invasive species introductions, gene pollution, regional and global toxification, desertification, and urban growth that has escaped the boundaries of healthy development. Others are not, of which I identify three[6]:

Biogeographic restructuring of the life of the land

Study of the geographic distribution of plants and animals shows very evident displacement, reduction, and extinction by deforestation, putting lands into agriculture, and urban expansion. Global climate change compels organisms into new biogeographic patterns and relationships as they move toward the poles or to higher altitudes. A recent analysis of 1,700 species, for example, shows global climate change driving plants and animals some 3.8 miles per decade towards the poles. Climate change is bringing earlier springtimes, with an average decadal advance of 2.3 days. Species driven to extinction by global warming include those that can move no farther north and no higher in altitude, and become de-synchronised from other species thereby threatening survival or removing population controls.[7] There still is hope here: that human beings will resolve to reverse habitat destruction and address global climate change.

Trophic restructuring of the life of the sea

The history of ocean fisheries shows that over-fishing and removal of filter feeders (oysters and clams), grazers (herbivorous fishes), and predators (car-nivorous fishes) have restructured oceanic food webs. Preferential removal of the largest sea creatures from the top trophic levels of the food web has caused smaller species to take the vacated top consumer role. As these in turn are over-fished or succumb to disease from overcrowding, the next lower trophic level takes top place, spiralling the system downward toward 'microbialization'.[8] This trophic restructuring is signalled by collapse of commercial fisheries. The cod fishery of the European Union for example, dropping from 270,000 tons in 1977 to 38,000 tons in 2002 now has less than half the population needed to sustain it. Earlier, in 1992, the Canadian Atlantic coast cod fishery collapsed and no longer has enough mature cod for needed egg production. Yet, there is hope: understanding of ocean food webs provides the basis for taking action for ocean and fisheries stewardship.[9]

Global carbon imbalance

Living creatures are based upon the element, carbon – their primary structural substance. In its oxidised form – carbon dioxide – it provides a basic raw material for photosynthesis, the process that produces fuels and building blocks for creating and multiplying living things and for transfers within trophic food webs. Carbon is cycled within the biospheric fabric in producing and con-suming, multiplying and diminishing, developing and decomposing. Carbon is conserved and can be accounted for in a 'carbon budget' within and among 'reservoirs'. Of four major reservoirs, the atmosphere, terrestrial biosphere, oceans, and ocean sediments, the atmospheric reservoir shows a continuing rise in carbon dioxide concentration. The longest continuous records, from Mauna

Loa, Hawaii, show a 21.6 per cent increase in the concentrations for the month of February from 316.5 parts per million in 1959 to 384.9 parts per million in 2007 – a 21.5 per cent increase in 48 years. Current atmospheric carbon dioxide levels are 27 per cent higher than at any point in 650,000 years. Because carbon dioxide is a greenhouse gas, this increase portends a warming of the earth, already underway. Immediate action is needed.

These three degradations join others to show that earth is now under human domination. Globalisation of human impact extends human responsibility to the whole biosphere, requiring a global response even as local and regional responses remain as important as ever. Various Christian traditions, locally and regionally, can contribute significantly, particularly by bringing our human economies into respectful accord with God's greater economy.

Safeguarding the garden and Creation's Economy

The biosphere – owned by God – is a great gift and trust that is conveyed to the children of Adam for service and safeguarding. We learn from Scripture:

> The Lord God took the man and put him in the Garden of Eden to work it and take care of it. (NIV)

> And Jehovah Elohim took Man, and put him into the garden of Eden, to till it and to guard it. (DBY)

> And the Lord God took the man, and put him into the garden of Eden to dress it and to keep it. (KJV)

> And Jehovah God taketh the man, and causeth him to rest in the garden
> of Eden, to serve it, and to keep it. (YLT)[10]

In these various versions of Genesis 2:15, the Hebrew word, *abad* is translated 'work', 'till', 'dress', and 'serve'. We know from experience that gardens (and the biosphere) serve us – with good food, beauty, flavourful herbs, useful fibre, healing remedies, pleasant microclimates, soil-making, nutrient processing, and seed production. The biosphere provides 'ecosystem services' – including water purification by evaporation and percolation, moderation of flood peaks and drought flows by riverine wetlands, development of soils from weathering of rocks, and moderation of local climates by large water bodies. Yet, Genesis addresses *our* service to the garden. Service from the garden *to us* is implicit; service *from us* to the garden is explicit. What is expected of Adam, and of us, is returning the service of the garden with service of our own: a reciprocal service – a con-service, a con-servancy, a con-servation. This reciprocal service defines an engaging relationship between garden and gardener; between the biosphere and its human safeguarders.

Biblical principles of stewardship in context

The con-servancy principle: We should return the service of creation to us with service of our own

- We can call this 'never taking from creation without returning service of our own' the *con-servancy principle*. Our love of God our Creator, God's love of the creation, our imaging this love of God – join together to commission us as con-servers of creation. As con-servers we become followers of the second Adam – of Jesus Christ. As such we come to recognise ourselves as children of Man, children of God, for whose coming the whole creation awaits with eager longing and eager expectation (Romans 8:19).

The safeguarding principle: We should safeguard the Lord's creation as the Lord safeguards us

In our reflecting on Genesis 2:15 in four translations above, we find that we are to con-serve the garden and also guard and keep it. We find the Hebrew word, *shamar*, – to 'take care of', 'guard', and 'keep' also in the blessing of Aaron: 'The Lord bless you and *shamar* you.' As we expect God to keep us, God expects us to keep the garden. It is a wonderfully dynamic way of keeping, the kind of keeping given to long-distance runners that are not kept in padded cells, but put through their paces.

The fruitfulness principle: We should enjoy the fruit of creation but not destroy its fruitfulness

Being a fruitful expression of God's love for the world, the garden bears good fruit. So do the birds, the fish, and human beings (Genesis 1:20, 22, 28). When the prophet Ezekiel asks,

> Is it not enough for you to feed on the green pastures?
> Must you also trample them with your feet?
> Is it not enough for you to drink the pure water?
> Must you also muddy it with your feet? (Ezekiel 34:18)

he is speaking to this principle by saying that the creation's gifts are to be enjoyed, but not destroyed. Highly expressive of this is Noah, who with obedience and great effort safeguarded animal lineages, saving them on the Ark. From the Torah, we learn, 'When you lay siege to a city, you must not destroy the fruit trees' (Deuteronomy 20:19–20) – a basis for the Jewish teaching of *bal taschit* – 'do not destroy'. We must preserve creation's fruitfulness.

The Sabbath principle: We should provide for creation's Sabbath rests with no relentless pressing

'When you come to the land that I will show you, the land must keep a Sabbath to the Lord …' Knowing the importance of Sabbath each week, we also must know its importance for the land. Thoughtful reading of Exodus 23 and

Leviticus 25–26 gives us powerful reasons for not relentlessly pressing fields and streams, valleys and mountains, flowering plants and creatures of the sea. All things must have and enjoy their Sabbath rest. The exemplar for Sabbath keeping is the Creator of the world who established and blessed it on the seventh day.

The biospheric and covenantal context of stewardship

The biblical principles of *Con-servation, Safeguarding, Fruitfulness,* and *Sabbath* are at the core of human safeguarding and fruitful enjoyment of the garden and the whole creation – at the heart of stewardship and a mark of Christian mission. For the garden, the dynamic interplay between garden and gardener fosters a robust stewardship that yields an increase in knowledge, understanding, and wisdom. This wisdom in time can produce a plan for the garden to be in greater harmony with the principles of garden economy. Harmonious engagement of the garden's economy through interactive service is the essence of stewardship. Stewardship of the garden dynamically shapes and reshapes human behaviour in the direction of maintaining sustainability for garden plants and the garden over the generations.

Much as we strive to be stewards of the garden, we also strive to be stewards of God's creation. As our plan reflects the garden's economy, so God's plan reflects Creation's Economy – 'God's plan or system for the government of the world'.[11] Creation belongs to God:

> The earth (*'eretz*) is the Lord's, and the fulness thereof; the world (*tebel*), and they that dwell therein. (Psalm 24:1, KJV)

> The earth (*ge*) is the Lord's and the fulness thereof; the world (*oikoumene*), and all that dwell in it. (Psalm 24:1, LXX)[12]

In contrast with other great faiths, Christianity derives its pervasive influence by translation of God into the flesh in Jesus Christ, and of Holy Scripture into various languages in various cultures.[13] Psalm 24:1 is a case inx point, where the Hebrew words *'eretz* and *tebel* are translated respectively in the Septuagint (LXX) as *ge* (the root of the word *geology)* and *oikoumene* (from which we get the word, *ecumenical*). Placed into contemporary scientific context, *oikoumene* (οἰκουμένη) is translated *biosphere* – the contemporary name for the habitable earth with all its inhabitants. We can say then that the biosphere, owned by God, is the *biophysical global context* of human action and habitation in the world – it is the *biophysical global context* of stewardship.

This context joins with the *theological and covenantal context* toward development of a full and robust stewardship. The canon of Christian Scripture, 'both recounts the history of God's covenantal dealings with humanity and regulates God's ongoing covenantal relationship with his people' and, as the 'supreme norm for Christian life and thought', provides 'the abiding theological witness to God's pattern of communicative action in Israel and in Jesus Christ'.

Archbishop Rowan Williams, in his reflection on these quotations from Kevin Vanhoozer has us 'locate ourselves' within the 'set of connections and engagements, the history of Israel, called, exiled, restored, and of Jesus crucified and risen and alive in the Spirit within the community ...'[14] Located both within the canon – 'the instrument through which the Spirit of God ministers and administers the covenant ...' and within the biosphere – our principal source of knowledge on its workings and degradation by human action – followers of the Christ, are informed and equipped to do every good work in the world God loves. As the biosphere is the biophysical context, the canon is the theological and covenantal context of every human action and habitation in the world. Moreover, Jesus Christ, translated into the flesh by the Father's love for us, and upholding Creation's Economy as its Creator and Reconciler, is the Servant, whose service as the second Adam invites and inspires us also to serve. This is the contemporary context of the fifth mark of mission.

Our places of living and doing may be forests, prairies, ancient agricultural landscapes, and any number of other biomes and ecosystems. And so at the local and regional ecosystem level – in *ecosystem context* – our stewardship will be additionally defined and shaped. This will join with a global stewardship that gains and acts upon understanding from other stewards world-wide – stewards of tropical rainforests, montane ecosystems, lakes and streams, prairies and steppes, estuaries and oceans among them. While 'tending the garden' on a local scale, our global impact also requires our 'tending the creation' on a global scale. Our stewardship needs to operate locally, regionally, and globally to establish the conditions for healing and restoring the integrity of degraded ecosystems and the global ecosystem – the biosphere. The wisdom gained from the dynamic interplay between creation and us as stewards can be developed to bring our stewardship into accord with Creation's Economy. We can conclude that: Stewardship of the creation dynamically shapes and reshapes human behaviour in the direction of maintaining sustainability for ecosystems and the biosphere over the generations in biophysical and covenantal context.

The word made flesh

As we locate ourselves within the canonical drama of Adam and on through Israel to Jesus crucified, risen, and commemorated in the Holy Eucharist, we come to understand that Adam of Eden was 'the first Adam'. This Adam, prefiguring 'the second Adam', Jesus Christ, is envisioned by Milton in his wonderfully beautiful and inspiring Eden, singing at sunrise in Eden with dear Eve,

> Ye Mists and Exhalations, that now rise
> From hill or steaming lake, dusky or gray,
> Till the sun paint your fleecy skirts with gold,
> In honour to the world's great Author rise;
> Whether to deck with clouds the uncoloured sky,
> Or wet the thirsty earth with falling showers,
> Rising or falling still advance his praise.[15]

Yet, in the midst of immense beauty, fruitfulness, and pleasantness of Eden, Genesis tells of their dissatisfaction with the limits of the garden's economy. They yielded to the tempter's temptation – gaining such freedom from the garden's constraints that in another day the sons of Adam would proclaim, 'Come, let us build ourselves a city, with a tower that reaches to the heavens, so that we may make a name for ourselves …' (Genesis 11:3). They would now do things *by themselves, for themselves*. They made bricks *by themselves*, made a tower *by themselves* and *for themselves*. They made names *for themselves*. Believing themselves to be successful in breaking through the limits of Creation's Economy – conceiving it to be subservient to *their own* – they brought themselves to believe they were making new things that were 'bigger than life'.

Ever since, as the canon tells, people continued their pursuit of 'freedom' from God's economy – from creation's life-giving principles and wholesome constraints. Human gains in 'freedom' came at the expense of increasingly losing the life-giving service – ecosystem services – of Creation's Economy. This 'success' brought 'freedom' to take direct charge over things in creation that once produced free goods and free gifts of God's grace; people became the producers, as they also became creation's consumers.

As Adam was tempted, so was the Son of Man. And whereas the first Adam yielded, the second Adam resisted and overcame temptation, conquered death, and vindicated creation in his resurrection.[16] He appeared to Mary Magdalene as the gardener, ushered in the new Eden – the new creation – and fulfilled creation's eager expectation for the coming of the children of God (Romans 8:19).

The Word made flesh, dwelling among us (John 1:14a) became the focus of divine action in the world. As the Logos through whom all things were created, Jesus Christ, 'the hermeneutical key… to the history of the whole world, and hence to the meaning of life …'[17] initiated and led the process of undoing of the degrading works of the first Adam; initiated and leads in doing what the first Adam was supposed to do; and reconciles all things to God. The Word incarnate, expressing God's profound love for the world (John 3:16–17) comes liturgically into the sanctuary and the Holy Eucharist, moves into creation to open the shackles of enslaved peoples and creation, breaks the chains of sin, oppression, degradation, and bondage, and renews the life of the earth. Jesus Christ – the hope of the world.

> He is the image of the invisible God, the firstborn over all creation. For by him all things were created: things in heaven and on earth, visible and invisible, whether thrones or powers or rulers or authorities; all things were created by him and for him. He is before all things, and in him all things hold together. And he is the head of the body, the church; he is the beginning and the firstborn from among the dead, so that in everything he might have the supremacy. For God was pleased to have all his fullness dwell in him, and through him to reconcile to himself all things, whether things on earth or things in heaven, by making peace through his blood, shed on the cross. (Colossians 1:15–20)

Principles on the care of creation, gleaned from the canon, reverberate in Jesus Christ – the Logos through whom the whole creation has its integrity. Adopting the mind of Christ (Philippians 2:5–11), we take on his humility, not counting ourselves divine, but servants (Philippians 2:6–9). As was expected of Adam, achieved by Noah, and taken on by Christ, we also become servants – servants of the garden, of humanity, of the whole creation. Adopting his mind, we come to know him and participate in him incarnate in the Holy Eucharist.

The Holy Eucharist

As we eat the bread and drink the wine in the Holy Eucharist, we thereby become participants in Christ's crucified body and shed blood. As this fleshly participation brought his disciples to know him following his resurrection (Luke 24:30–35), so it is for us.[18] Christ's hospitality – 'a hospitality once and for all established as indestructible by the cross and the resurrection ...' – makes what Christ has accomplished to be 'done constantly in the history of the Church'.[19] Recognising his broken body and shed blood in the fruits of the garden, and also in their preparation by the gardener – the wine-maker and baker[20] – we experience a reciprocal service, a reciprocal communion, between garden and gardener. We experience a reciprocal service between the grain and grapes of the garden and ourselves as adopted children of the second Adam. The material food and drink, broken and poured out as Christ's body and blood, affirms the good creation and good steward of God's gift of creation.

Stewardship of reconciliation and renewal

With the now clear and abundant scientific evidence of adverse restructuring and transformation of creation's *oikoumene* by adverse human actions in the world, there is the clear and vital need for gaining substantial knowledge and understanding of the biosphere and for developing moral and spiritual courage and resolve to examine the message of the Christian church in the light of our global biospheric and covenantal context. The church needs to do what it can do best: 'to proclaim the full truth about the environmental crisis in the face of powerful persons, pressures and institutions which profit from concealing the truth'; and to strive for reform and replacement of practices and institutions that degrade God's creation.[21] The joyful task and honourable privilege of the church and of every member is to strive to safeguard the integrity of creation and sustain and renew the life of the earth – meeting creation's eager expectation for the coming of the children of God.

To do this↑ :
watch ¨ conspiracy¨

5. To Strive to Safeguard the Integrity of Creation and Sustain and Renew the Life of the Earth (ii)

Dave Bookless

The current series of ecological crises – of which human-induced climate change is merely the most obvious – is causing missions not only to react, but also to re-think at the deepest level. We live in a world today where our interactions with nature are having a profound effect not just on our environment, but on us as the human species, such that they call everything we do in mission into question.

An illustration from eastern India serves to illustrate how environment and mission are not separate spheres which occasionally collide, but that nature is both the context for all human existence, and a vital focus in mission. In the Krishna river delta of Andhra Pradesh, the Full Gospel Churches of India had been working for many years in evangelism and church planting. They began with an inherited Pentecostal understanding focusing exclusively on the first mark of mission – seen as 'saving souls'. As they travelled to remote coastal villages, the evangelists were shocked by what they found. The villagers were poor, illiterate, disease-ridden, eking out a living from saline soil, and, crucially, destroying the coastal mangrove swamps on which a whole ecosystem depended. Forced to rethink their missiology, the Full Gospel Churches of India eventually set up a 'Christian Coastal Development Project' (CCDP) during the 1990s. Starting with church planting and discipleship, the work grew to include education, medical help, and rural development (the second, third, and fourth marks of mission). Then the problem of the mangroves was diagnosed. Most villagers had lost relatives in floods caused by storms in the Bay of Bengal, and the once extensive local mangrove forests had disappeared in many places. The CCDP researched the possibility of a mangrove regeneration project, and, with funding both from the Indian Government and international development agencies, has now seen over 100 hectares regenerated. When, at an international mangrove consultation, they were asked how they achieved their remarkable success rate, they replied simply: 'We pray for every seedling when we plant it.' By restoring the natural environment, the needs of a community of people were also being met, and there was receptivity among villagers to the Christian message. Interestingly, the missiological response of the CCDP, motivated by compassion, came long before any real theological underpinning. So it was some years after the project began that I was privileged to lead a two-day workshop, translated into Telegu, on 'A Biblical and Practical Approach to the Environment' for about 50 workers from the Full Gospel Churches and World Vision. One of the staff commented that now at last they had a theology to explain what the Holy Spirit had led them into doing! As Martin Kähler stated in 1908, 'Mission is the mother of theology'.[1]

Today, not just in eastern India but across this fragile globe, each of the first four marks of mission is having to be re-examined as we wake up to the obvious truth that nature is the context for all we do and are.

- **Evangelism** (proclaiming the Good News) needs to grapple in its apologetics with the accusation that Christianity has nothing helpful to say about today's biggest question – how to have a sustainable relationship with planet earth. Indeed we also have to overcome the widely held perception that Christianity is to blame for the ecological crisis, through placing humanity as 'the image of God' on a pedestal above the rest of nature. It is a claim that is straightforward to refute theologically, but will people listen unless they see practical evidence of Christians taking care of the earth?

- **Discipleship** (teaching, baptising, and nurturing) must move beyond resourcing people's relationship with God and neighbour, to include our relationship with the land and the fellow creatures whose welfare we have been entrusted with.

- **Responding to human need in loving service** is increasingly becoming a self-defeating task unless we address the root causes of those human needs. As Bangladeshi relief worker, Nazmul Chowdbury bluntly states: 'Forget about making poverty history – climate change will make poverty permanent.'[2]

- **Transforming the unjust structures of society** must mean addressing not only the global injustices which prevent the poor from accessing development, but also questioning our very aspirations of development towards lifestyles we now find to be unsustainable. At the launch of the Stern Review on 'The Economics of Climate Change' it was rightly commented, 'The impacts are inequitable: poor countries will be hit hardest and earliest, when it is the rich countries responsible for three-quarters of greenhouse gases currently in the atmosphere'.[3] Yet, the nettle that nobody will grasp is this – while we believe in justice and a better life for all and support the aspirations of developing nations, there is simply not enough to go around if all earth's citizens want to live at the levels the West considers 'normal'. Statistics vary from country to country, but if everybody wanted to live at the levels of the average UK citizen, we would need more than three planet earths to support the world's current population. Justice must look not only at increasing access for the majority, but at drastically reducing the living standards of the wealthy western minority.

Historical perspective

Before examining some contemporary expressions of environmental mission, it is important to consider the allegation that this is simply an attempt to be relevant, with no historical or biblical basis as part of mission. This is a serious charge, and superficially carries weight, but ignores some crucial points:

- Mission histories often underplay the diversity of mission involvement. For example, the campus of Serampur College near Kolkata, set up by William Carey – the 'founder' of the modern Protestant missionary movement, is littered with large native fruit trees. Carey is often painted simply as an evangelist and Bible-translator, but he was also an accomplished botanist and passionate naturalist. His success as a missionary did not come out of a focus on evangelism alone, but from his healthy interest and curiosity in all areas of life. It was this that enabled him to find points of contact with his educated Hindu neighbours. Carey was by no means the only example of a missionary who cared for creation as well as for people.

- Mission histories often underplay the contribution of 'native' Christians. In many cases, the local knowledge of habitats, ecosystems, and soil types were actually preserved rather than destroyed by missions, and particularly by local converts. For example, St Joseph's Roman Catholic College in Tiruchappali, in Southern India, has founded a pioneering herbarium and helped to catalogue, study, and protect many rare plant species across South India.

- Mission needs to be seen as more than the story of the last 250 years. The modern missionary movement was itself influenced by the Enlightenment. Enlightenment rationalism enabled the industrial and scientific revolutions, precisely because it objectified nature, seeing it as something to be understood, described, and exploited for human progress. It was profoundly anthropocentric, putting human thought and development firmly at the centre, so it is not perhaps surprising that the modern missionary movement of the past 250 years has often reflected that anthropocentrism. If we look before and beyond 1750 in America and Europe, we find other, richer understandings of mission. Luther, Calvin, and other Reformers all had a more positive view of our relationship with nature than is often realised. Going back further, St Francis of Assisi redefined mission in his day, understanding humanity as part of a wider creation community, and according to legend preaching to the birds and animals. Before St Francis, the whole tradition of the monastic movement, which was the great missionary movement of the

Due Date Receipt

Name	Rubi Lopez
Call Number	BV2061.3 .M5 2008
Title	Mission in the twenty-first century : exploring the five marks of global mission /
Item Barcode	39844001423843
Due Date	12/04/2017 11:59:59 PM

Enjoy your materials, and please return them on time. Thanks for visiting your library

mediaeval era, was one where the relationships between land and people were closely integrated and intertwined. The same could be said of the Celtic missionaries, who (while often romantically interpreted through the eyes of the modern Celtic revival) saw God's self-revelation through nature as central, and who embodied a missiology that saw nature as God's greatest evangelist.

- Finally, mission that excludes the non-human creation stems from a biblically deficient definition of God's mission for humanity. This is a far-reaching claim, but not hard to substantiate. The over-emphasis on the 'missionary mandate' of Matthew 28:19–20, 'Go into all the world and make disciples', forgets that Christ's Great Commission is slightly different in each gospel, and in Mark 16 speaks of preaching the Gospel 'to the whole creation'. There is a simple equation of mission with humanity which does not stand up to biblical scrutiny. In fact, within the whole sweep of Scripture, we must remember that the first 'Great Commission' is the creation mandate of Genesis 1:26–28 – the call on human beings to be God's representatives and stewards in serving and preserving the non-human creation. Jesus would have seen this as the context for our entire mission, and so must we. The clearest illustration of this is in Genesis 6–9, where the familiar story of Noah's ark needs to be rediscovered missiologically. Like the whole of Genesis 1–11, this is paradigmatic for our understanding of God's creating and saving purposes, and shows the mission of humanity and the purposes of God directed in saving, covenant love towards the whole creation – almost marginalising human beings in the central emphasis on the preservation of biodiversity. Noah's missiology had no room for anthropocentrism!

Contemporary expressions of environmental mission

Today, there is a rapid, significant and often spontaneous movement towards ecological mission both around the world, and across the main Christian traditions. This chapter, while seeking to describe some diverse examples, is neither comprehensive nor representative, as it is inevitably flavoured by the author's own experience – as a CMS (www.cms-uk.org) partner, seconded to *A Rocha* (www.arocha.org) – the international Christian conservation agency. In particular there is a deliberate focus here on how the more theologically conservative parts of the Christian church (those who might categorise themselves as evangelical, Bible-based or charismatic) have been moving into practical expressions of environmental mission. While, as in any new movement, some projects with hindsight will be seen as knee-jerk reactions or ill-considered responses, there are also new models of mission emerging which are among the most creative and integrated examples of twenty-first-century mission.

Example: Boise Vineyard, Idaho
Environmental mission sometimes appears in unexpected places, and a good example is Boise Vineyard Fellowship in Idaho, USA. Generally, newer church

movements arising in the charismatic or Pentecostal traditions, such as the Vineyard churches, have not been the first to focus on environment. When, in the late 1990s, Pastor Tri Robinson decided to preach on 'Creation Care' out of a deep and growing conviction that this was both biblical and something prompted by God's Spirit, he was aware of the backgrounds of dispensationalist theology and political conservatism that many of his church would be starting from. As he says, 'I know that there are a lot of pastors and Christians who are very apprehensive about this message.'[4] To his amazement, his passionate message received his first standing ovation in 25 years of preaching, and rapidly led to a range of 'creation care ministries' undertaken by the church. These have grown to include a major recycling project, wilderness camps for high school pupils, partnerships with the Forest Service and the Boise Parks & Recreation Department, including trail maintenance and 're-leaf Boise', and a community garden, where food is grown in raised beds and then distributed among local socially disadvantaged families.

The environmental projects undertaken by Boise Vineyard have become an integral part of the church's overall mission. A television advertisement entitled 'Let's tend the Garden' led to the church gaining substantial numbers of new members from the local area. In terms of apologetics, some of the prejudices people have had against Christianity as irrelevant in a time of ecological crisis, have also been challenged. For instance, the church has received very positive coverage in the secular environmental media – such as an article on 'TreeHugger.com' which praised the church saying, 'One finds an evangelical vision of the environment and human beings' relationship to it that's both complex and nuanced.'[5] Moreover, the ministries undertaken by Boise Vineyard have deepened the church's involvement in all aspects of their local community – including issues of social deprivation and political engagement. This is not an 'add-on' to mission – it has become an essential part of the mission of God's people. As Pastor Tri Robinson says: '"Tending the Garden" is not a new commission to many Christians; it simply has been neglected by the Church. However, the Church can't just "take it back"; we have to earn it back. At Vineyard Boise we have acknowledged our shortcomings, have repented of them, and will endeavour, through our actions and ministry, to earn back the right to own this vital, biblical commission.'[6]

Example: Dronfield, England

A somewhat different example of environmental mission is found in the small town of Dronfield on the Derbyshire-Yorkshire borders in northern England. Here, the vision began with Norman Crowson, for years a keen birdwatcher, and also a committed lay member of his local Baptist church. Discovering that the new minister of his church was a botanist, they planned 'bird and flower walks' into the beautiful hills of the nearby Peak District, as part of their outreach into the local community, and to nurture fellowship among existing members (the first two marks of mission). Through contact with *A Rocha*, Norman was encouraged to consider linking his enjoyment of God's creation with our God-given responsibility to steward and protect the earth. This led to some church Bible-

Due Date Receipt

Hey girl - 2017

Name

Jessica Denham

Call Number

BV2061.3 .M5 2008

Title

Mission in the twenty-first century : exploring the five marks of global mission /

Item Barcode

39844001423843

Due Date

12/09/14 11:59:59 PM

Call Number

BS1375.6 .P68 F78 2004

Title

The decree of Esther : changing the future through prophetic proclamation /

Item Barcode

39844001255740

Due Date

12/02/14 11:59:59 PM

Enjoy your materials, and please return them on time. Thanks for visiting your library

studies based on Bishop James Jones' book *Jesus and the Earth,* and in turn to an 'eco-weekend', hosted by Dronfield Baptist Church. The weekend consisted of an environmental exhibition in which many local organisations participated, an evening with a talk explaining a Christian understanding of environmental responsibility followed by a panel with open questions, and a special creation-focused guest service on the Sunday. The church found itself in contact with a whole range of new environmentally concerned people, many of whom had previously regarded it as unhelpful or irrelevant. The next stage was both more ambitious, and also revealed a growing theological understanding of environmental work not simply as a method of reaching people, but as an integral part of Christian mission in its own right. Norman and his Baptist minister spoke to a local ecumenical grouping of 17 churches (Churches Together in Dronfield and District) suggesting that as part of a forthcoming 'town mission' there should be an environmental project. The project was to clean up an overgrown and rubbish-strewn urban river valley, and to manage it for wildlife and people. It was an ambitious project requiring substantial volunteer labour, co-operation with local government and conservation agencies, and an on-going commitment from the churches to maintain what they had begun. The results, though, have been beyond anybody's hopes. The Lea Brook Valley was cleaned and restored, with new nest boxes, a nature trail for schools, and improvements in biodiversity. In addition, the project was front page news in the local newspaper, churches had an improved relationship with their local council, there was a tangible demonstration of 'good news' for the local community, and both Christians and others were encouraged to re-think the scope of the Gospel.

Example: A Rocha Portugal – Cruzinha

Perhaps one of the most significant stories of the fifth mark of mission has been the remarkable world-wide development of *A Rocha*,[7] and so it is worth examining the roots of *A Rocha*'s vision and ethos in a little detail. In the early 1980s, a British couple, Peter and Miranda Harris, arrived in the Algarve region of Southern Portugal as missionaries with the Anglican agency Crosslinks (then known as BCMS). Peter is an Anglican clergyman, and the Harrises arrived in Portugal with an expectation that their primary missionary task was one of evangelism and church-planting in association with the Lusitanian Church (sister to the Anglican Church in Portugal). As most Lusitanian ministers also had 'tent-making' jobs, it was agreed that Peter's somewhat novel idea of a Christian-based Bird Observatory & Field Studies Centre might be a suitable 'way in' to ministry in the Algarve. Their story, told in Peter Harris' book *Under the Bright Wings*[8] carries many of the marks of classic first-stage mission – working to understand the language, culture, and community of the place they were in and to find bridges of relevance for the Christian Gospel. However, they also arrived with the beginnings of a more comprehensive vision, of the relevance of the Gospel to the environmental pressures that were facing the Algarve. The concept of a Field Studies Centre was not an excuse for evangelism, but stemmed from a growing awareness that creation provides the context for all our relationships, and community-living is a powerful (if risky) way of sharing the truth that the Gospel transforms all our relationships. The vision eventually took shape in an old farmhouse, Cruzinha, which became *A Rocha*'s first project, and the inspiration for what has now become a global network of diverse Christian conservation projects.

Over the last 25 years Cruzinha has seen a large amount of detailed scientific research – studying the ecosystems of, and the growing human impact upon, the Alvor estuary – the last 'unspoilt' estuary in the western Algarve. In an area surrounded by the marks of mass tourism – golf-courses, hotels, marinas, and apartment complexes – the headland, marshes, and estuaries surrounding Cruzinha have received growing recognition through *A Rocha*'s work, for their importance to threatened species varying from birds (little tern, Kentish plover) to plants (camphor thyme) to a small moth new to science. This has led to legislative protection for the site right up to European level (Europa 2000), and the recognition of *A Rocha*'s work by national and international conservation agencies. At the same time, threats to the site still remain, and there exists a fragile uncertainty as to whether the overwhelming pressures of development can continue to be resisted. Alongside the patient scientific study and occasional campaigning, other key strands at Cruzinha have been environmental education among local schoolchildren, and a strong emphasis on community living – embodying an integrated Christian vision of 'life together'.

This stems from an understanding that everything – and mission in particular – is about relationships. Ecology is the study of relationships between organisms and their physical environment. Mission is about the restoration of broken relationships between God, human beings, and the natural world. What is significant about the vision that has emerged and evolved at Cruzinha, and is now finding expression in *A Rocha* projects across six continents, is the way that it brings together all five of the 'Marks of Mission' in a naturally integrated way. People of very varied backgrounds visit *A Rocha* projects as volunteers, students, or simply as visitors, sharing a common desire to explore and study the natural world. They arrive with all the usual preconceptions and prejudices about Christianity, and are often relieved to find they are not 'preached at' but rather accepted and welcomed simply as fellow human beings. In *A Rocha* centres (and a residential field-studies centre is a feature of many well-established *A Rocha* projects), Christian faith is never hidden – prayer takes place before meals, and there are regular times for Bible-study and worship to which anybody is welcome. Neither, however, is Christian faith imposed, but rather it infuses every aspect of life – from cooking and washing up, to the standards with which scientific studies or financial accounting are conducted, to the value given to people as whole persons, and to every other aspect of creation. There are no splits between the five marks of mission – and evange- lism arises naturally out of relationships rather than becoming a task to be accomplished.

There is much that is 'classic mission' about *A Rocha*'s *modus operandi*. National *A Rocha* organisations are encouraged to follow Henry Venn's principles of being self-supporting, self-governing, and self-propagating. There are strong emphases on prayer and biblical reflection, on cultural contextualisation and national leadership, and on servant leadership and sacrificial ministry. Yet there is also much that challenges traditional missiological approaches. Peter Harris speaks of *A Rocha*'s DNA as consisting of five commitments – Christian, Conservation, Community, Cross-cultural, and Co-operation. 'Christian' and 'Cross-cultural' are standard in mission agencies, and 'Community' has been explored above, but it is worth examining briefly *A Rocha*'s understanding first of 'Co-operation', and of 'Conservation', as these have not often been part of modern Western missions.

A Rocha works in *co-operation* with other organisations and individuals for the protection of the environment. This means partnerships with secular conservation or environmental organisations, and sometimes with groups from other faiths. Rather than seeing these partnerships as compromising *A Rocha*'s Christian integrity, they are seen as ways of building bridges of trust, upon which lasting relationships can be constructed, and the Gospel can be shared. For instance, as well as partnerships at a local project level in terms of practical conservation, at a global level *A Rocha* is unique as a faith-based member of IUCN, the World Conservation Union. This gives an opportunity to influence the global environmental debate in terms of values and beliefs. Many are currently questioning the whole basis of modern environmentalism, with its faith in humanity to 'do the right thing' once enough research and education is done. There is a growing realisation that environmental issues are moral and ethical, and call into question our whole understanding of human nature, and of the value and importance of nature. Due to its practical track-record, and its patient relationship-building, *A Rocha* is uniquely able to contribute to this debate. Perhaps there is something about beginning with a theology of creation that allows *A Rocha* to accept people as created beings first, rather than categorising them immediately as 'atheist', 'Muslim', 'New Age', or whatever. Thus, instead of mission being a raiding party to bring people back into the safety of a Christian compound or ghetto, it becomes, as biblically it always should be, a participation in God's mission in transforming the world – people and the wider environment – into a Kingdom fit for the King.

This leads on to *conservation* – which in *A Rocha*'s terms has never been about the preservation of some mythical natural status quo, but rather about active involvement in studying, managing, and restoring a fragile and precious creation. As we saw earlier, the first 'Great Commission' in Scripture is not Matthew 28:19 but rather Genesis 1:26–28, the creation command to humanity to rule over and look after the earth and its creatures. In Genesis 2:15 Adam is told to 'tend and keep' the garden, words well translated as 'serve and preserve' – and this well describes *A Rocha*'s understanding of conservation. Environmental mission involves careful science in cataloguing and analysing species in their ecosystems, leading to management strategies that seek to enhance the earth's fruitfulness and biodiversity, not forgetting that human beings are part of the natural system and also have needs and aspirations. As Peter Harris says, 'In conservation terms *A Rocha*'s vision is quite wide really, because it's to see ecosystems restored, but it's also to see the well-being of those human communities that are dependent upon them; so you're talking about restoration ecology, but sometimes you're also talking about developmental economics, or sustainability.'9

Other examples of *A Rocha*'s work: Kenya, India, UK

A Rocha's integrated model of mission as starting with creation (while always including salvation), and including God's purposes for all creation (not only but including people), has now taken root in some very diverse settings and eco-systems. A few examples help as case studies to demonstrate the adaptability and contextualisation of this model.

In **Kenya**, *A Rocha*'s main base is at Watamu on the northern coast, and adjacent to a number of internationally important biodiversity areas, including the Arabuko Sokoke Forest. There are a number of critically endangered species of mammal and bird in the forest area, and threats from illegal logging for wood-carving and fuel. As well as conventional scientific studies and en-vironmental education, *A Rocha* has focused on the dilemmas posed by a growing economically deprived human community living alongside a dis-appearing ecosystem where species are threatened with extinction. It is a fascinating case-study in mission, because whereas conventional approaches (based on the first four marks of mission) would probably have focused entirely on the spiritual, social, and economic needs of local people, *A Rocha* has tried to take all these into account while also studying and protecting a threat-ened ecosystem. There is a deeply biblical but very simple logic to this – if God has made everything in a given area, and has provided enough resources for all, then surely our task is, with justice and integrity, to seek ways of meeting all these needs together? In the case of *A Rocha* Kenya, this has led to encouraging responsible eco-tourism, whereby Western visitors see rare wildlife while bringing much-needed money into the local economy. Agreements with local hotels and tour companies paying into an *A Rocha*-managed fund[10] have made it possible for local families to apply for bursaries for their children's secondary education. For local people it means their chief cash-need is being met, while simultaneously the pressures on the forest are lessened as people see it providing towards their livelihood.

In the enormous city of Bangalore, **India**, *A Rocha* has established a base and project led by Dr Vijay Anand, an expert in Indian elephant conservation. Once again, the competing demands of human and animal populations in a fast-developing country have provided the context, in this case the issue of human–elephant conflict. As Bangalore expands, and India's population con-tinues to soar well over 1 billion, there is inevitable pressure on land for farming, buildings, and transport. On the edge of Bangalore, Bannerghatta National Park provides a wildlife refuge, and the start of semi-contiguous forests that stretch for hundreds of miles. Elephants are no great respecters of fences, fields, or boundary posts, and will travel large distances at certain times of year, search-ing for food and water, or simply following ancient migration routes. *A Rocha* India has worked with the state Forest Department, with local village communities, and through direct field-based research, in order to understand the complexities of how humans and elephants can continue to live alongside each other. As in Kenya, holding together a solid scientific approach with a sympathetic understanding of local issues, has won considerable respect, and various methods are now being studied that can minimise harmful interactions between people and elephants.

Perhaps *A Rocha*'s most unexpected project setting is the heavily urbanised suburbs of Southall and Hayes, in London, **England**, but here too, the issues of how people and wildlife interact have become a focus for integral mission. Southall is one of the most diverse places in the UK, both ethnically and religiously, with huge Sikh and Muslim communities, but it is also a place that suffers urban deprivation. A poor environment and local people who do not relate well to their surroundings are factors in a vicious circle of deprivation. This has been recognised by Southall Regeneration Partnership: 'There is a lack of greenery, open space, clean air and environmental awareness – all of which contribute to a lack of confidence and pride in the area.'[11] As vicar of one of Southall's Anglican parishes from 1993 to 2000, I observed the complex interaction between people and their environment, and saw how a lack of connection to the land, the seasons, and God's creation contributed to both psychological and spiritual poverty. Having had prior involvement in *A Rocha* for some years, a vision slowly emerged of a Christian environmental project in the heart of the city. In explaining this, I found that certain phrases communicated this vision in ways that both local churches and mission organisations, and also secular political, environmental and educational bodies could relate to. This project was to combine 'environmental renewal and community transformation', aiming at 'making the urban desert bloom'. The tangible focus of the project was on transforming 90 acres of formerly derelict and rubbish-strewn land belonging to the local council, into the Minet Country Park and nature area, a good place for people and wildlife, and then supporting this with environmental education, practical conservation, and community projects. All of this was accomplished during 2001–2003, and *A Rocha* continues to work with the local council and the community in these areas. However, behind this transformation of the land was a wider vision of integrated mission. Not only is the Minet Country Park now a place of biodiversity and fecundity, but it has also become a symbol of hope at an individual and community level. People say things like, 'Now I believe things *can* change around here – before this I never thought they could!' The project has led to greater co-operation between local churches, a higher profile for Christians in a largely 'other faith' area, and many, many individual faith-sharing conversations. Generations of schoolchildren are now receiving opportunities to run up and down green hills, to pond-dip for tadpoles, and to simply enjoy wide open spaces. None of these are the whole Gospel on their own, but undergirded by prayer, good relationships, and the on-going work of local churches, they contribute to 'signs of the Kingdom' for individuals and the wider community.

Conclusions

As this chapter has tried to illustrate, the 'fifth mark of mission' is not an optional extra, or simply a contemporary reaction to our current environmental crises, but rather a genuine recovery of a biblically integrated understanding of mission. Mission is ultimately the *'missio Dei'* – God's mission to his world including both the human and non-human elements of that world. Our commission is to participate in God's mission, as ambassadors of Christ, who is not only the Saviour of the world, but the 'One in whom all things hold together' (Colossians 1:17) – the Creator and Sustainer as well as the Saviour. Mission that ignores creation will always present too small a vision of God and his purposes. Mission that encompasses caring for creation – as long as it always keeps Christ central and makes him known – provides a message of hope and of life in all its fullness. The good news of the Kingdom of God 'on earth as it is in heaven' is good news for people, communities, and for a groaning creation.

SECTION TWO:

Issues in Mission

---

1. 'Whose Religion is Christianity?'[1] Reflections on Opportunities and Challenges in Christian Theological Scholarship: The African Dimension

Kwame Bediako

Introduction: seeing Christianity afresh

In an article published in the centenary issue *of African Affairs – The Journal of the Royal African Society*, April 2000, I suggested as follows:

> What much of the study of Africa appeared to miss, perhaps because of a persisting Eurocentrism, was that the very conditions of Africa, as well as developments within the continent, were steadily making it into a privileged arena in some important areas of scholarship. For our present purposes, what is most striking is the enhanced place of Africa in the modern transformation of Christianity in the world, as, indeed, in the renewed significance of religion as a social force in human affairs more generally.[2]

Since then, the prospect that the majority of the world's Christians will be Africans[3] – either on the continent or in the diaspora – has attracted two contrasting reactions. One is that it will constitute 'the next Christendom', a relocation of power from Western churches and therefore a 'global' threat to the West.[4] The other reaction to this new reality of the Christian world is that it is the emergence of a positive 'polycentrism', in which the many centres have an opportunity to learn from each other.[5] On this understanding, the situation in which 'the centres of the Church's universality are no longer in Geneva, Rome, Athens, Paris, London, New York, but Kinshasa, Buenos Aires, Addis Ababa and Manila', as John Mbiti noted over twenty years ago,[6] indicates a decidedly post-Western phase of Christianity. It also makes it possible to explore pathways in Christian theology that take as their primary matrix the new theatres of Christian vitality. Accordingly, the new Christian reality in the world enables a fresh understanding of Christianity itself, so that African (as well as Asian or South American) perspectives can have relevance beyond their immediate settings.

Appreciating the significance of the African field

Christian theology as public discourse will relate primarily to the fortunes of Christianity in any given time and context. This fact makes it of crucial importance for any credible African Christian theological scholarship that one should appreciate the significance of the African evidence within the new Christian reality of the world. At the risk of flogging a dead horse, or at least a dying one, it cannot be stressed enough that the continuing influence of the stereotype of Christianity as the religion of the West, and of the West as 'the Christian West', means that no serious tradition of Christian theological scholarship will take off in Africa without adequate recognition of 'the Gospel beyond the West' (the subtitle of Sanneh's book referred to earlier).

It does not require exhaustive investigation to demonstrate that the history of Christian expansion from its origins is not marked by inexorable, uniform, and cumulative growth in every context of its manifestation. Through the successive shifts in its centre of gravity and relocation of its heartlands – from the Jewish to the Hellenistic world, to the Barbarian world of northern and western Europe, and into its present heartlands in the southern continents of South America, Asia, and Africa – the evidence of Christian expansion shows that both accession and recession belong within Christian religious history. This itself qualifies as a unique feature of the Christian religion: among all major religions, the Christian religion presents the unusual characteristic of being comparatively marginal in the land of its birth. One could reasonably conclude that there is no such thing as a permanent centre of Christianity. Every centre is a potential periphery, while every periphery is a potential centre.

As a result of the relocation of its centre of gravity to the southern continents, Christianity as a world religion now lives through other cultural, historical, linguistic, social, economic, and political categories than those that are dominant in the West. To persist with a so-called 'Western' paradigm in seeking to understand Christianity, therefore, could be positively distorting and disabling. This is so because the new phase of Christianity presents opportunities as well as challenges that are not generally available in the Western context. But perhaps more important, these opportunities and challenges have taken Christian theological scholarship 'into new areas of life where Western theology has no answers because it has no questions'.[7] This implies that if our knowledge of Christianity should continue to be shaped predominantly or exclusively by the more recent Western intellectual and cultural experience of it, we may be ill-equipped to recognise the opportunities and to deal with the challenges. Two elements of significance for the African field readily come to mind: the factor of religious pluralism and the factor of living data with which to pursue Christian theological scholarship afresh.

The factor of religious pluralism

In what was probably the last published work under his name, the late Adrian Hastings commented on the predominant presence of Christianity as a religion on four and a half of the world's six continents and concluded: 'One could reasonably claim that it is, in historical reality, the one and only fully world religion.'[8] However, what Adrian Hastings' observation conceals is the fact that Christians are now more dispersed than ever before. The new configuration of the Christian phenomenon in the world has brought to an end the notion of territorial Christianity, of Christendom. This development in the West, the supreme achievement of Charlemagne (742–814), endured in Europe and in the extensions of Europe, until relatively modern times. In Africa, two attempts to create Christendom in an 'ontocratic' arrangement that involved an effective union of throne and altar – in imperial Ethiopia and in apartheid South Africa – have both collapsed.

Now virtually all Christians the world over live in plural societies, comprising persons of diverse religious faiths or of none. How persons in such situations may live in harmony and contribute to a common human intellectual space has become a crucial testing of the public theology of every religious faith.

In this connection, so far as religious engagement in a pluralist setting is concerned, the modern West has less to offer than may be readily recognised. There are two main reasons for this. The prolonged experience of Christendom in the West meant that Western Christian thought lacked the regular challenge to establish its conceptual categories in relation to alternative religious claims, while the secularised environment that followed the Enlightenment has tended to suggest that specifically religious claims are no longer decisive. As a result of this two-fold Western handicap, the encounter with religious pluralism may lead to either religious polarisation, or else the diminishing of religious conviction. It is what Lamin Sanneh elsewhere describes as 'a situation that tolerates people to be religiously informed so long as they are not religious themselves'.[9] The African field presents some rather distinctive features with regard to Christian expansion. In the majority of cases, the expansion has taken place in the presence of other religious faiths. This situation has compelled modern African Christian thought also to establish its categories in the interface of African Christian convictions on the one hand, and the local alternatives, in particular the perennial spiritualities of the African primal religious traditions, on the other.[10]

This must mean that the experience of African Christianity has some unique contributions to make towards the development of a Christian theology of religious pluralism. However, because the 'Western' paradigm that was used in the interpretation of Africa by Western theology, including its missionary wing, for so long regarded the African primal traditions as 'primitive', with little or nothing to contribute, their theological significance remained obscured. And yet it is a new appreciation of the African evidence that has led to the increasing realisation that there are genuine religious affinities between the primal and Christian traditions. As a consequence, primal religions are now seen to constitute the sub-structure of the faith of the majority of all Christians of all places and periods in Christian history so far.[11]

There is a further dimension to this African evidence as it relates specifically to the articulation of Christian thought in a plural intellectual environment. In the post-Christendom West, religious pluralism has become an issue for discussion, with persons of other faiths seen as the 'irreducible other'. The early development of African theology, on the other hand, shows that religious pluralism was quite often the normative experience, and Christian identity was the major issue to clarify and articulate.[12] While in the Western Christendom paradigm, in which possible alternatives are presumed eliminated from both the context and theological existence itself, the development of African theology has shown that religious pluralism does not lie outside of theological existence and that an acknowledgement of the faith of others does not need to mean a denial or a watering down of one's own. In the Western Christendom paradigm, there is little that a Christian theologian can say about his or her faith to a person of another faith without becoming adversarial, while a person of another faith cannot encounter the Christ of Christianity, except on the terms of a Christian theology whose categories have been established with little reference to the faiths of others.

The factors that have shaped Christian thought in Africa have compelled a subversion of such a paradigm. After half a century of development, African Christian thought is yet to produce a 'confessional' or denominational theology. One early commentator rightly observed that African theology was 'not primarily an intra-ecclesiastical exercise'. Rather, it was a 'communicative' discipline, in which the overriding question remained: 'How can we best do our theology so that the Gospel will touch Africans most deeply?'[13] When extended into the realm of a Christian theology of religion, this question can become: 'How can we best articulate our Christian affirmations so that they express also the truth of those who inhabit other spiritual worlds?'[14]

The factor of living data

In relation to the second factor of living data with which to pursue Christian scholarship afresh, the recognition of the far-reaching significance of the African evidence for theological research was articulated most clearly thirty years ago, by the late Harold W. Turner. Turner, a New Zealander who studied theology in Edinburgh, Scotland, made his most notable contribution to scholarship following a deep exposure to, and study of, African Independent Churches.[15] In a volume of essays in honour of Harry Sawyer of Sierra Leone, *New Testament Christianity for Africa and the World*, Turner contributed an article on 'The contribution of studies on religion in Africa to Western Religious Studies'.[16] I have interacted with Turner's argument in my *Christianity in Africa – The Renewal of a Non-Western Religion*.[17] However, I recall it at this point, because I am not aware that Turner's ideas have been sufficiently farmed and followed up in much subsequent African theological research. But conceivably, that could not happen until there was an adequate and courageous recognition of 'the Gospel beyond the West'.

In that article, Turner argued that in all the regular Christian religious disciplines, ranging from Biblical Studies and Christian History to Systematic Theology and Christian Ethics, as well as in the Phenomenology and History of Religion, the African field threw new light on old issues because it yielded data that were both vital and contemporary. The particular focus of Turner's study was the African Independent Churches (AICs). With regard to Biblical Studies, Turner pointed to the ability of the AICs to penetrate into, and participate in, the reality of the biblical world in their modern situation. The evidence from the AICs indicated a new appreciation of the Bible as 'indeed a book for all cultures', in Turner's view. Thus when the Bible ceases to speak to 'our [Western] culture, we learn more about ourselves than about the Scriptures'.[18] Regarding Christian history, the AICs gave new insights into earlier and parallel movements in Christian history. Obviously operating with an organic view of Christian history, Turner drew the conclusion that areas of earlier Christian history that are poorly documented might benefit from the study of living manifestations of similar phenomena in modern times. With regard to Systematic Theology, Turner noted the tendency among AICs towards an ecclesiology that stressed the church as a community of the Holy Spirit, organised around Christ as source of life and power. Thus they raised the question as to what is meant by the marks or criteria of the church.

Turner thus commended the African evidence 'to all the Western religious disciplines not merely as a highly specialised field of enquiry, but as a field pregnant with new ideas, new methods and procedures, new categories and points of view, for use throughout their work'.[19]

Perhaps one needs to make clear that Turner's hermeneutic of the AICs soon became applicable to the broad spectrum of Christianity in Africa, as the AICs were in point of fact indicating the direction in which African Christianity was moving. But it is also important to note that Turner was not projecting the ascendancy of African Christianity in a triumphalistic way, nor was he uncritical about the evidence he was commending. I share both aspects of his approach. It is therefore important to understand fully the basis of his commendation:

> Theology as a science depends upon access to its appropriate data in their most authentic and vital forms. If we regard the data of theology as being the revelations and acts of the Divine, the post-biblical and contemporary manifestations of these data will occur less vividly in a dispirited Western Church with declining numbers and morale. On the other hand, the data will be more evident and accessible ... where the living God is taken seriously as present in the healing and conquering power of the Spirit, with a gospel-generated growth and a spiritual creativity and confidence. Here at the growing edges of Christianity in its most dynamic forms, the theologian is encouraged to do scientific theology again, because he has a whole living range of contemporary

data on which to work. It is not that these dynamic areas of the Christian world are free from imperfection; but being full of old and new heresies, they need theology and offer it an important task.[20]

I consider that what Turner wrote then was, and still is, important for African Christian theological scholarship. It is important to maintain that there are properly theological categories, methods, procedures, and perspectives for elucidating and making intelligible developments on the plane of history that find their ultimate source in 'the revelations and acts of the Divine'. Nowhere does Turner suggest that a diversity of approaches is not admissible, but the important methodological principle that Turner sets forth is that the field of study itself provides the most appropriate methods for its investigation.

Opportunities and challenges: some pointers arising from the significance of the African field

Doing theology afresh

If one dimension of the significance of the African field is that 'Here at the growing edges of Christianity in its most dynamic forms, the theologian is encouraged to do scientific theology again' – to do theology afresh – to investigate, elucidate and make intelligible 'the revelations and acts of the Divine', then what might be the challenges that attach to these opportunities?

But perhaps a prior, fundamental question is not out of order. Does theology have a place and a role in public discourse, bringing its unique contribution to the shaping of a commonly shared human intellectual space? Or, in the face of the opportunities of the African field, will theology be tempted to succumb to what has been called, in the context of the post-Christian West, 'Christian theology's false humility'? This is 'the tendency to allow its social contribution to be shaped and defined by the secular disciplines of political science, economics and sociology', as Katongole has written.[21] Drawing upon Stanley Hauerwas in his 2001 Gifford Lectures, *With the Grain of the Universe: The Church's Witness and Natural Theology*,[22] Katongole continues:

> It is this tendency that gives rise to the project of natural theology, which in effect amounts to an attempt to divorce Christian claims about the world from the concrete practices, characters, and stories in which those claims are embodied; such claims can then be displayed as the truth of anyone. In *With the Grain of the Universe*, Hauerwas sets out to show that the project of natural theology is misconceived. Natural theology, he argues, 'divorced from a full doctrine of [and practice of] God cannot help but distort the character of God and accordingly of the world in which we find ourselves'.[23]

Within the limits of this paper, I am not able to pursue to the full all the details of the argument as Katongole advances it. And yet it seems that the main point is made and has relevance for us. In the cultural world of Africa, where arguments of the proof of the existence of God are largely pointless, because there are no doubts about God's existence, if theology should demur from a full-orbed Transcendence, then might theology as a discipline be in danger of losing its soul? What is meant here is not the uncritical supernaturalism that Kwasi Wiredu rightly criticised.[24] Rather, what is being urged is an appropriate recognition, as Kwame Gyekye has shown, that the African perception of the universe is that of a spiritual reality. 'What is primarily real is spiritual.'[25] In *Christianity in Africa*, I have argued that by courageously drawing upon this prevailing African 'primal' sense of the holistic, fundamentally spiritual character of the universe, African Christian theological scholarship can hope to regain a unified and organic view of the knowledge of truth, and so avoid the destructive dichotomies in epistemology which, since the European Enlightenment, have gradually drained the vital power out of Christian theology by shunting its affirmations into the siding of mere opinion.[26]

If, then, theology can face up to the challenge of its own self-image in public discourse, then it could reasonably be expected to face also the challenges that attach to the factors that demonstrate the significance of the African field that we have identified.

A new approach to religious pluralism

In his *Theology in Africa*, Kwesi Dickson posed the question:

> Is the theologian adequately defined as a spokesman for a particular religion, that is, Christianity? Or is the theologian one whose understanding of the revelation of God has been tempered and enriched by an insight into God's self-disclosure in other religious traditions? Is the term theology fully meaningful when used in relation to the life and thought of strictly one group of people, that is, Christians?[27]

In these questions, to my mind, Dickson was framing the results of African Christian thought having had to learn to establish its theological categories in the interface with the vital realities of African religious life. For, by all indications, in African theology, it is religion and the findings in the history and phenomenology of religion that have become the handmaid of theology. Indeed, Dickson expressed himself quite emphatically on the point:

> The theologian who fails to recognise the structures of religion as revealed by the historian of religion ... may not notice the absence of religion from his/her theology.[28]

Here, might the opportunity offered by the African evidence entail therefore the challenge of a new approach to religious pluralism that reaches beyond mere conversation and discussion on the topic, to serious inter-religious and inter-faith engagement?

A recent article by Tahir Sitoto, a Muslim scholar in the School of Religion and Theology, University of KwaZulu-Natal, is an indication of what might be possible.[29] Writing on 'The ambiguity of African Muslim identity with special reference to Christianity', Sitoto makes use of my own attempt to articulate an African Christian identity. After quoting from my *Christianity in Africa* to the effect that,

> An important dimension of Africa's role as the 'laboratory' for the world may ... include the vindication in the modern world of the viability of Christian religious discourse, as not outworn and to be discarded, or about which to be embarrassed, but rather as fully coherent with human experience and fully meaningful within the history of world redemption.[30]

Sitoto then comments:

> Although Bediako has attracted some criticism from African theologians and other scholars in African religion, what is discernible from a reading of Bediako here is that his perspective is located squarely in an articulation of a Christian identity that is boldly African in outlook. For Bediako, it is the acknowledgement of the African character of Christianity, which makes Christianity a truly universal faith. In other words, without an African identity, Christianity remains provincial.[31]

Sitoto's article and its demonstration of genuine inter-faith engagement illustrates how, in fact, Christian theology in Africa, in the context of the new Christian reality of the world, without denying its commitment to its own received tradition, may put its findings to service within a larger framework of a commonly shared intellectual discourse.

The challenge of living theology

In relation to the factor of living data, African theological scholarship will confront perhaps its most demanding challenge to maintain an alertness and a vigilance over its criteria, methods, procedures, and categories of description, analysis, and interpretation. Because theological categories are unlikely to constitute the dominant frame of reference in public discourse, here the temptation is at its most acute to succumb to a 'false humility'. And yet, the essential point has to be made: theology may not lose its soul. Harold Turner, whom I cited above on the contribution of the African evidence to Western religious studies, wrote in another connection:

> Cultural, anthropological, psychological, sociological, political and other models have proved their value in the elucidation of the interaction between religions and their milieux. Religion, however, cannot be equated with culture, society, morality, psychic processes or political systems and the distinctive features of religion escape us if we reduce it to any or all of these other categories, no matter how intimately it is

interwoven with these aspects of the total reality. We need therefore a religious model for the study of the 'religion' of African religions.[32]

The important thought here is that 'the nature of the field of study must provide the major control over the methods employed'. If this is a sound principle, then categories derived from Christian life, history, and thought will provide the major control in Christian theological scholarship.

A case in point is the role of post-coloniality in the investigation of Christian phenomena.[33] It is futile to deny the colonial entanglements with the Christian phenomenon in Africa; and yet it also remains true that from the actual evidence on the ground, the nature and the significance of African Christian life reach beyond the Western colonial connection. This means that the post-colonial paradigm can be restrictive and, when used exclusively, can be distorting. The early studies of AICs provide a good illustration of this. Many of the early investigations tended to focus on their sociological and political causes, as protest movements against the colonial arrangement. Rarely were religious and properly Christian factors taken into account. Only later did it become more widely acknowledged that the Christian faith in Africa had, in fact,

> had a liberating effect, setting men free, free from fear, fear of witches and the power of darkness, but above all conferring a freedom from an inner dependence on European tokens of grace or favour, to aim for higher things and a finer sensitivity.

The words are those of Bengt Sundkler in his book, *Zulu Zion and Some Swazi Zionists*.[34] Part of the process I am referring to of eventual acknowledgement of religious and properly Christian factors in understanding independency is reflected in the difference between his pioneer study, *Bantu Prophets in South Africa*[35] and the later *Zulu Zion*. Anyone interested in understanding Sundkler's interpretation of the AICs needs to study the two books together, noting the differences between them. It is possible to show that the post-colonial perspective may sometimes fail to reach beyond the perspective of *Bantu Prophets in South Africa* to the realisation that Sundkler came to in *Zulu Zion*.

The need for a larger intellectual framework

If, therefore, one will have to reckon increasingly with 'the Gospel beyond the West', this will make it all the more important to arrive at a larger intellectual framework than post-coloniality for describing, analysing, and interpreting African Christian history, life, and thought. As it has been shown that the c-oming of African political independence from Western colonial rule proved a 'relatively insignificant factor' for African Christianity,[36] it is important to take seriously that Christianity has now entered a post-Western phase. This makes the category of 'post-missionary' a larger framework, in fact, since it recognises that the Christian faith in Africa is not ultimately determined by Western paradigms of interpretation.

Related to the importance of a larger intellectual framework than post-coloniality is also the factor of African indigenous languages. It is now widely recognised that at the specific level of religious experience, African Christianity is lived largely in African indigenous languages, rather than in the colonial languages, which, admittedly, have also become African languages. This means that the impact of African indigenous languages as reflectors of African experience of reality, cannot be treated as marginal to African Christian interpretations of existence. In this regard, it is perhaps significant that in many African languages, God-talk is non-sexist.[37] It could be revealing if this characteristic of African languages were to be more fully explored in African women's theology. At least, it would have the advantage that one could be drawing on African indigenous resources in critiques of African patriarchy, and so be less inclined to resort to the re-invention of the assumption or presumption that male violence was somehow intrinsic to Africa. The non-sexist character of African indigenous God-talk, in turn, could have its own impact upon the understanding and interpretation of biblical material, when the latter is passed through the prism of African indigenous languages. Thus scriptural exegesis may stand to gain from African indigenous languages.

From the standpoint of theology as the fruit of the engagement of the Gospel of Christ with culture, the failure to draw upon these and other indigenous resources will mean that the impact of the Gospel upon African life, thought, and action might become blunted. Paradoxically, therefore, by learning to become more African in inspiration and methodology, African Christian theological scholarship will be making African Christianity less provincial but instead more truly universal!

Conclusion: a twist in the tale?

We noted earlier on that one reaction to the new Christian reality of the world has been to see it as a 'global' threat to the 'old' Christendom, the hitherto 'Christian West'. And yet it is self-evident that the new heartlands of the Christian faith are in the economically and politically more vulnerable regions of the world. When Walbert Buhlmann wrote *The Coming of the Third Church*,[38] in which he commented on the southward shift of Christianity's heartlands, his view was that 'the migration of the Church towards the Southern hemisphere' meant among other things that the Church was turning towards the poorer peoples of the earth and there to find the opportunity not only to be in a real sense the Church of the poor but also to have some experience of the goodness, humanity, simplicity, and integrity of poor peoples.[39]

Does it matter, theologically, that this has occurred while 'the levers of global economic and political power have remained located in the post-Christian West'?[40] Is there any symbolic significance for theology that the new configuration of the Christian world globally recalls the social origins of Christianity in the New Testament? Does this constitute an opportunity for theology to investigate afresh the mind of the Crucified and Resurrected Saviour who is the Lord of history, according to Christian theology, and who taught: 'Blessed are you poor [not because you are poor but] because yours is the Kingdom of God' (Luke 6:20)?

However, the poor themselves may prefer prosperity and so desire a theology of prosperity![41] Theology has the option of following these desires of the poor and so of rewriting its agenda along secular lines, or else of discerning here a heresy, which therefore gives theology an important task. If it should pursue the latter course, it could well come upon a strange divine irony: God chooses the lowly things of this world to confound the mighty. Theology then retains a distinctive prophetic voice in public discourse.

In the Scriptures of the Christian church, the foundation documents of Christian tradition of divine self-revelation, prophetic discourse about God and the world was always public discourse, offered in a commonly shared human space. Perhaps the greatest opportunity and challenge for African Christian scholarship in the new Christian reality of the world is to seek to restore theology to its rightful place in the public domain.

This article was first published in *Journal of African Christian Thought*, Vol 9 No 2, December 2006. It is reproduced here with the permission of the author.

2. Migration and Mission: The Religious Significance of the North-South Divide

Jehu J. Hanciles

> The *migration model* that has functioned admirably through the centuries is also an avenue for mission in our days. Migrants from poor countries who travel in search of economic survival carry the Christian message and missionary initiative with them … This missionary presence and activity has been significant though it seldom gets to the records of formal institutional missionary activity.
>
> Samuel Escobar, *A Time for Mission* (2003)

Few factors are as consequential in the history of the human race as migration. Migrant movement, stimulated by myriad factors and considerations (including sheer survival), is intrinsic to the human condition. Indeed, migration has been described as 'an irrepressible human urge'.[1] Within a wide range of possible modes of interaction and reactions, human migration has the capacity to expand cultural diversity and significantly alter demographic, economic, and social structures. Large-scale migration has been, and remains, integral to the processes of globalisation; and the contemporary world order, including the global religious landscape, was fashioned to a significant extent by extensive migrant movements. The link between migration and global religious expansion remains profound and inextricable and, importantly, both phenomena have intensified in recent decades. It has also becoming increasingly clear that (as in previous eras) current patterns of migration will potentially have an incalculable impact on religious interactions in the course of the twenty-first century.

Such is the extraordinary upsurge of people movements since the 1960s that the present period has been termed 'the age of migration'.[2] According to UN estimates, international migrants totaled 191 million in 2005. This number, which represents 2.95 per cent of the world population or roughly the size of Brazil's population, may seem inconsequential. Yet it means that one in every 34 persons on the planet lives outside his/her land of birth or citizenship. It is also no small matter that the number of international migrants in the world increased by 150 per cent in the last four decades and more than doubled in the 30-year period from 1975 to 2005.

But to understand why international migrations have escalated in volume, velocity, and complexity in the last half a century requires careful study of the global impact and legacies of European colonial expansion. For four and a half centuries (roughly 1500 to 1950), international migration was shaped by the needs and purposive designs of European imperialism. European initiatives and movement fomented a new world order, one characterised by advanced communication technologies, new modes of travel, an interstate system, unprecedented global interconnectedness, and menacing economic inequalities. In these complex developments lie the principal explanations for the direction and extraordinary upsurge in international migratory flows that typify contemporary experience.

European colonialism, migration, and mission

From the late fifteenth century, Europeans appropriated and occupied vast territories in the Americas, Africa, Asia, and Oceania. Europe's colonial project and mercantile needs, centered on the establishment of plantations for the large-scale cultivation of sugar, cotton, coffee, and tobacco, was the principal driving force behind trans-regional migratory movement. Between 1500 and 1800, only a relatively small number of Europeans – perhaps several hundred thousand – migrated as settlers, artisans, entrepreneurs, and administrators. But plantation economy was labour intensive and the insatiable demand for cheap labour became the motivational force for the organised and wholesale transfer of millions of non-European people. The most remarkable of these involved the enslavement and forcible transfer of some 10–12 million Africans to the Americas. In sheer numbers the movement of Africans exceeded that of European out-migration within the same period by about five to one.[3]

However, European migration intensified from 1800 to 1925. An estimated 50–60 million Europeans moved to overseas destinations during this period.[4] By 1915, 21 per cent of Europeans resided outside Europe and Europeans effectively occupied or settled in over a third of the inhabited world. This, the most remarkable human migration on record, was instigated by a combination of industrialisation, massive population growth in Europe, and colonial expansion.

But migrations of non-European peoples remained significant. The abolition of the grossly exploitative system of African slavery in the nineteenth century did not eliminate the ravenous needs of Europe's massive empire. African slavery was gradually replaced by the use of indentured workers recruited (often forcibly) as the chief source of labour for plantations, mines, and railway construction in Europe's imperial projects. Once again, European economic needs and political ventures accounted for the forcible or coerced intercontinental transfers of non-European peoples from and to areas under the direct or indirect control of European powers.

In 1865 when slavery was officially abolished in the United States there were about 4.5 million Africans in that country – the largest African population to be found outside the continent. According to one estimate, the indentured system involved 12 to 37 million workers between 1834 and 1941.[5] Indentured labour not only compensated for the loss of slave labour but also involved huge migration movements in which Asian peoples featured prominently.[6] Between 1830 and 1916, for instance, 1.5 million Indians were shipped to far-flung areas of Britain's growing empire as semi-free indentured workers.[7] In short order Indian populations emerged in East and South Africa, the West Indies, and the South Pacific. By the end of the twentieth century roughly 9 to 10 million Indians were living outside their county.[8] Well over 2 million Chinese were also contracted and shipped to the Americas, South-East Asia, and South Africa in the course of the nineteenth century.[9] Thus, for an almost unbroken period of 400 years, European economic growth and industrial expansion was serviced to a great extent by the blood, sweat, and lives of non-European peoples throughout its extensive colonies.

The missionary impulse

Intimately intertwined with the extraordinary swell of European migrant movements and imperial action were equally unprecedented missionary initiatives. By 1500, Europe was the heartland of the Christian faith. European identity and self-understanding were defined and shaped by 'Christendom', a religious-political construct in which Christianity was understood as a territorial reality. The understanding and mentality that flowed from this concept informed European colonial expansion and missionary enterprise. European nations, both Roman Catholic and Protestant, believed that their greatly superior military and technological powers, as well as their vast territorial appropriation, reflected God's providence and purpose. They were also convinced that imperial acquisitions were providentially ordained for the expansion of the Gospel of salvation. These beliefs, codified in the doctrines of 'divine providence' and 'manifest destiny', exemplified the explicit acceptance of the link between empire and Christian mission.

The implications were paradoxical. While the conversion of non-European peoples to the Christian faith was taken quite seriously, missionary action became fettered to political aggression and economic exploitation; and while European missionaries often made extraordinary sacrifices in their efforts to preach the Gospel in distant lands, the missionary project was blighted by attitudes of cultural and racial superiority. The link between colonialism and mission was complicated but undeniable. The Western missionary project not only derived considerable impetus from the expansion of Western prestige and power, it also spearheaded the spread of Western knowledge, culture, and values. Colonial structures and initiatives came to be regarded as vital for effective missionary enterprise on account of what colonial presence guaranteed: the establishment of law and order, safeguards for religious freedom, and unlimited access to new regions. Instances of international co-operation notwithstanding, foreign missionary operations were energised and defined by nationalist fervour and allegiance; and foreign missionaries typically looked to their home government for political protection in the same way that they depended on their home country for sustenance.

All this is not to suggest that missionary initiatives were wholly motivated by imperial designs or that the link between the two was inevitable. The missionary impulse is intrinsic to the Christian faith and missionary activity. For this reason, mission often outdistanced the reach of empire – as in the case of Jesuit efforts in China and Japan or later Moravian initiatives in Greenland. During this period also, some missionary initiatives embodied *anti-empire*; notably the transatlantic movement of American blacks, whose emigration to West Africa in significant numbers from the late eighteenth century represented a counterfoil to colonial missions. Nineteenth-century faith missions were also partly motivated by 'a determination to operate in isolated and unfamiliar territory, as far as possible beyond any European influence or colonial rule'[10] – though this aspiration overlooked the possibility that the distinction would be lost on non-Western peoples.

Surprisingly, the critical role which the rising tide of migration played in the nature and scope of the Western missionary movement is little recognised. The migration element is arguably one reason why the two European projects (missions and colonialism) largely coincided in geographical extension and historical existence. The Western missionary represented a segment of the massive tide of European migrations which characterised the period under review. The tide and flow of missionary activity was an undercurrent in the much broader sweep of migration movements. As noted above, one in five Europeans migrated between 1800 and 1925, the largest migration movement in history. This period also coincides with the most dominant phase of the Western missionary movement, when it achieved its greatest spread and impact. The overlap in the timing and extent of these two extraordinary movements is hugely significant. To the extent that European missionary movement reflected larger migration trends, its shape and size were also affected by migrant flows. The two ebbed and flowed together.

Global migrations from the 1960s

In the long run, Western initiatives and migration movements helped to create a new world order and stimulated the global spread of Christianity. Typically understood or assessed as one-directional in its impact, this process had many unintended consequences. In particular, it unleashed powerful forces of change which have acted back on the Western world and now impact the new world order in significant ways. The unprecedented rise in non-white migration is one of the most prominent examples. In this regard, it is worth bearing in mind that these migratory flows 'generally arise from the existence of prior links between sending and receiving countries based on colonisation, political influence, trade investment and cultural ties'.[11] Furthermore, in the same way that earlier European migrations were attended by a massive missionary movement, the recent and even more voluminous migration movements are also marked by tremendous missionary activity, with equally far-reaching implications for the global religious landscape.

Contemporary international migrations are unanticipated products of European colonial expansion, and the new world order fashioned by it, in two important ways. First, colonialism established the transnational structures, interstate system, global networks, and economic order that frame (as well as distinguish) the present era of global migrations. Second, the dismantling of European colonial structures from the late 1950s unleashed powerful forces within the non-Western world which have triggered phenomenal migration movements. Britain provides, perhaps, the best example of this historical connection.

By the early twentieth century the British Empire encompassed almost a third of the earth's inhabited surface and roughly a quarter of its population (well over 500 million people).[12] Mass immigration from the colonies to Britain had already begun by the late 1940s and was galvanised by the attraction of labour opportunities in Britain in the wake of the Second World War.[13] Even so, the dismantling of this global empire precipitated a flood of workers and aspiring citizens from far-flung lands. The migrant influx from struggling democracies and impoverished economies in former territories in Africa, the Caribbean, and Southeast Asia was unprecedented. Pushed out by troubled postcolonial economies, many Commonwealth subjects emigrated *en masse* to Britain to seek work and a new future. By 1981, there were 1.5 million non-European immigrants in Britain (60 per cent from Africa and South Asia). In 1972, when Ugandan dictator General Idi Amin expelled 80,000 African Asians – people whose settlement in East Africa was a direct result of British imperial policies – the British government faced a major crisis. Many of the deportees held British passports. Amid feverish public debate, Britain admitted 28,000 in two months – the largest intake of the decade.[14]

At the height of British colonial rule, also, the Queen of England had more Muslim subjects than any Muslim ruler. And colonisation of Muslim lands also opened Britain to Muslim migration and settlement from the late nineteenth century.[15] But the most significant growth of the Muslim population came from successive waves of post-Second World War immigration. The partitioning of India (and the creation of Pakistan) caused massive displacements, which coincided with the guest worker programme and stimulated huge migrations to Britain, especially from the Punjab.[16] Additionally, British universities attracted a growing foreign student population from oil-rich Muslim countries, from the 1960s. Overall, the Muslim population surged from roughly 21,000 in 1951 to an estimated 369,000 in the early 1970s.[17] By 2006, they numbered 1.6 million (almost 3 per cent of the total population).[18]

The great reversal
From the 1960s, international migrations have escalated into a truly global phenomenon no longer dominated by European needs and initiatives. But the direction and composition of migration movement has radically altered. Until the late 1950s international migration chiefly involved movement from the highly developed, politically powerful, nations to areas in the non-Western world characterised by agrarian (or pre-capitalist) systems and relatively weak

political institutions. Since the 1960s, migrant movement has been predominantly from areas with weak economic and political systems to the centres of global dominance and advanced industrial growth. The vast majority of migrants now come from the non-Western world and the main destination countries include the European nations that have previously been the main emitters of international migrants.

But demographic patterns and economic considerations remain unchanged. Now, as then, international migration flows are from densely populated parts of the world to areas of relatively low population density. Just as millions of Europeans once braved perilous conditions and horrible dangers to seek a better future and fortunes outside Europe, millions of non-Europeans are now desperate enough to endure all manner of hardship and even imperil their lives in a bid to reach Europe and North America. In a world where the richest 1 per cent receive as much income as the poorest 57 per cent,[19] the inverse relationship between demographic growth and economic development is a potent catalyst in the build-up of pressures which stimulate mass migration. In the poorer developing nations of the South, demographic expansion, anaemic economic conditions, and socio-political turmoil generate intense pressures for migrating to the much wealthier, stable democracies in the North where low fertility has also created huge labour demands.[20]

The reverse flow of international migrations coincides uncannily with the onset of population stagnation and decline in Western societies. According to the Population Reference Bureau, the rate of population growth in more developed countries 'peaked during the 1960s, at about 2 per cent annually, and has declined since'.[21] By the early 1990s it was already clear that the vast proportion of all future global population growth would take place in developing countries (of the South): over half in Asia and one-third in Africa.[22] By 1999, 82 million people were being added every year in less developed countries compared to about 1.5 million in more developed countries.[23] With Africa, Asia, Latin America, and the Caribbean accounting for more than 80 per cent of the world's population, the pattern and volume of international migrations are unlikely to change any time soon. Of particular interest here is the fact that South-North movement constitutes a major component of contemporary trends.

South-North migration movement

In the last half century, South-North migration, involving swelling tides of guest workers, labour migrants, asylum seekers, political and economic refugees, as well as family reunification, has been a dominant element in international migration. South-to-North migration is clearly rooted in global realities, primarily the daunting economic divide, demographic imbalances, and increasing global connectivity. To reiterate, it is impossible to account for the massive upsurge in international migrations from the late twentieth century without reference to the systems or structures erected by wealthy Western nations.[24] Quite frankly, the combination of global integration and the ever-widening divide between the wealthy industrial North and the nations of the 'developing'

South has transformed the former into a veritable magnet for migrant movement. Since the 1960s, migrants from the South have accounted for an increasing percentage of immigrants in wealthy developed countries.

In the US, the proportion of migrants from the developing world rose from 40 per cent in 1960 to 90 per cent by 1990.[25] In Canada and Australia, the rise in the proportion of migrants originating in developing countries (from the early 1960s to 1990) was even more striking because it was relatively low in to begin with – from 8 and 12 per cent to 70 and roughly 52 per cent, respectively.[26] Although data incompatibility bedevils analysis, European countries have also experienced a dramatic rise in the number of migrants originating in the South.[27] In Britain, where the proportion of migrants from developing counties has remained fairly high (compared with most European countries), a general decline in numbers from around 64 per cent in the late 1970s to 48 per cent in the late 1980s has been followed by a sharp rise.[28] Non-Western migrant inflows to Britain more than tripled from 43,790 in 1991 to over 114,000 in 2004 – one of the most significant increases of any developed country.

Overall, the last four decades have witnessed a massive upsurge in South-North migrations. In Canada, Britain, and America, non-Western migrants constituted on average 70–80 per cent of all immigrants between 1994 and 2004. Between them, Europe and North America had 96.9 million migrants by 2000 – more than half of the estimated 175 million migrants world-wide. The dismantling of the Soviet Union and the redefinition of borders are contributing causes to the massive increase in Europe's migrant stock, but the most important factor has been the dramatic rise in South-North immigration.

Until a little over a century ago Western Europe was dealing with the effects of overpopulation and the burdens of imperial expansion. It exported tens of millions of its peoples, along with its religion and culture, to much of the non-European world. Now, with its native population steadily shrinking at a rate that will see a further 3.5 per cent reduction over the next decade, its need for substantial immigration is enormous. Yet, far from being a welcome presence, non-European immigrants have been met with xenophobic hostility and rejection. Growing anti-immigration sentiments in Europe, fuelled further by acts of terrorism, have seen a fierce backlash against immigration and immigrants, compelling European governments to implement increasingly restrictive immigration policies. But the impulses stimulating mass migration are often too strong for restrictions to be fully effective. Non-white migration (legal and illegal) has proven to be largely unstoppable.

The religious implications: a brief word

Contrary to a popular assumption within the globalisation discourse, Western civilisation is not sweeping all before it. Paradoxically, the global spread of socio-economic modernisation may be contributing to a widening of cultural disparities between the West and non-West. In Western societies, the process of modernisation has witnessed distinctive cultural changes associated with the secular ideal of liberal democracy: notably, stronger individualism, a greater push for gender equality, sexual permissiveness, a weakening of the institution of marriage, as well as greater tolerance of divorce, abortion, and homosexuality. Non-Western societies are not static, but they remain resistant to secularisation (at least Western forms of the phenomenon) and retain strong allegiance to religious systems and traditional values. Present trends indicate that this cultural cleavage will steadily widen as younger generations in the West become more liberal and secular while their counterparts in the non-West (especially within the Islamic societies) remain deeply traditional.[29] Rapid population growth within strongly religious non-Western societies combined with stagnant or negative demographic patterns within increasingly secular Western nations will also contribute to this divide.

This widening gap in religiosity between the West and non-West is supremely relevant to any assessment of the potential impact of non-white (South-North) migration on Western societies. Due to the pervasive religiosity of the non-Western world, the South-to-North migration movement arguably translates into a religious movement. This is to say that, in addition to the economic and cultural benefits which the new immigrants bring, they are also impacting Western societies in fundamental ways related to religious life. Generally speaking, their communities and ways of life represent a visible alternative to the hedonism and libertinism of secular society, and their cultural values have contributed to fresh debates within Western countries about cherished liberal democratic principles like freedom of (religious) expression and individual rights. The dilemmas posed by radical Islam, for instance, have already 'forced plenty of Western countries to sacrifice some liberties in the name of security'.[30] In a word, contemporary global migrations implicate the West as a site of new religious interactions which portend long-term transformations of Western societies.

It is also significant that Europe is confronted with the growing presence of immigrants (predominantly Muslims) 'at precisely the moment when the historic religions in Europe are losing control of both the belief systems and lifestyles of many modern Europeans'.[31] Largely due to immigration, Islam now represents Europe's fastest-growing religion and its second-largest faith. The number of Muslims on the continent has tripled in the last 30 years – estimates in 2005 ranged from 20.5 million (or 5.4 per cent of the European population) to 51 million (roughly 7 per cent) – and an even higher rate of growth is forecast for the near future.

To the bewilderment of highly secular Europeans, religious devotion and affiliation among Muslim groups remains strong decades after settlement within modern industrial society. Assessments of the level of religiosity among Europe's Muslims tend to be conflicting: prominent Islamic scholar Tariq Ramadan asserts that less than 40 per cent of Europe's Muslims attend Mosque frequently[32]; yet, one survey found that 80 per cent of Muslims in London attend Mosque regularly.[33] Even Ramadan attests that some 70 per cent of Europe's Muslims fast during the holy month of Ramadan. The point at issue is that Europe's Muslims by their presence and growth signify the resilience of religious vitality and the endurance of religious commitment. And it is the fact that avid religiosity flourishes practically unchecked within modern industrial society – not only among less modernised, or 'backward', groups but also among urbanised European-born Muslim youths and the highly educated[34] – which troubles fundamental assumptions about secularisation and European visions of the future.

But while the growth of Muslim populations in Western societies commands the most attention, recent shifts within global Christianity and the concomitant rise of a non-Western missionary movement – inextricably linked to South-North migrations – have equal, if not greater, significance for long-term religious trends within the West.

Recent shifts within global Christianity and the making of a non-Western missionary movement

It is now a commonplace that global Christianity experienced an epochal demographic shift in the last half a century. The shift is the product of two extraordinary trends: massive recession from the faith in Western societies (the traditional heartlands) and phenomenal growth in non-Western societies within Southern continents (notably Africa, Latin America, the Pacific, and parts of Asia). According to the *World Christian Encyclopedia* (2001), roughly 2.7 million church attendees in Europe and North America cease to be practising Christians every year (an average loss of 7,600 every day).[35] Throughout Europe, the Roman Catholic Church (Europe's largest Christian constituency) has declined by more than 30 per cent in the last 25 years.[36] Harvard political scientist Robert Putman estimates that church attendance in America had fallen by roughly 25 to 50 per cent in the last four decades.[37] Meanwhile, massive numbers of adherents are joining the church or renewing their commitment to Christianity in Latin America, Africa, and the Pacific. In Africa alone the net increase is estimated at 23,000 new believers a day.[38]

It is possible to argue that explosive population growth in the non-Western world skews Christian growth trends. But it is worth bearing in mind that similar demographic changes in Europe and North America coincided with downturns in religious vitality, partly because existing church structures were ill-equipped to cater for the attendant surge in migrations.[39] In the event, by the dawn of the twenty-first century, more than two of every three Christians (65–70 per cent) lived outside the West, compared to less than 5 per cent two centuries ago.[40] In 2006, there were almost as many Christians in Latin America as there were in the entire world in 1900. By 2025, according to one estimate, Africa and Latin America will together account for at least 50 per cent of the world total Christian population,[41] underlying their status as the new heartlands of the faith. This southward 'shift', which has seen the emergence of Christianity as a non-Western religion, represents one of the most profound religious transformations in the world within the last half a century.

The timing of the transformation points to the strong possibility that it is intimately linked to the same historical processes that have shaped the current era of global migrations. It is intriguing that this historic shift in global Christianity's centre of gravity coincides with the equally momentous change in the structure and composition of global migrations. Both have profound implications for global religious interactions; both signal the critical (and historic) link between migration and mission which has driven Christian expansion since unnamed migrant refugees preached the Gospel to non-Jews in Antioch (Acts 11:19–20).[42] To put it explicitly, the fact that the direction of inter-regional migratory flow is now primarily South to North and East to West, where it was once primarily North to South, preserves the vital association between missionary enterprise and migratory flows from the heartlands of the faith.

Precisely because the heartlands of global Christianity are now in the South, contemporary South-North migrations form the tap-root of a major non-Western missionary movement. Western missionary initiatives remain the most visible but are no longer the most dominant or consequential. Through migrant movements, Christian missionary activities are criss-crossing the globe in unprecedented fashion, mainly through trans-national networks. Among the swelling tide of guest workers, students, labour migrants, asylum seekers, political and economic refugees, and family members of previous migrants are innumerable Christians, each one a missionary in some sense. As Samuel Escobar recognises, Haitian Christians have ended up in Canada, Filipino Christian women have gone to Muslim countries, and Latin American evangelists can be found in Japan, Australia, Spain, and the US.[43] African migrants, he may well have added, have dispersed throughout the Western world. Western missionary agency – which chiefly targets impoverished countries in southern continents – continues to dominate missiological analysis. Yet, the growing presence of non-Western immigrants and proliferation of immigrant churches implicates the largely post-Christian West as a new frontier of global Christian expansion.

Post-Western Christians and the post-Christian West

In sheer numbers America has been the chief Western missionary-sending nation since the Second World War,[44] and the US remains a major missionary-*sending* nation.[45] Yet, America is the quintessential immigrant nation. By the early 1980s some two-thirds of all legal immigrants world-wide came to the United States[46]; today, one in ten Americans is foreign born and, as noted above, the vast majority of its new immigrants come from developing countries in the South. The impact of recent non-white immigration on America's religious landscape is far-reaching.[47] Among other things it has transformed it into a major missionary-*receiving* nation. It may also be providing a significant counterweight to the downturn in Christian observance and church attendance.

Data from the New Immigrant Survey (2001) indicates that the majority of America's new immigrants (some 65 per cent) claim to be Christian – of whom 42 per cent identified themselves as Catholic and just under 19 per cent identified themselves as Protestant.[48] These figures mean that the new immigrants include a higher percentage of Catholics than the native population (22 per cent). And among Catholic immigrants, Hispanics constitute the vast majority. By 2000 one in four American Catholics was Hispanic,[49] and Mass was being celebrated in Spanish in some 3,500 Catholic parishes throughout the US.[50] Massive Hispanic immigration is a major reason why the Roman Catholic Church in the US has avoided the fate of Catholicism in Europe – even if one must allow for large post-immigration defections of Hispanic Catholics to vibrant charismatic churches. By 1998 there were 7,000 Hispanic/Latino Protestant congregations nationwide, most of them Pentecostal and/or evangelical.[51]

In major American cities where Hispanic, Korean, and Chinese congregations have proliferated vigorously, the religious landscape looks less and less European.[52] Recent research confirms that the new Christian immigrants 'are expressing their Christianity in languages, customs, and independent churches that are barely recognizable' to ordinary Americans.[53] To be sure, immigrant churches in America (and elsewhere in the West) mainly attract and cater for immigrants. But, in a context where multiplicity of choices is valued, their presence multiplies the spiritual 'options' available to potential converts, and, most important, many are increasingly adopting strategies aimed at reaching across cultural/ethnic/social divides.[54] Furthermore, immigrant churches and pastors often find that being in the US affords them ample resources for international missionary outreach unavailable to them in the impoverished economies of their home countries.

In Europe also, the new immigrants include large numbers of Christians whose presence has contributed to an explosive growth in the numbers of churches. Largely confined to major metropolitan centres, these immigrant congregations display extraordinary spiritual vigour and dynamism, in startling contrast to most churches within the older denominations. The number of African Christians throughout Europe is estimated to be in excess of three million.[55] A 2005 assessment of church growth and attendance in England reports that non-white groups accounted for 58 per cent of churchgoers in London (outside London the percentage drops to 31).[56] In Europe, too, the face of Christianity is increasingly non-white. A century ago, Charles Spurgeon's 5000-seater Metropolitan Tabernacle at Elephant and Castle (south London) was the largest Baptist church with thousands of white English worshippers; today the largest Baptist church in Britain is composed of African immigrants.[57] The Nigerian-led Kingsway International Christian Centre has the largest congregation (over 10,000) in the entire United Kingdom, while the Redeemed Christian Church of God (a Nigeria-based movement), which established its first church in Britain in 1989, had grown to 141 churches with a total of 18,000 members by 2005.[58]

Perhaps the most powerful testimony to the dynamism and drive of contemporary African Christianity is the fact that the largest single Christian community in all of Europe is the Embassy for the Blessed Kingdom of God to All Nations (in Kiev, Ukraine), founded by Sunday Adelaja, a Nigerian pastor. Established in November 1993 as a Bible study group of seven people meeting in Adelaja's apartment, the new group registered as a church three months later with only 49.[59] Yet, by 2002, after adopting an outreach strategy which focused on the marginalised groups within Ukrainian society, the church had grown to 20,000, with an overwhelmingly Ukrainian membership. Indeed, over one million Ukrainians have reportedly been converted to Christianity as a result of its ministry.[60]

Never before has the course of missionary movement been this multi-directional, disparate, and global. The emergence of the non-Western missionary movement in conjunction with global migratory flows represents a major turning point in the history of Christianity. While the movement has an official or institutional segment evocative of Western initiatives – the best example being the South Korean international missionary force which has exploded in numbers from about 100 in 1980 to 10,745 in 2002 and about 19,000 in early 2006[61] – this aspect represents at best a small fraction of its capacity. The movement remains fundamentally unstructured, spontaneous, and clandestine. For this reason, analysis of its scope and potential impact remains complicated, and its largely inchoate nature also means that even the best assessments will remain partial and provisional for some time.

But even now it is emphatically clear that the emerging non-Western missionary movement diverges sharply in crucial respects from the Western missionary movement which preceded it.[62] Among other things, the global forces, cultural assumptions, and spiritual outlook associated with the current movement differs from the Western missionary movement in significant ways. Prominent features associated with the Western missionary project are largely absent, including the entrenched territorial (and one-directional) structure of missions, the instrumentality of para-church mission societies, the complicated relationship with colonial dominance, and the projection of cultural superiority. Preliminary research indicates that the burgeoning South-North element is church-based, self-evidently incarnational in its witness, and closely exemplifies New Testament patterns (demonstrated in its dependence on individual inventiveness, emphasis on spiritual power, use of house churches, reliance on tent-making ministries, and disconnect from empire).

In other words, the non-Western missionary movement is not simply an extension of previous Western missionary initiatives. Assessments which depend on categories and concepts derived from the Western experience are liable to mislead and befuddle. Even so, the past furnishes two basic lessons: first, that attentiveness to the nature and composition of human migration is crucial for understanding the possibilities and potential of Christian missionary endeavour; second, that in much the same way that the Western missionary movement proved decisive for the current shape of global Christianity the future of global Christianity is now intricately bound up with the emerging non-Western missionary. The case for giving it full attention could not be stronger.

3. The Church and its Missionary Vocation: The Islamic Frontline in a Post-Christian West

Lamin Sanneh

Prophet with secular honour

The post-Western Christian awakening today stands in striking contrast to the religious recession in Europe, requiring us for once to refocus attention on the new Christian margins of the West. One response to the decline has been to see the secular West as a new mission field, with the West's growing pluralism a challenge and an opportunity for the churches. Writers such as William Gladstone, John Henry Newman, C. S. Lewis, and T. S. Eliot, for example, have examined the nature of a Christian society, but not until recently has there been an attempt to look at the post-Christian West in the light of post-Western Christianity. Lesslie Newbigin (1909–1998) attempted such a reappraisal, and so it would be appropriate to assess his proposals for the church's contemporary mission. Newbigin was an important link between the rising awakening and its bearing on Europe's rapid religious recession.

Newbigin served as a missionary in India where he became a bishop of the Church of South India from 1947 to 1957, and was subsequently appointed general secretary of the International Missionary Council, before returning to India for the final time as bishop from 1965 to 1974. He retired to England where he went on to publish a number of studies on mission to Western culture.

Newbigin sought to map onto the secular West the outlines of a reinvigorated Christianity by responding to the doubts and reservations about Christian mission and re-examining the intellectual and cultural forces that have affected contemporary Christian attitudes. According to Newbigin, the West was now in a totally different situation from the period before 1914 when people assumed that the influence of European nations was identical with the influence of Christianity. The Western world has had to be recognised once again as a mission field, Newbigin wrote in 1963. Thanks to the lifting of the barriers of travel and communication, thriving religious pluralism has transformed the West, enabling Muslims to become a critical part of the pluralism overtaking the

West. In correspondence with the present writer in May 1995, Newbigin said one of the major issues facing the West was the challenge of Islam to Western culture, and to Britain in particular. He said many people who spoke of a multicultural Britain assumed that Britain was a secular society, that is, a society with no controlling beliefs, in which all religions were allowed to co-exist peacefully.

Newbigin disagreed. He said Gladstone was correct in pointing out that the Roman Empire gave equal tolerance to all religions because the empire was adamant about something much more important for it than religion.[1] That, he said, was also true of a secular Britain. It happens, however, that accelerating global forces were set to erode that secular assumption. Newbigin said the signs were that Max Weber's theory of irreversible secularisation as the fore-ordained future for human society, a theory on which the champions of a secular Britain seemed to pin their hopes, was proving untenable in respect of Islam specifically. While under the secularisation theory each person is free to choose his or her own personal supernatural, as Lawrence Friedman expresses it,[2] radical Islam has challenged that freedom and the choice it fosters. In any case, religion has asserted itself onto the global stage, and 'is now a much bigger factor in world politics than it has been for 200 years'. In that larger picture Islam offered a model for society of law, state, economics, culture, science, which challenges the West's secular norms. Contemporary British society is incapable of meeting, or even of understanding this challenge – as the episode of (Salman Rushdie's) *Satanic Verses* demonstrated. We can no longer evade the question: 'What Kind of Society?' If 'secular' is breaking down, and Islamic (society) is not what we want, can we evade the question, 'What would it mean to work and hope for a Christian society?'

Newbigin sketched out three responses to that question. First, there is the response of racists, open or covert, who saw the large concentrations of Muslims from Pakistan, India, and Bangladesh in major cities as a threat to the British way of life. Even those immigrants who were born and bred in Britain were regarded as not really British by these racists. Second, there was the attitude of sensitive and educated elites in the churches who hated racism and who wished to show Christian love and sympathy with Muslims in their many difficulties. These elites supported dialogue and condemned as intolerance any attempt to preach the Gospel to Muslims. Third, there was a small company of people, mostly of a conservative-evangelical stripe, who were actively in touch with Muslims and were seeking to communicate the Gospel to them.

These three positions, however, did not deal with the question of how the neutrality of a secular society could allow for accommodation with Islam and its anti-secular posture. In a prophetic pointer to the attacks by radical British Muslims on the London transport system in July 2005, Newbigin warned that secular Britain would be defenceless against the forces of rising Islam. Government could deal with actionable deeds, perhaps, but not with the diffuse culture of radicalism that bred them. In respect of that challenge, Newbigin offered the opinion that the marks and values of a Christian society would be required to engage – not to combat – Islam, and so he embarked on delineating the general features of such a Christian society.

In two draft manuscript essays, Newbigin presented a cogent view of the historical trajectory of the course of the West's Christian development, culminating in the momentous outcome of a coherent Newtonian universe. Isaac Newton's *Principia Mathematica* offered a brilliantly clear and comprehensive picture of how things were, a picture that in principle was capable of explaining the mysterious movements of the heavenly bodies as well as the events of everyday life. It was a winner. Even Newton's avowed humility could not disguise the revolutionary secular consequences of his discovery which freed religion from the determinism of mysterious hidden forces, including Newton's own mystical fascination with the *una res*, the one thing which generated everything. It also freed religion from the territorial principle of cultural absolutism. Religious freedom and personal belief were the checkered fruits of Newton's discovery.

Yet, Newbigin contended, those fruits were steadfastly rejected by Islam, and in that rejection Islam set itself not only apart from the West but in open confrontation with it. 'For that reason it is becoming increasingly clear that the attempt to establish liberal forms of the state in cultures which have quite different roots is proving to be very problematical. When it is introduced into societies shaped by other traditions the graft tends to be rejected – even when grants from the IMF and the World Bank are conditional upon its acceptance!'

The idea of a Christian society: faith and the new realism

Newbigin postponed discussion of Islam to return to his central concern, which was and remains the recovery of the West's Christian heritage as embodied in the church to be a safeguard of the West's liberal gains. In a *tour de force* Newbigin described how the liberal triumph of the West emboldened it to adopt a combative stance towards its Judaeo-Christian heritage. He urged loyalty both to the heritage and to its fruits, though he offered little by way of instructions on how a reintegration was possible. He gave a few hints. Newbigin agreed with secular critics that we could not go back to Christendom, but he also agreed with religious advocates that we could not at the same time stand still. He said it was one of the perplexing features of contemporary liberal societies that the moral high ground was claimed by movements of protest rather than by the political parties governing or aspiring to govern. Presumably, political parties should claim the moral high ground, though that still left the question of how political authority could incubate a Christian society without smothering it. Political authority is by nature contractual, while moral authority is personal. How to unite the two has been a flash point since the time of Saul and Samuel, and is the fundamental issue for Newbigin's theological project. King and prophet are not each other's keeper.[3]

Newbigin acknowledged the tension when he observed that contemporary liberal Christianity was marked by a strong Manichaean streak which regarded all power with suspicion, suggesting how moral influence might remain such only by abjuring power, with the idea of a Christian society belonging in the sphere of the church's teaching and exemplary influence. Newbigin confessed that power tended to corrupt, but insisted that it was equally the case that without power it was impossible to do any good. Furthermore, the potential to do any good with power increased if those in power acknowledged realities greater than themselves. This is similar to Aquinas' idea that authority does not derive its moral legitimacy from itself. In other words, the tendency of power to corrupt is an argument against adopting it for the moral life. Even in political life government is not immune to wrongdoing. However indispensable for order and safety, government is not above God's law.

The role of religious faith here is crucial, for religion comprehends the life of politics without being exhausted in it. For example, the Christian knows authority in the church as well as authority in the state, though the difference cannot be more fundamental. God's authority is qualitative and moral – it is original and relational, while political authority is quantitative and remedial – it is expediential and instrumental. Jesus said anyone who saved his or her life would lose it, and anyone who gave her life to God would save it. God's rule gives life abundantly, but not so the arithmetic of power, unless power is inspired by revealed ethics, as Augustine insisted. A democratic state and the rule of God converge in the enterprise of good and productive citizens, yet only the rule of God points to a higher truth.

Here we are thrown back to the grounds of the case for a Christian society and its liberal political safeguards. Bearing in mind the challenge of radical Islam, Newbigin considered how religious moderation may provide a common bond. Muslims in general consider anarchy to be the enemy of God's design for human society, yet seem relatively complacent about authoritarianism as a fall-out of Sharí'ah law. Tyranny is not the solution of sin any more than anarchy is the corollary of freedom. To the extent that we cannot be exempt from the consequences of our action, moral accountability in religion echoes the principle of democratic responsibility. As such, moral persuasion, including the rule of conscience, points to consent as a divinely sanctioned tribunal. In so far as liberal society operates by persuasion rather than by arbitrary use of power, Christians must accept to live in that society not as exceptions but as full participants even when as a group they do not get their own way. The Islamic caliphate and the Byzantine Christian empire, for example, were similar in their view of power as a divine mandate, showing little appreciation for a culture of persuasion, and in both cases a democratic society, not to say the teachings of Jesus, could not be more alien. It was with good reason that Jesus never founded an earthly kingdom.

This view of limited power to which Christians became reconciled had compromise written all over it, supported by cogent theological reasons. In spite of Newbigin's claim that it is not possible to do any good without power, much good, in fact, has been accomplished by Christians and others active in voluntary and benevolent organisations as well as in education, medicine, and social work. Much of that civic activism has been sustained by the charity and benevolence of ordinary people without political power. In the event, such charitable work helped to humanise power.

In lectures delivered in Bangalore, India, in 1941, Newbigin cautioned against blueprints, saying they were charters of blind optimism that did not solve real-life problems. How may Muslims be persuaded to accept that view of power? Is such a liberal understanding of power derived from Christian sources? What institutions and structures would you entrust with Christian warrants in a liberal society? How would Muslims fit in? Ensconced still in its historic heartland, can the Islam of immigrant Muslims be reformed from the new margins of the secular West?[4] Or is the secular West itself a new breeding ground of radicalism? Except by conceding the religious ground, what is the secular defence against religious contradiction?

Understandably, if unsatisfactorily, Newbigin was slow in answering these intractable questions, and in broaching the hoary issue of how a Christian society is related to a Christian state. One reason for this may be because Newbigin was looking for a theological solution to a non-theological problem. When he framed his Christian apologetics to prescribe for a post-enlightenment West, he side-stepped the issue of the radical Islamic prescription for public order. As a religion with a world mandate Islam is hard to fit into the minimalist religious frame of a post-Christian West, and Newbigin conceded that in the course of defending the reconciliation of Christianity with a Newtonian universe, which he said Islam rejected.

In that regard, Newbigin called for taking a long historical perspective and for looking afresh at the idea of a Christian society. 'There is simply no question of seeking a return to the territorial principle which has been discredited and rejected in the Enlightenment. That move is surely irreversible, and it is simply an evasion of the issue we confront to suggest that it is the only alternative to the present model of a secular society. However difficult it may be, we have to try now, in the light of all we have learned through this long history of Christendom's attempt to relate the Gospel to public affairs, to learn what it would mean to affirm the Gospel as public truth.'[5] At this point Newbigin gave us a molehill instead of the mountain we expected.

T. S. Eliot and the bounds of Christian liberalism

In his very thoughtful comments on the subject, T. S. Eliot argued that the idea of a Christian society touched on three related aspects: the Christian state, the Christian community, and the community of Christians. The Christian state, he explained, was the kind of state with which the church could have the sort of relation that was not a concordat or a reciprocal one. That could happen only if the rulers had a Christian education to enable them to think and act in Christian categories without compelling belief. 'What the rulers believed, would be less important than the beliefs to which they would be obliged to conform.'[6] The Christian community, Eliot observed, was constituted of the parish, though that was in serious decline, thanks to urbanisation and sub-urbanisation. Like Newbigin, Eliot did not think that a utopian retreat to the past was possible, or that an expedient surrender to the world was desirable, any more than that a neutral state was feasible. A Christian community must be one which recognised the primacy of ethics and a code of Christian conduct and behaviour.

When he turned to the community of Christians, Eliot defined that as the composite and cumulative effect of the influence of Christian persons, lay and clerical, living and working in the different areas of society, in education, in the arts, in science, in government, and so on. 'The mixture will include persons of exceptional ability who may be indifferent or disbelieving; there will be room for a proportion of other persons professing other faiths than Christianity.'[7] For Eliot the community of Christians fits well with the demands of what Jacques Maritain called a 'pluralist society'. For such Christians it 'will be their identity of belief and aspiration, their background of a common system of education and a common culture, which will enable them to influence and be influenced by each other, and collectively to form the conscious mind and the conscience of the nation'.[8]

Eliot's reflections made much of the idea that too great a strain must not be placed on Christians in terms of a feeling that there was an unbridgeable gulf between a Christian and a non-Christian view of society. A way of life that required an unremitting conflict between what was easy or normal and what was Christian was not sustainable. If Christian behaviour was restricted to a cloistered way of life, then the rationale for a Christian society would be diminished.

Eliot's observations impinge directly on the importance of a Christian society having a wide margin of flexibility to enable virtue to flourish, but without becoming intolerant by suppressing all error and indifference. The point for Eliot was that we should not think of the wrongs or evils of society as having causes wholly beyond the human will and, therefore, to think that only other non-human causes could change society. As long as society was established on Christian foundations, Eliot argued, solutions to the problems of society would not be hostile to Christian aims.

Among those aims were the freedom, dignity, the sense of accountability of human beings, and the existence of educational institutions where those aims were nurtured. State jurisdiction in such a Christian society would reflect the ethos of Christian teaching. In a Christian society power flowed through numerous rivulets which had their source in a view of human possibility that was religious in origin. Thus, Pius XII developed the idea of power as a theological principle. Speaking on Christmas Eve in 1944, he said human beings as free persons were endowed with inalienable rights and bound by mutual obligation; such persons were the irreducible core of a free society. Genuine state authority must reflect a measure of the dignity with which God endowed human beings at creation. A Christian society in both Eliot and Pius XII's view was not a utopia or a blueprint for nihilism, but a transformative process.

Comparative horizons

The problem of reconciling religion and secularism, however, persists. The historical options that we know as lived practices were the caliphate and Christendom in their time, and secularism in ours. The caliphate and Christendom failed in their turn, while, in spite of tragic setbacks, secularism has remained the reigning option. Against that secular option, the argument of a Christian society in a pluralist age has been unpersuasive, not because

Christian teachings cannot be effective as public policy but because compulsory godliness is undemocratic as well as violative of religion itself. That has left secularism as the default logic. Because of his theology of religious freedom, including the idea of the primacy of conscience, Newbigin found himself undermined in his stated objective of instituting a Christian society.

In his reflections on a similar problem, Roland Allen, for instance, was correct that it was wrongheaded to think of introducing Christian social conditions apart from the Christian faith. Christian faith works as a leaven to transform society and its structures, as is evident in educational work, medical work, agricultural work, social work, environmental work, and the work in human rights as domains of legitimate Christian activity. In so far as these activities are based on the persuasive and philanthropic principle they are legitimate vehicles of the obligations of Christian citizenship. In their civil character, they are non-sectarian and non-partisan. Yet they are emphatically political in their impact and challenge. A proliferation of such civil agencies may be the way to work for the values and purposes of a 'Christian society', rather than a bid for power.

Although Newbigin did not cast his ideas in the terms just described, they are in harmony with his views. He wrote: 'This belief [of applying Christian teachings in the public realm] carries with it the implication that part of our Christian obedience is the acceptance of our share of responsibility for the life of our city, our nation, the world. This is not an option which one may choose or reject. To ignore it is a dereliction of duty.'[9] He went on: 'It is through the presence and activity of committed and competent Christian men and women in the various areas of the common life of society that a Christian society could come into being and be sustained in being ... The reality of the reign of God, hidden from the eyes of [non-believers], is to be made visible to the world through the obedience of believers in the midst of their daily work.'[10] That would necessitate collaborating with people who were not Christians and who did not necessarily share Christian motives or goals.[11] Newbigin called attention to the history of Roman Catholic social work developed in the past one hundred years, saying it was a great resource for nurturing the roots of a Christian society.

Newbigin would also concur with the view that it is the responsibility of Christians to invest in the holding stock which yields the dividend of a culture of freedom and persuasion. Christian structures and institutions exist for the benefit of the wider society. Thus, ordination in terms of a professional warrant, can provide a class of dedicated persons to serve exemplary roles in society, though ordination cannot be a requirement of public office. Irish monks, for example, gave dignity to work of the hands without state sponsorship. The state as such could not manufacture virtue or anoint the conscience; at its best, it could only utilise works of virtue and of civic enterprise. The state might not use the argument of privatised religion to obstruct the beneficial work of churches and synagogues lest it undermine the whole basis of a liberal society. State imposition of religion, such as a theocracy, would be no less harmful than state prohibition of religion, such as a Marxist state. Prescription and proscription are two sides of the same coin, and their authoritarian nature conflicts with the nature of the moral life.

We may conclude that religion and the state share a mutual interest in each other's integrity, but for different reasons. The state's interest is one of pragmatic expedience, for the liberal state works through pragmatic channels. But religion's interest is pragmatic and moral at the same time. Caesar's authority shares in Caesar's finitude, as Tertullian affirmed. 'Never will I call the emperor God, and either because it is not in me to be guilty of falsehood; or that I dare not turn him into ridicule. To call him God is to rob him of his title. If he is not a man, emperor he cannot be,' Tertullian asserted. Political authority, like religion, serves the higher ends of order, peace, security, and justice, though, unlike religion, politics, as the fear and reverence for magistrates, is not for the cure of souls. Pointing beyond the material sphere, religion's infinite reach attests to humanity's undying spiritual nature. Nevertheless, religion also ministers to the cause of a free and just society, and therein acts as an ethical constraint on power. It is not just thick walls that make a stout city.

Secular canopy and sacred horizons

As it stands, ordination cannot be a prerequisite of public office; typically it is a bar, and as such a symbol of what secular people find objectionable about religion. It is not just the religious office that should be excluded from the public domain; religious faith is considered at best a social indiscretion and at worst a social menace, whether or not any wrongful act has been committed. One definition in the *Encyclopedia of Religion* (2005) speaks of secularism as a process of decline in religious institutions, activities, beliefs, and ways of thinking, indicating a comprehensive rout of the practice and idea of religion, not just the giving up of state sponsorship of religion. As the French Jesuit, Henri de Lubac, pointed out, it is not true that man cannot organise the world without God. What is true is that, without God, man can only organise the world against man.[12] Accordingly, Europe has gone through paroxysms of Christophobia, i.e., intolerance of any convictions suspected to be of Christian origin, even when the behaviour, conduct, and assurances of those affected fall squarely within the law.[13] The secular canopy imposes a restricted view of human possibility.

The result is religious discrimination, and the repudiation of any chance of co-operation between the political and religious spheres. It is the dictum of *was soll nicht sein, kann nicht sein*, 'what should not be, cannot be', and it violates the rule of *cuius participatio eius in id ipsum*, of each sphere having a share in the other.

The perfection that the religious sphere holds before society is at the same time a demand for political statesmanship to strive for the general good within the bounds of our common imperfection and failings. Religious ethics may affect for good personal standards of transparency, honesty, civic responsibility, and voluntary good works, and thus constitute the kind of renewable national resource and social capital which are pillars of the public good. That is part of what makes a nation great, as John Henry Newman contended. Without an idea of perfection, without moral norms, our imperfection becomes our peril, and the political craft its own reward and hostage. Political corruption becomes inevitable and insoluble. As Christopher Fry once wrote in *The Lady's Not For Burning* (1948), echoing Tom Paine, in our plain defects we already know the brotherhood of man. If it is based on nothing higher than our lowest nature, the conduct of public affairs would lead us into a Leviathan upheaval of permanent conflict, with authoritarianism as fallout. In function church and state may be a split-level edifice, but in terms of the unfettered conscience they share a common foundation of freedom and obligation.

That reality led Newbigin to argue that it was state prohibition of religion that has been a more common threat than state imposition of religion. In an aggressively secular Europe, public stigma attaches easily to religion, with harmful results for civil rights. The argument of Marx is relevant here, that although the secular state might abolish distinctions of religion, birth, rank, and education, yet that did not deny the truth of those fundamental distinctions. The state exists only by presupposing their reality. Marx continued: 'Where the political state has achieved its full development, man leads a double life, a heavenly and an earthly life, not only in thought or consciousness but in *actuality*.'[14] By proscribing religion the state would have committed an act contradicting its political nature, and assumed a religious nature – the state would have become dominated by a preoccupation with religion, as in the case of China. Marx aptly called it one of the most serious of secular contradictions, and warned against ignoring its consequences. For classical Marxism religion was the attribute of the conscience under siege.

Christians and Muslims can ill afford to fall for the view that the extremism of proscription can be remedied by the corresponding extremism of imposition. The Manichaean religious suspicion of power that Newbigin describes may in fact be useful as a cautionary warning about political extremism. Society is protected when religion is a constraint on power – when conscience is not set aside – but society is imperilled when power is a constraint on religion, as when, as Marx noted, the state claims jurisdiction in matters of faith. Newbigin suggests that managing their relationship in a balanced way is one solution to the commoditisation of religion and to the religious manipulation of government. That balance is necessary to maintain political accountability and religious integrity. It is, perhaps, Newbigin's way of recognising that, with no viable alternative to a liberal democracy, it is necessary to prune and tend the vine of Christian teaching so that the branches in terms of accumulated social and moral capital do not stray too far from their taproot in religion. A Christian society should recognise the necessity of a rule-based regime of incentives and constraints as the barrier to lawlessness and anarchy, as well as the importance of a faith-based social conscience for the production of common values and social ethic. Caesar and God are separate precisely because they are unequal.

The interfaith frontline

The post-Christian West is firmly committed to the principle of religious pluralism, and to its corollary of the rejection of Christianity as entitled to any special or exemplary role in the West. The pressing question critics had put to

Christians, says Newbigin, is whether by continuing to insist on the uniqueness and finality of the revelation of God in Christ, the church is not incapacitating itself to play its proper part in healing the divisions of the human family. Humanity must learn to live as one community or suffer injury. Once, when humanity was divided into distinct cultural groups, and effectively separated by distance, religion played a crucial role as an integrating factor making for coherence and stability.

There is no more separation today, and so the role of religion has changed fundamentally. To take the religion of one of the great cultural groups, even if that religion now has a foothold in all parts of the world, and claim for it that it is the proper faith for all humanity, is simply to prove oneself blind to the realities of the concrete human situation. It is to invite a religious civil war just at the moment when humanity needs above all to find civil peace. This brings Christians to the position of having to ask: 'Are we so sure as our predecessors were that there is salvation for humanity only by the explicit acceptance of the Name of Jesus Christ?' Newbigin asks. Is Jesus Christ alone the Lord and Saviour of humankind, the king and head of the race?[15]

That challenge threw down a gauntlet Newbigin took up. The challenge for Newbigin, however, is whether it is a theologically defined gauntlet, and whether his response would be heeded at all. The chances are slim if the basis of the new pluralism is a pragmatic sociological imperative, as it seemed to be. Newbigin assumes the basis to be philosophical, in which assumption I think he was partly correct. What he calls the knee-jerk reaction to his proposals indicates he is faced with a *fait accompli*.

Newbigin issued many eloquent and persuasive statements on the subject, but their value lies not so much in their power to shift attitudes in the cultural mainstream as in their capacity to equip the churches to live in a post-Christian West without too much defensiveness or without the need for a radical dis-avowal of religion. Christians do not need to be in denial in a world of rampant secularism because they have unacknowledged allies in the post-Western resurgence. Newbigin was the apostle of a confident Christianity in an ascen-dant post-Christian West. As the title of one of his books put it, he was proposing an 'honest religion for secular man'. We should appreciate his ideas against that background.

Newbigin was insistent that God's unique and matchless revelation in Christ carries the obligation to proclaim the Gospel in mission and service, whatever the demands and limitations of religious pluralism.

On the matter of other religions, Newbigin was sensitive to the calls for racial tolerance and cultural acceptance. In the presence of Hindus, Buddhists, Muslims, and Sikhs, he said, we are reminded that our societies have become more diverse and different, and in these circumstances many people in the churches are calling for an abandonment of the policy of converting people of other faiths. The Christian faith may be true for those who were Christians already, but it is not necessarily true for others. The Christian confession of Jesus as Lord and Saviour and their worship of him in the language of the church are right and proper. But Christians have no right in a pluralist, multicultural society, critics urged, to say that there is no other name given under heaven by which people are to be saved.

The empirical situation flatly contradicts such a claim. Modern historical consciousness, these critics said, must disallow Christian claims of uniqueness.[16] Newbigin was aware that many theologians claim that for Christians to offer Christianity as the only answer to the global nuclear and environmental challenge is preposterous. These theologians maintain that the challenge to affirm the validity of the other great religions of the world has become a necessary part of the struggle of their people to emerge from the spiritual and cultural humiliation of colonialism. Furthermore, some of these critics speak of the astonishment of a Hindu at the idea that God has had only one incarnation. They insist the Christian attempt to place the event of the incarnation in only a first-century historical record is nothing short of folly. Critics point out that it is incontestable that people are all part of one global society more and more dependent on one another, and that is the radical new fact of our time.[17]

While Newbigin agrees that there is much truth in these criticisms, he responds that it does not mean people are not all in search of truth and salvation, or that in that search they should not possess a reliable clue into universal meaning and history. It is not true that all roads lead to the peak of the same mountain. Some roads are false short cuts, and even if they do not lead over the precipice, they leave people self-centredly entangled. For Christians, the ultimate clue, the rock of ages, is Jesus, the one God chose to honour and to glorify the divine name, and who has gone before them in honour and faithfulness.

Newbigin makes the point with some force that religious pluralism, in the sense of competing truth claims as well as of simple numerical multiplicity, does not exclude claims of absolute uniqueness. Without some sense of objective truth people will become totally imprisoned in subjective relativism. Religion can become relativist only by turning into an ideology, in which case tolerance will become a relative value as mere expedience. There would be no independent basis for it.[18] That is why truth claims are not convertible currency that give people personal advantage; they are not a question of will power, à la Nietzsche: you want in this case a liberating creed, so you produce the sacrosanct truth of the infallibility of revolutionary relativism and smash your way to victory by gutting truth claims, any or all of them. Will power can only produce a wilful world based on power. Its truth claim leaves no room for difference or variety, or for openness and tolerance.

Yet mission here cannot go to the other extreme and turn into religious fundamentalism. In Newbigin's hands mission is not about attesting to biblical inerrancy, about the Bible as a manual of correct beliefs. It is about Jesus and his redemptive life, and about the church's role in witnessing to that truth. Those who think that Christian mission is the uncritical assertion of religious truth claims are wrong, because mission is not about the finality of this or that theological clarification but about the finality of God's irrevocable act in Jesus. In any case, critics who range against mission wrapped in the mantle of infallible realism do so because they are committed to their mission of liberal realism, which is quite exclusive in its own view of truth. The liberal agenda of the equality of all religions captures the mood of the post-Christian West, but it does not reflect the reality of humanity's religious crisis. The bounds of liberal Christianity have shrunk, with no signs of gaining ground anywhere else. Given his extensive ecumenical missionary experience Newbigin was all too aware of the fact that abroad Christianity had taken root in diverse societies whose religious core remained intact. Those societies show the perennial appeal of the Gospel; it is the secular West that seems out of step.

Is Christianity necessary? Commitment and tolerance

The challenge with which religious pluralism confronts Christians is how the necessity of Christianity can be upheld if Christians wish to honour other religions. Newbigin felt that Christians must respect and honour the religious traditions of others because they respect and honour their own tradition. Respect of others is not at the expense of respect of oneself. To assume that is to settle for a beguiling notion that to concede truth to the other side somehow represents an advance on mutual tolerance when in fact it only triggers an unintended domino effect: the fall of Christian uniqueness would be followed in turn by the fall of all the other claims of uniqueness. Fewer generalisations would be possible until all religions are excluded – a most unsatisfactory state of affairs in which the generalisation of exclusion, not pluralism, would be left ascendant.

In mitigation, we may revert to the truth claim about seeking the honour and favour of God as consistent with the desire of seeking the honour and favour of other religions. If Christians put the honour and favour of God first; if they hallow truth before means and tactics, then they would find other religions worthy of their honour and favour. It is when Christians trust God to value their efforts at faith and obedience that they most persevere against the odds and often in spite of themselves in seeking and doing right by others.

At this point we come upon an impasse in which the necessity of Christian commitment is locked in a head-on collision with the necessity of tolerance of pluralism. Christian truth claims requiring faithfulness to God in terms of God's sovereign truth would seem to infringe on the imperative of solidarity with others, and to impair the Christian obligation to be neighbours to others. Yet, the impasse is only apparent. Deep down, the faithfulness involved in seeking God's honour and favour is productive of communities of mutual esteem. As a medieval Muslim theologian put it, the more we love God the more we are relieved of the *consciousness* of performing the divine command, including the command to love and honour others. The command here is a call to tolerance and self-giving. A religious motive of faithfulness to God, then, involves the act not so much of regarding oneself as infallible and exclusive, as of uplifting God as an act of pure love, and the neighbour as made in God's image. Even the zeal to earn the approval or goodwill of one's neighbours cannot in this theological view be the cause for loving God, for that would reduce God to a form of goodwill, or the zeal for it. Love of God is primary and fundamental – love is God's unalloyed attribute rather than a question simply of means and tactics. In all of this, a confessional stance, a commitment to what is true and worthy of God and of honouring the neighbour, however indebted to perspectivalist concerns, seems inescapable for all communities of faith. Commitment here safeguards religious distinctiveness, and that in turn promotes interfaith responsibility.

The oft-repeated secular case for pluralism rests on the view that a new society fashioned out of religious truth claims stripped down and applied in equal measure is necessary in the interests of equality, fairness, justice, and tolerance. Such a view recognises that faith communities emerged once in isolation but that in the modern West they have been plunged in a new milieu of critical synthesis, with the requirement of a radical reconstitution of their roots and identity.

Yet as the reservoir of new religious influx, a hybrid Western culture remains merely experimental and morally expedient. Thus, a secular Europe finds itself wanting to respect values of diversity but without a core commitment to the West's formative legacy. Europe is caught between the spectre of cultural fragmentation that Enoch Powell said in his 1968 Wolverhampton speech would be the grim outcome of immigration, and, on the other hand, an unaligned multiculturalism of incongruous parts as endorsed by the government. The suggested compromise of 'common values' put forward by Trevor Phillips, chairman of the Commission for Racial Equality (CRE), begs the question about the roots and ownership of those common values.[19] In order for it to continue to be a positive force, as Eliot argued, Western society must resonate in an organic way with its Christian heritage rather than rely on an ad hoc multicultural patchwork to give it a sense of direction and coherence.

In this regard, Newbigin spoke challengingly of a troubling reversal and denial among modern critics of the claims the Bible makes about God. When critics speak of the Copernican revolution, of a move that amounts to the crossing of the Rubicon of religious pluralism where it is no longer feasible or convincing to assert Christian uniqueness, they do so on the view that humanity is moving towards a common ideal and a shared historical consciousness, which is the transformation of human life from self-centredness to God or Reality-centredness. Newbigin said this is an illusion, because to claim all human beings as united in their desire and search for salvation is to leave human beings holding centre-stage, shifting the focus from God, or Reality so-called, to human needs and desires, in fact to a prescriptive market view of religion. It is, according to Newbigin, a reversal of biblical teaching, a move that is the reverse of the Copernican revolution. 'It is a move away from a centre outside the self, to the self as the only centre,'[20] deflecting Christian theology from its concern with the saving acts of God to religious experience. An argument of human determinacy is thereby given primacy over claims of revelation and salvation.

Newbigin argues that Christian mission should proceed from the tension between the amazing grace of God and the appalling sin of the world, with confidence only 'in the infinite abundance of [God's] grace'.[21] It is better, Newbigin contended, to see and judge cultures by the criterion of the Gospel than to allow each culture to be itself the criterion by which it judged others. We often hide this uncomfortable fact from ourselves by pretending that modern historical consciousness has abolished the need to judge others and has left us with the recourse of subjective retreat, a retreat that avoids the arrogance of imposing our views on others, but that, objected Newbigin, is an illusion. 'To affirm the unique decisiveness of God's action in Jesus Christ is not arrogance; it is the enduring bulwark against the arrogance of every culture to be itself the criterion by which others are judged.'[22] The cultural criterion is not a guarantee of tolerance and acceptance of others. It only makes the problem more acute in a non-religious way. As a general claim, cultural relativism is the seedbed of ideologies of ethnic cleansing.

Newbigin was careful to separate his opinion from the question often posed about whether the non-Christian can be saved, whether, that is, the non-Christian will go to heaven after death. That question is God's alone to answer. Furthermore, the question is a mere abstraction, abstracting the soul from the full reality of the human person as an actor and sufferer in the ongoing history of the world. The question is not, 'What will happen to this person's soul after death?' but 'What is the end which gives meaning to this person's story as part of God's whole story?'[23] A third difficulty with that question is its focusing on the individual need to be assured of ultimate happiness, not on God and God's glory. 'The gospel, the story of the astonishing act of God himself in coming down to be part of our alienated world, to endure the full horror of our rebellion against love, to take the whole burden of our guilt and shame, and to lift us up into communion and fellowship with himself, breaks into this self-centred search for our own happiness, shifts the centre from the self and its desires to God and his glory.'[24]

Thus, Newbigin rejects the exclusivist position that all who do not accept Jesus as Lord and Saviour are eternally lost. In witnessing to the non-Christian, the Christian advocate takes as a starting point the non-Christian experience of the hearer without which there can be no way of communicating. That fact makes it impossible to affirm a total discontinuity between the Christian faith and other religions.[25] In fact, it compels rejection of exclusivism while demanding recognition of common ground. Unless Christianity is anticipated it was not Christianity. This is a point Newbigin's critics have been slow to recognise, yet he was not a child of the ecumenical age for nothing.

The diversity of religion and the asset of human unity

Accordingly, Newbigin insisted that it is not our business to say who can or cannot be saved. 'I confess that I am astounded at the arrogance of theologians who seem to think that we are authorized, in our capacity as Christians, to inform the rest of the world about who is vindicated and who is to be condemned at the last judgment ... We have to begin with the mighty work of grace in Jesus Christ and ask, How is [God] to be honoured and glorified? The goal of missions is the glory of God.'[26]

This sentiment of Newbigin's is supported by Vatican II in its document *Gaudium et Spes* which affirmed God's solidarity with the peoples of the world, saying the church was resolved to embrace the world without threats and sanctions. In another document, *Nostra Aetate*, the Council endorsed other reli-gions in strong affirmative terms, leading John Paul II to insist on the unity of the human family. He said the words of the Council were in tune with the con-viction of the existence of the so-called *semina Verbi* (seeds of the Word), which were present in all religions. In the light of that conviction, the Church has sought to identify the *semina Verbi* present in the great traditions in order to iden-tify a common path against the backdrop of the needs of the contemporary world. But, like Newbigin, John Paul II noted that Vatican II was 'inspired by a *truly universal concern*. The Church is guided by the faith that *God the Creator wants to save all humankind in Jesus Christ*, the only mediator between God and man, inasmuch as He is the Redeemer of all humankind.'[27]

The future of history and the new dawn

Secular champions have objected to Newbigin's vision and, instead, have argued that the Gospel carries the limitations of its European captivity, and that if Christians accept as their own the enlightened liberal gains of the West they must allow Christianity to accompany Europe in its retreat from the role of the world's moral tutor. Critics recognise the rise of world Christianity as a delayed fruit of the work of Western missions, but suggest that a historical lag behind the secularisation that has overtaken the post-Christian West will in time, like day following night, also overtake the post-Western awakening. The time fuse of modernisation has been lit by the raging forces of globalisation, bringing remote and exotic societies within range of a transforming uniform impact, it is claimed.

According to the canon of modernisation, the current evidence of vital life in the post-Western resurgence, of dynamic, imaginative movement in thought and practice, that evidence will be altered to conform to the secular logic of an open, cumulative future. To secular champions, Newbigin's hope that a bridge exists, or can be coaxed into existing, with the post-Western religious resurgence is the shrinking, brittle shell of the secular chrysalis. Only delusion would make Christian die-hards think they can survive in their fuzzy religious cocoon. As Newbigin himself observed many times, he seemed to cause a knee-jerk reaction by his proposals, although the post-Western resurgence he encountered in his missionary work seemed to be spreading to the new Christian margins the West had become.

Seeing himself as a bridge between post-Western Christianity and a post-Christian West, Newbigin strove to re-attach a post-enlightenment West to its spiritual roots in the church and in the Christian heritage. He said a condition for a missionary encounter with the waning religious horizon of the West is to look for help from the frontier Christianity of Asia and Africa so that the West might see its own culture 'through Christian minds shaped by other cultures. The fact that Jesus is much more than, much greater than, our culture-bound vision of him can only come home to us through the witness of those who see him with other eyes.'[28]

Asian and African Christians received the Gospel from European and American missionaries, and in that way saw Jesus in the way European and

American culture necessarily formulated him. But Asians and Africans have logically gone on to make Jesus a figure of their own cultures. The West needs their witness to correct its picture of Jesus in as much as it is to a Western Jesus that they first came. There is now a new urgency, however. 'At this moment our need is greater, for they have been far more aware of the dangers of syncretism, of an illegitimate alliance with false elements in their culture, than we have been [of syncretism in the West].'[29] It is impossible and unacceptable, Newbigin pleaded, for the church to undertake an effective mission in its own Western homeland unless the church is willing to hear what God is saying to the West through the witness of post-Western Christians. The movement of missionaries must now be multidirectional, with all churches both sending and receiving.

Postscript: Can Europe be saved?

In his book, *God's Continent: Christianity, Islam and Europe's Religious Crisis*,[30] Philip Jenkins notes that many in today's Europe worry that it is no longer an idle or implausible question to ask whether the rapid pace of dechristianisation will push Europe to the fringes of the Muslim world as 'Eurobia', whether, for example, Spain will revert to Islam. Will Britain become North Pakistan, France the Islamic Republic of New Algeria, Spain the Moorish Emirate of Iberia, Germany the New Turkey? Will Octoberfest now feature a German Biergarten flush with glasses of sweet mint tea? With its 20 per cent Muslim population will Brussels and Belgium become Belgistan? Will Italy and Albania merge to become a new Albanian Islamic Federation? As the Libyan President Qaddafi asserts, 'there are signs that Allah will grant Islam victory in Europe without swords, without guns, without conquests. The fifty million Muslims of Europe [allegedly] will turn it into a Muslim continent within a few decades.'[31]

Qaddafi is alluding not only to the statistics of precipitous religious decline in Europe but to serious low fertility rates across Europe. A Norwegian Muslim leader, Mullah Krekar, says jubilantly, 'Look at the development of the population of Europe, where the number of Muslims increases like mosquitoes. Each Western woman in the EU produces, on average, 1.4 children'. 'By 2050 thirty percent of the European population will be Muslim,' he predicts.[32] Michael Novak and George Weigel concur with that grim Muslim assessment and predict a dire cultural meltdown, as does Niall Ferguson who declares, 'The greatest of all the strengths of radical Islam ... is that it has demography on its side. The Western culture against which it has declared holy war cannot possibly match the capacity of traditional Muslim societies when it comes to reproduction.'[33] It is as if a strange moon has appeared in the firmament like a circulating anti-aphrodisiac and is lulling Europe into self-negation.

There are other forces eating away at Europe's resolve, and none is more intentional than the secular liberal hostility to Christianity. Bruce Bawer's book, *While Europe Slept: How Radical Islam Is Destroying the West from Within*, presents gay rights and same-sex marriage as fundamental components of European values. Bawer compared Islam to Christian fundamentalism. 'The main reason I'd been glad to leave America was Protestant fundamentalism,' he says with a flourish. Bawer does not grant the existence of any religious or conservative moral critique that he does not stigmatise as 'fundamentalist'. It does not help him to appreciate any distinctions.

In a fantasy novel, *The Flying Inn* (1914), Chesterton describes Islam over-running England. It begins with the secular liberal commendation of Islam as progressive: it is intellectual, rational, devoid of priestcraft and mystifying rituals, and is strongly anti-alcoholic. Chesterton is making the point that secularism is itself a form of rigid religion with an intolerant outlook, and as such paves the way for authoritarianism. Jenkins agrees. 'Secular liberalism, it seems, is a self-limiting project; unlimited libertarianism brings its own destruction.'[34]

This secular hostility represents the reigning orthodoxy of Europe, though it is not limited to that continent. In a review article in the *New York Times*, Stephen Metcalf writes without any provocation: 'If the spirit should finally move me, and I answer the call to care for my fellow man unconditionally, the biggest challenge will be extending my newfound caritas to the religious zealots, for it is the zealots – more than the child molesters, petro-dictators or certain on-air personalities of the Fox News persuasion – whom I despise above all.'[35] That heap of sauerkraut is the measure Metcalf offers to offset the chocolate he says religious people use to stop the mouth of those who ask about why God allows evil. Such secular disdain seems fodder for an awakened Islam.

Jenkins picks up this theme in his final reflections on the fate of Europe. For two centuries, he says, many of Europe's intellectual debates have been shaped by the encounter with secularism and scepticism, a milieu that conditioned Christian attempts to make the faith compatible with modernity. 'But what happens when the main interlocutors in the religious debate operate from assumptions quite different from those of secular critics, when the rivals assume as a given the existence and power of a personal God who intervenes directly in human affairs, and seek rather to clarify the nature of His revelation?'[36]

For Jenkins the choice is between acknowledging the Qur'án as the true revelation, and with it the authority of Muhammad which excludes all rival claims, on the one hand, and, on the other, the Qur'án as a historical text subject to the demands and limitations of the circumstances of its creation. In the first case we would have a concession that is tantamount to submission to Islam, and would allow the demands of radical Islam, and in the second, we would let stand at best a sterile confrontation with Islam. 'If there is a third course – to accept some prophetic status for Muhammad while maintaining belief in the Christian scriptures and the church – it is not yet apparent,' Jenkins argues.[37]

However we define and in other ways set out the marks of mission today, we face a new situation with the church now occupying the new Christian margins in the West and facing stiff competition from activist Muslim organisations, networks, and movements. Amid the new ferment, the old standard line of secular accommodation seems out of date, at least as an avenue for conversion and renewal.

In the secular scheme a professional pastoral counsellor once defined the ideal church in highbrow middle-class terms as 'a well-organized psychiatric unit' distinguished 'by acceptance and tolerance; equality; commitment to honesty; meaningful rituals; and mutual helpfulness'.[38] That was precisely the fate Virginia Woolf saw for religion as it emptied itself into the cultural reservoir. How, then, might the church be re-equipped to missionise in the post-Christian age? Does the Christian awakening among new wave immigrants, what Jenkins calls the 'southernization of Christianity',[39] offer scope for re-evangelising the West? Whatever his limitations, Newbigin in his time raised questions highly pertinent to the role of the church in a religiously reawakened world. The ascendancy of radical global Islam may provide the incentive to move beyond a moribund dechristianised Europe by inspiring a recovery of Europe's own religious heritage. In that sense the twenty-first century may turn out to be a post-secular century, thus showing Newbigin's observations to be prescient.

4. Reading the Bible in the Non-Western Church: An Asian Dimension

Moonjang Lee

With the expansion of Christianity into the non-Western world, we have seen new expressions of the Christian faith in the global context. However, as has often been pointed out, the expansion of Christianity has not always been accompanied by the necessary expansion of theology, which is the natural outcome of the direct interface between the Gospel and the local community. As the Gospel encounters people in a specific culture for the first time, a new understanding of the Christian faith by the receptors seems inevitable because they approach the Bible within their own framework of thought and worldview. Any interpreter of the Bible has his or her own cultural blind spot that makes an exhaustive understanding of the Bible within one cultural group implausible. It is now widely recognised that culture plays the role of a hermeneutical filter, and what we bring to the biblical text is bound to affect the way we read, understand, and interpret the text. Their existing traditional concepts and the elements of their culture affect the way people understand the Gospel.

Although this is widely recognised in principle, the discourse of academic biblical studies has been slow to negotiate with the receptor cultures. The various interpretative tools devised in Western biblical scholarship still dominate the way the Bible is studied in the non-Western world. There seems to be a widely held assumption that the interpretation of the Bible should be carried out in the traditional Western academic style, and only after that is the cross-cultural communication of the interpretation to be considered. This hermeneutical stance is observed even in the setting of the ministry. The assumption is that the preacher should first establish the interpretation of a Bible passage by the traditional academic approach, and then seek the most convincing way to apply the message (or the interpretation of the message) to the local context. In such a milieu, there is very little space for a non-Western hermeneutical or exegetical model.

A small but significant number of scholars in the non-Western world are now questioning the relevance and effectiveness of the Western methods of reading Scripture. Their discontent comes partially from their consciousness of the long history of Asian interaction with Asian literary, philosophical, and religious texts, and their awareness that this rich traditional heritage has not been incorporated into the discourse of biblical interpretation.

In this paper, I will reflect on some prominent issues that arise in reading the Bible through the eyes of an Asian Christian scholar. We identify at least four main issues: (1) biblical authority, (2) the goal of Bible reading (3) Asian interpretative method, and (4) the various perspectives – or lenses – available.

The authority of the Bible

The issue of biblical authority has been a much-debated issue in the West from the time that historical and cultural relativism began to affect the academic and intellectual climate in which biblical scholars operated. Scholars at the more radical end of the spectrum emphasise the historical and cultural difference between the Bible and the modern world. They assert that the Bible cannot be the norm for modern people and is necessarily subject to critical academic research.[1] At the other end of the spectrum are those who argue for the eternal relevance of the Bible on the basis of the belief that the Bible is the word of God. They resort to the inner evidence of inspiration, and some speak of the inerrancy and infallibility of the Bible as the word of God. A more recent contribution has come from those forms of Liberation Theology that propose a 'hermeneutic of suspicion' in reading the Bible. What is entailed here is a shift in the idea of biblical authority. The Bible is regarded as a book that contains conflicting ideological traditions, the tradition of the oppressors and the tradition of the oppressed.

In an Asian discourse about biblical hermeneutics the issue of the authority of the Bible takes a different form. One stream of questioning derives from the multi-scriptural nature of the Asian environment. The gist of this argument is that the authority of the Bible cannot be maintained because the Bible is only one of the multiple sacred Scriptures in Asia, and can claim no superior status over the others. The following remark by Archie Lee well expresses this view:

> The encounter between the biblical text and the religiosity and spirituality expressed in the sacred texts of the living faiths of Asia will readdress the whole question of scriptural authority and absolute truth claims of the Christian faith.[2]

It seems legitimate, therefore, to attempt to redefine the status of the Bible in Asia, for this has significant implications for the way that Christianity is practised and Christian theology formulated in Asia. We need to articulate the authority of the Bible in Asia in Asian languages in light of Asian religious and cultural experience, for the perception of the nature of the Bible is linked with the identity of Christianity and Christian theology.

The critical attitude that Christian theologians have toward their own sacred Scripture reflects the collapse of Christendom and the failure of Christianity in the West. The authority of the Bible may be in crisis within Western Christian scholarship, but the authority of other sacred texts in other communities of faith is simply not a question.

In the religious and intellectual tradition in Asia, however, those writings given the name of 'sacred book' (*gyung* in Korean; *ching* in Chinese) are accepted as writings that contain fundamental truths about the universe. They thus have eternal relevance transcending the limits of time and space and those in the faith community believe that their sacred Scriptures contain Truth (the Law or the *Tao*) that must be studied and practised. Muslims have the *Qur'an*; Hindus their triple canon of *Upanishads*, *Bramasutra*, and *Bhagavadgita*, Buddhists the *Tripitaka*, Confucianists and Taoists their books. And, as the other communities readily recognise, Christians have the Bible. The place of the sacred texts within the respective faith communities is given due respect. The authority of Buddhist sacred books is upheld in the Buddhist community; the authority of Confucian classics is not questioned by Confucian scholars; the status of the Qur'an in the Muslim community cannot be challenged at all. All accept without question that the Bible is the sacred text of the Christian faith community.[3]

Religious commitment in Asia entails the acceptance of the authority of the sacred books of one's community, whether it is Christian, Buddhist, or any other. It would therefore be unusual to see a theologian-scholar who belonged to a faith community challenging the authority of the sacred books of that tradition. To question the authority of the sacred books would be to indicate abandonment of the teachings of the tradition. A Buddhist scholar-monk who openly rejected the authority of Buddhist sacred books would be expected to take off the monk's robe and to leave the Buddhist faith community. With this traditional understanding of sacred books in Asia, we can see why the authority and eternal relevance of the Bible is not usually questioned or challenged among Asian Christians, except by those under outside influence from training in Western critical scholarship.

Nor does the plurality of Asian Scriptures necessarily serve to relativise the authority of the Bible over against the authority of other Scriptures. It is well observed that 'in a multi-religious community there are different scriptures which are accepted as authoritative by their respective adherents'.[4] It may not be wrong to argue that the Bible must be treated as 'one of the sacred scriptures' in Asia; but we should not misunderstand the religious implications of this statement. It guarantees rather than relativises biblical authority in the Asian religious milieu.[5] Within the Christian faith community, the Bible cannot be regarded as 'one among many references in the search for truth'.[6] The Bible is seen as normative for Christians as the other sacred books are normative for their respective adherents. The Asian contribution to the reading and study of the Bible begins with its authority as the normative sacred book of the Christian community of faith.

The purpose of biblical studies: becoming like Christ

Why do we read the Bible? What expectations do we have in studying it? The reasons need to be revisited and clarified from a non-Western perspective; for what makes many Asian readers discontented with the academic interpretative tools forged in the West is not the inherent flaws in the reading methods *per se* but the misplaced goal of the reading.

Since coming to teach in the West I often ask my seminary students why they read and study the Bible. Strangely I find that for most, the goal of their biblical studies is not clearly defined. Most Christians read the Bible hoping to become familiar with the teachings of the Bible. Those who decide to be trained in theological schools expect to become effective ministers of the Word. Preachers desire a deep interface with the biblical text to perceive God's wisdom for the present time. Different people approach the Bible with different intentions. What is the ultimate Christian goal in reading the Christian sacred text?

Asia has a long tradition of scriptural interpretation. In its different religious traditions people have studied the teachings contained in their sacred text with certain goals. In the Taoist tradition, people trained themselves to be Taoist masters. In the Confucian tradition, scholars pursued personal discipline to become the Sage. In the Buddhist tradition, people strove to attain Buddhahood through the various steps of self-discipline.

The ultimate objective in reading the Bible should be to upgrade ourselves and become like our Master, Jesus Christ. We are to follow Jesus and achieve the likeness of Christ. Becoming like Jesus should be the single goal and objective for all who read the Bible for all its worth. The person desiring to become a martial arts master, having learned all the skills from teachers, must then spend time and energy in practice. Through practice the person will experience a personal transformation, growing to the master's level in the art. The same principle applies to the study of the Bible. To become like Jesus, our interaction with the Bible should focus on two major areas. First comes perception of spiritual insights through awakening and enlightenment. There follows the embodiment of those insights through meditation, personal application and practice to achieve personal transformation – to become like Jesus Christ in our thought, word, and deed.

Personal reading: enlightenment

Reading the Bible (a sacred text) should be different from reading a literary work or a historical document. The purpose of reading a sacred text is to gain personal knowledge and insight, not simply to amass objective knowledge. The barrenness of much Western biblical scholarship derives from the fact that the intended audience of biblical interpretation is the academic guild. The purpose of biblical interpretation in the academic community is thus to provide answers to questions that interest scholars. From an Asian perspective the defect of Western biblical studies is the lack of the personal dimension.

In Asian hermeneutical traditions, the primary concern was not 'how to read' but 'what to read'. This approach is the basis of traditional Asian scholarship and the philosophy formed within the Asian epistemological world. Stanley Samartha well captures the thrust of the Asian hermeneutical quest when he states: 'The question in Asia is not so much rules of interpretation as the perception of Truth or *Sat* or Reality or *Dharma* or the *Tao* itself. How Reality is to be perceived is a concern prior to questions of rules of interpreting the scriptures.'[7] Western reading methods characterised by 'a-political detachment, objective literalism, and scientific value-neutrality'[8] are alien and foreign to Asian readers. The hermeneutical interest of an Asian reader lies in perceiving the *tao* through the sacred text, which is contrasted with 'the academic barrenness of scientific exegesis'.[9] In reading the Bible, we are to endeavour to obtain personal knowledge in four crucial areas: (1) personal knowledge of God that will deepen our intimate relationship with God; (2) personal knowledge of the way to die to our fleshly nature; (3) personal knowledge of God's ways; (4) personal knowledge of the power of the Holy Spirit.

Non-dualistic embodiment: practice

After gaining personal knowledge and insight from the Bible, a reader should meditate on and put them into practice through non-dualistic engagement in order to embody what has been learned. Non-dualistic engagement means that there is no dichotomy between the subject of the reading (the reader) and its object (what is read). This is what we may call academic study – Asian style. In this sense, the act of reading the Bible is fundamentally practice-oriented.

Reading the Bible with multiple perspectives

We bring multiple perspectives to the biblical text. A reader of the Bible may bring his or her interests and concerns to the biblical text, and expect the Bible to answer these questions that arise from the reader's context. Biblical scholars have traditionally brought their own theological and academic questions and themes to the text: salvation, the plan of God, covenant, people of God, historical Jesus, Pauline theology – the list is infinite. It is a legitimate enterprise to read the biblical text with these various themes in view. These themes can help to illuminate various aspects of the Bible and enhance our understanding of the biblical text. The critical response of Asian scholars arises from the awareness that these themes, however helpful in illuminating the biblical text, cannot answer contemporary questions and the pressing concerns of local people.

Theologians in Latin America, Asia, and Africa brought a critique of 'neutral' and 'objective' approaches to the biblical text by introducing contextual concerns and perspectives. Asian theologians were among those attempting to read the Bible from socio-economic and cultural-religious perspectives. The cultivation of local perspectives in order to construct local theologies is now encouraged, another aspect of the search for viable Asian perspectives in biblical hermeneutics. We are now familiar with various contextual perspectives from Africa, Asia, and Latin America affecting our reading of the Bible: partisan love for the poor and oppressed, social justice, political justice, preservation of the environment, realisation of *minjung* reality, nation building, feminist concerns, post-colonial discourse, religious pluralism, and many others.

We should remember, however, that not all perspectives are useful to unlock the biblical text. Some perspectives may be endorsed by the biblical text, but others may distort its message. Therefore, the reader should be ready to be corrected by the biblical text while seeking answers to the contextual issues and questions.

A new reading method: an Asian exegesis

George Soares-Prabhu, an Indian Jesuit, has pointed out that a reading method devised to obtain exact information is not helpful in interpreting a sacred text that aims at 'personal transformation of the reader through his response in faith'.[10] Once the authority of the Bible as the sacred book for the Christian faith community is respected and we approach it to get insights to become like Jesus Christ, we may need to devise a reading method that will measure up to the intention of the biblical text. We may interact with the biblical text in two steps.

Step One: Perceiving the reality in, behind, and beyond the text

- Re-enacting the text:
  The first step in reading the Bible is to re-enact the biblical reality. A reader should be able to reconstruct in a three-dimensional way the biblical reality that was once as alive as our own reality today is alive. A reader needs to enter into the biblical reality through repetitive reading and historical imagination. In the biblical text, we encounter all the components of life – people, nature, animals, music, buildings, clothes, food, business, and many others. In the process of the three-dimensional re-enactment of the biblical text, a reader should be able to participate in the biblical reality.

- Reading inferentially:
  To facilitate our full participation in the biblical text, we may undertake an inferential reading. This involves inference based on the information given in the text, and thus excavating various aspects of behind-the-text or beyond-the-text realities. A reader may infer further from the inferences already made. In other words, serial inference is possible. Let us attempt an inferential reading of Genesis 1:2a:

  > And the earth was formless and void, and darkness was over the surface of the deep.

  This verse describes the condition of the earth before the creation of light . We may infer from the reading of the text that if there was darkness over the surface of the deep it must have been extremely cold at that time.
      An inferential reading may well be the most significant aspect of the Asian approach to the biblical text. However, there is a hermeneutical condition for using the inferential reading method. What a reader infers should be based on the given text, and others in the Bible-reading community should be able to accept the inference. Only if an inferential reading satisfies this condition, will it be acceptable.

- Reading interactively:
  Entering into the text and reading inferentially, we meet many people and

observe many different situations. In the Bible a reader encounters adults, children, males and females, disciples, prophets, kings, Jewish people, Romans, soldiers, farmers, tax-collectors, fishermen, sick people, and many others. They were once alive as we are alive and they were once moving on earth where the human and divine stories intersect. A reader should be able to be part of the lives of those persons in the text either as a spectator or as an actor.

- Observing the backgrounds: literary, historical, and spiritual:
  The Bible is a historical document written in human languages. Thus a reader should pay attention to the literary aspect of the Bible. The Bible has its own historical, cultural, social, economic, political, and religious backgrounds. We cannot and should not simply ignore these backgrounds of the Bible. At the same time a reader should be mindful of the spiritual background of the text as the Bible testifies to the intersection of spiritual (or trans-historical) realities with the historical process of human life.

Step Two: Perceiving God's ways (or spiritual insights)

A reader enters into the biblical reality, re-enacts the behind-the-term reality and observes that reality through an inferential reading. However, the inferential reconstruction of the biblical reality is not the ultimate goal. Our hermeneutical interest is to perceive God's ways – spiritual insights for our personal knowledge and personal transformation. We may call it the trans-temporal and trans-spatial principle, or meta-phenomenal truth that we attempt to retrieve from the text. A reader is to study the Bible to gain biblical insights and teachings that will help us: (1) to develop our intimate relationship with God; (2) to die to our flesh on a daily basis; (3) to perceive God's ways that we are to follow in our daily lives; and (4) to actualise the spiritual gifts and powers written in the Bible.

The Bible and Asian resources

Another issue we need to address is the use of Asian resources along with the Bible. Archie C. C. Lee suggests a cross-textual hermeneutics as the most appropriate approach to the Bible in Asia.[11] He dismisses the 'text-alone' approach and the text-context interpretative mode in the multi-religious context of Asia. He holds that the cross-textual hermeneutics will solve what he calls the dilemma of Asian biblical interpretation. The dilemma is linked with the theological premise that God has been present in the histories, religions, and cultures in Asia. Thus Lee argues that we need to accept the Asian religious text (text B) along with the biblical text (text A). The hermeneutical task in Asia necessarily includes two sides:

> On the one hand, [cross-textual hermeneutics] affirms the cultural-historical point of view in order to understand its form and setting-in-life. The text is then applied to and interpreted in a contemporary context. It is assumed that the text can enlighten our context. On the other hand,

our Asian perspectives must also be brought in to shed light on the interpretation of biblical text.[12]

In another article Lee proposes a creative inter-penetration between the Gospel and the Asian cultural text as the guiding principle in cross-textual hermeneutics.[13]

We find similar suggestions in other Asian theologians. In his article, 'The Bible and its Asian readers', Sugitharajah surveys the hermeneutical trend in Asia that creatively employs 'divers textual expressions of human-divine encounter' in the interpretative process.[14] He argues that 'it amounts to a religious bigotry to claim the uniqueness and superiority of one religious tradition over others, and the Christian scriptures should be regarded as only one among many references in the search for truth, recognising the definite limitations of the closed Christian canon'.[15] Wesley Ariarajah's *The Bible and People of Other Faiths* espouses the same idea.

What we see behind the proposals for cross-textual or comparative textual studies is the presuppsition that God has been present in Asia before the advent of Christianity. We cannot fail to notice that this theological presupposition has affected the contours of Asian biblical hermeneutics. In fact, this emphasis on God's presence in Asia is linked with the shift in the Christian attitude toward other religions.

Asian Christians' experience of religious plurality is to be correctly described. In Asia, each religion is a comprehensive system to perceive humanity, nature, and the universe, and maintains its own religious identity with its own faith community. Hinduism, Buddhism, and Confucianism each have their unique religious identity and teachings.

But the cultural identity of an Asian needs to be differentiated from his or her religious commitment to a particular religion. An Indian may be Hindu by culture, but that does not always mean Hindu by religious commitment. A Korean may be a Shamanist, a Buddhist, a Confucian, or a Taoist by culture, but not a Shamanist-Buddhist-Confucian-Taoist by religious commitment. Asians carry the traditional religious elements in their body, but multiple simultaneous commitment to various religions is something alien to the experience of religious plurality in Asia.

If the reader's religious identity by commitment is Christian, it is not right to demand that he or she be 'open to different religious and cultural insights in the matter of interpreting the texts'.[16] In the same way, it is not imaginable to advise a Buddhist scholar-monk to be consciously open to the Christian insights in reading the Buddhist sacred books.

Summary and conclusion

As Christianity expands into the global South, our understanding of the Bible will be enriched, for there are teachings of the Bible yet to be discovered. We should realise that the hermeneutical environment in the non-Western world is rather different from that in the West. Some hermeneutical issues that have emerged in Western Christian circles can benefit from the critical reflection of non-Western Christian scholars. Informed by Asia's ancient religious traditions and cultural ethos, readers of the Bible in Asia will bring fresh eyes to biblical interpretation. Biblical authority may have to be re-conceptualised; the goal of the biblical studies may have to be re-defined; and Bible reading methods may have to be re-designed. As the effectiveness and validity of the traditional way of reading the Bible is currently in serious question, a new reading method that will measure up the intention of the biblical text can be implemented.

5. Worship is Nothing but Mission: A Reflection on Some Japanese Experiences

Ken Christoph Miyamoto

The centenary of the historic World Missionary Conference held in Edinburgh in 1910 is now approaching. For the last several years, a project called 'Towards 2010' has been going on, preparing for a 2010 centenary conference planned to be held in the Church of Scotland Assembly Hall where the 1910 conference was also held.

The purpose of the 2010 meeting is not only to celebrate the centenary but also to seek the direction for Christian mission in the twenty-first century. The project has identified nine mission themes to be discussed for Edinburgh 2010. A document dated 7 June 2006 entitled, 'Towards 2010: Mission for the 21st century', lists these themes as follows:

- Foundations for mission
- Christian mission among other faiths
- Mission and postmodernities
- Mission and power
- Forms of missionary engagement
- Theological education and formation
- Christian communities in contemporary contexts
- Mission and unity – ecclesiology and mission
- Mission spirituality and authentic discipleship.[1]

These themes cover major areas of concern in today's Christian mission. One may, however, be struck by an important omission: that is, there is no mention of worship among them. A hundred years ago, Edinburgh 1910 deliberately set aside the question of worship to focus on practical issues, knowing that the question would raise controversies over faith and order and perhaps deter important components of the Christian world from attending. It was, however, soon recognised that the question was central both to mission and unity, and the Faith and Order Movement initiated under the leadership of Bishop Charles

Brent became one of the three major components of the ecumenical movement, an undoubted product of Edinburgh 1910. Today, no one would deny the vital significance of worship in the Christian life. The church ceases to be the church when it ceases to worship. By the same token, mission ceases to be Christian when it is separated from worship. One may therefore wonder why such a central dimension of the Christian life has been omitted from the proposed themes for Edinburgh 2010. It would seem that there has been no real progress in this respect during the century since Edinburgh 1910.

In fact, this omission is rather common. Following the Lambeth Conference of 1988, the Anglican Consultative Council (ACC) in 1990 identified the so-called 'Five Marks of Mission' as:

> To proclaim the Good News of the Kingdom
> To teach, baptise, and nurture new believers
> To respond to human need by loving service
> To seek to transform unjust structures of society
> To strive to safeguard the integrity of creation and sustain and renew the earth.[2]

On this list Paul Avis comments saying:

> This summary has proved serviceable in many arenas of Church and inter-Church life. But we can see at a glance that it is deficient ... [T]here is no mention of worship offered to God and particularly of the Eucharist as the centre and summit of worship.[3]

This comment is to the point. A more recent ACC statement indicates a development in the direction of taking the missiological significance of worship more seriously. It states that 'worship is not just something we do alongside our witness to the good news: worship is itself a witness to the world'.[4] This is a healthy development. Why should we leave worship out of our discussions of Christian mission if we believe that the church is the community of God's people, whose life centres on the ceaseless act of prayer and worship?

When the centrality of worship is forgotten, Christian mission may suffer a grave distortion and its effectiveness may be seriously endangered. One finds an example of such a problem in the practices of Christian education at many of the universities and colleges that Western missionaries founded in Japan many generations ago.

A Westerner who is interested in Japan from a missiological perspective tends to pay attention to its traditional religions and to interfaith dialogue. However, Japan's urban areas, such as Yokohama and Kobe, where I have spent much of my life, are dominantly post-religious and highly secularised. Indeed, most urban Japanese still live with the rites of passage that came from Buddhism, Shinto, and Christianity. They often like to celebrate holidays (including Christmas and even St Valentine's Day), which derive from these religions. They give, however, little attention to these religions as such in their daily lives, and are almost totally ignorant of what these religions are all about. When asked about their religious affiliation, the average Japanese would describe themselves as *mushukyo*, that is, non-religious. Of course, they from time to time raise the questions of the meaning of life, and in this sense they are still 'religious'. Such questions are, however, usually expressed in secular languages and concerns. In many ways, Japanese urban life is quite similar to the life in cities of the post-Christian West.

In my observation, Christian colleges in urban Japan (I teach undergraduate courses on Christianity at one such college in Kobe) are no exception. Japan has many Christian universities and colleges founded by Western missionaries many decades ago. Although these schools still cherish the memory of their Christian heritage, most of them have in fact become very secular, as has happened to so many universities and colleges of Christian origin in Europe and North America. There are not many Christians among their faculty members. Having grown up in today's secular society, students are mostly indifferent to religion in general and do not believe that religions can offer them anything substantial. The contemporary international situation also contributes to their indifference and even suspicion of religions since so many people are dying every day due to religious conflicts all over the world.

As I engage in teaching introductory courses in Christianity (some of them required by the curriculum) to young people, I constantly wonder what the real purpose of teaching such courses is. Our hope is partly that the knowledge of Christianity as one of the world religions will help students get a better understanding of human culture and history. We have, however, a greater hope. We hope, whether directly or indirectly, explicitly or not, that the knowledge they gain will lead them some day to a personal encounter with God and eventually to a confession of faith in Jesus Christ as Lord and Saviour.

Our students, however, have no motivation for taking the courses in Christian studies. Generally speaking, there appears a profound, pervasive disenchantment among young people with the academic knowledge that modern higher education offers them. It is part of the contemporary disillusionment with modernity. Japan has indeed achieved a high level of modernisation; this apparent success, however, has failed to assure the population of the meaningfulness of life, and in recent years more than 30,000 Japanese annually have committed suicide out of despair. The Japanese are today less confident than before that modernisation, supported by the accumulation of scientific knowledge, will really solve problems in their lives and bring about a further betterment of society.

Such wavering is natural in the case of the value of knowledge about a religion that young people do not believe in. Students begin without motivation; they take the courses simply because they are required to do so by the curriculum of their school. A few, perhaps, show interest in the subject as the course proceeds, but the majority finish the semester confirmed in the belief that Christianity is simply boring and without relevance for their lives. They conclude that they stand to gain no benefit from knowledge about the ancient writings called the Bible, nor the obscure ancient figure named Jesus Christ, nor an unintelligible imaginary being called God. It is a difficult task to help them understand the life-giving quality of Christianity, even though this task is extremely important if we are truly concerned with Christian mission in twenty-first century Japan.

Here we are seeing the breakdown of one approach to Christian mission that has been traditional in Japan, and once bore much fruit: 'through an education-al process dedicated to the imparting of rational knowledge' including the scientific knowledge of Christianity.[5] Christian colleges require their students to take the courses in Christianity because they still operate with the approach that sees the dissemination of the Christian knowledge as the primary way to evangelism. I believe that this traditional understanding has now become a major obstacle, and that we have to go beyond it to overcome the current impasse.

The fundamental question here is whether Christianity can be reduced to an intellectually teachable body of biblical and theological ideas, and whether the body of ideas can really serve as the gateway to Christianity. Probably it can – if it is not separated from the core of the Christian life, that is, the communal life of faith centred on common worship. The reality on the campuses, however, is that worship is very often pushed to the margins of life, and that teaching in the lecture room is cut off from the act of worship. As a result, most students hardly have a chance to experience the transforming power of the Christian Gospel taught in their classes.

The issue is not simply the question why we teach Christianity in secularised Christian colleges. There are more basic questions to be asked. Is the emphasis on rational knowledge appropriate as an approach to Christian mission or to Christian education? Does it truly conform to the fundamental character of the Christian life?

As I have said, Christian education at Christian colleges (particularly Protestant ones) is usually based on the approach to Christian mission that sees rational knowledge as the foundation of faith. This approach has its root in what Brian Stanley calls the 'unshakable confidence in the regenerative capacity of rational knowledge'[6] among the modern Protestant missionaries. Such a confidence came both from the Enlightenment trust in reason and from the Protestant understanding of Christianity primarily as God's self-disclosure in Jesus Christ. According to this view, the knowledge of God disclosed in Jesus Christ and witnessed in the Scriptures is considered as sufficient for salvation.

Theologically, this view presents no problem. Christianity is not, however, simply a sum of rational knowledge. It is primarily a way of life, a life centred on God. The knowledge of God's redemption in Jesus Christ needs to take a concrete form in a life grounded on the restored relationship between God and humanity, and such a life must be embodied in the life of a community centred on the worship of God. Doctrinal, theological, and biblical knowledge is important, and Christianity ceases to exist without it. Knowledge, nonetheless, becomes empty as soon as it is separated from the worship-centred life. In worship, the living God reveals himself personally to us human beings by means of the Word and the Sacraments, and we respond to God personally in prayer, thanksgiving, and offering. Thus, in the midst of worship an intimate encounter takes place between God and human beings.

This is not to deny the truth that God is redemptively at work in human history outside of the Church, as contemporary contextual theologians in the Third World have repeatedly insisted.[7] It is rather to affirm that God draws nearest to the world in the midst of worship, particularly in the Eucharist. There the broken relation between God and human beings is healed, and the right relation restored; human beings are transformed into the people of God; and the people of God are transformed into the true people of God. There the repeated personal encounter with God helps us internalise the divine grace and gradually nurtures our faith in God, and we thus develop a new identity as members of God's people.

This personal encounter with God is the true foundation for personal transformation. Contrarily, theological knowledge as such does not have such a transforming power although it certainly serves as a guide and framework. We therefore need to see a worship-centred life as the target of Christian mission. The church in mission is sent to the world as the locus where the worship-centred life takes place on earth. Inviting a friend of mine to Christianity does not simply mean inviting him/her to learn conceptually who Jesus Christ is and what God has done in him for our salvation. Nor does it simply mean an invitation to join an institute called the church. Inviting somebody to Christianity above all means inviting him/her to worship God together, to share the common life of 'celebration and thanksgiving'.[8]

For the average Japanese, the act of worshipping together is something quite new; there are so few occasions for it except for such occasions as weddings and funerals. Worshipping together, therefore, may initially cause a certain degree of perplexity and uneasiness. As they gradually get used to it, however, it starts to change their lives on the subconscious level, nourishing them spiritually just as good food nourishes the body and mind and helps it grow physically. They little by little internalise God's grace, identify themselves with Jesus Christ, and are eventually led to the confession of faith. Worship has a power to transform them and create in them a new identification oriented towards God.

A personal commitment to Jesus Christ thus arises from participation in the community of worship. There also Christian knowledge becomes truly alive and meaningful, and with this comes commitment. Avis argues correctly: 'Participation in community creates a sense of belonging, and belonging is the prerequisite for believing.'[9]

Because of this transforming power, worship cannot be seen as something additional to other activities in mission. It occupies and must occupy the central place in Christian mission as well as mission theology. While Lambeth 1988 considered the discussion of liturgy as 'inward-looking' and put it in the last section of the report, it nonetheless recognised that '[t]he Church's liturgy ... is bound up with her mission, and the renewal of her liturgy is bound up with the renewal of her mission'.[10] Worship is the place where God meets the world in the most intense way. Worship is never a private matter that only belongs to those who believe in God. It is rather a public matter where God directly challenges the unbelieving world, transforming it profoundly and taking it personally into the divine realm. Worship is the liturgy, *leitourgia*, public service offered by God in Christ to the world. It ultimately embraces the entire cosmos.

It is now widely recognised that mission and unity are inseparable. Only when the people of God are truly united in love is their witness to God authentic and effective. They present the divine love and grace to the world when they love each other and transcend the brokenness pervasive in the world. The world sees the divine presence in the Christian fellowship grounded on love, no matter how imperfect it is; it experiences the divine love personally through the mediation of the fellowship of those who daily struggle to love, following Christ's example. This does not exclude other possible ways to a personal experience of God's love, but there is no doubt that the fellowship of love centred on common worship plays a prominent role in Christian witness.

Sadly, however, the brokenness of the Christian community is most visible when Christians come together to celebrate the ritual core of their life, namely, the Eucharist. After a century of the ecumenical movement, Christians are now able to co-operate in various areas of their existence. As a consequence, the disunity at the Lord's Table is even more evident than ever before. In this sense, we have to admit that the ecumenical movement has not experienced any substantial breakthrough.

This problem has serious practical implications for mission and evangelism in a country like Japan where a small Christian minority is divided into numerous denominations. For instance, my college, though Christian, has fewer than twenty Christians among about 3000 faculty members and students. Though the college is affiliated to the Anglican Church in Japan (Nippon Sei Ko Kai), those twenty Christians belong to different denominations, Reformed, Baptist, Anglican, and Roman Catholic. This situation is neither exceptional nor unusual in Japan. We often encounter a similar situation whenever Christians get together outside their own congregations. In other words, we are often in an ecumenical fellowship when we meet other Christians outside our own churches, and when we are placed in a missionary context, sent into the wider, predominantly non-Christian society as witnesses to Christ.

And it is exactly at this point that our divisions become most visible, proving to be a grave obstacle to our witness. We of course accept each other as fellow Christians, but we are, sadly, neither able to come together to the Lord's Table nor to invite our non-Christian friends to it. The Eucharist, ironically, becomes the visible sign of our sin, brokenness, and failure to follow Christ's commandment though it is originally meant to be the sign of God's grace and human unity.

Needless to say, those who are not baptised are, in principle, not allowed to take bread and wine at the Eucharist. However, as is commonly practised in Anglican churches, the minister can invite them to the Lord's Table and communicate the divine grace to them by blessing them individually. This blessing

can be a unique spiritual experience for many and lead them to spiritual transformation. In the Eucharist, they are also offered a chance to witness the divine
mystery of redemption taking place at the heart of God's people. Consequently,
they are challenged and invited to take part in God's mission. Thus, the
Eucharist has a profoundly missiological significance. When we fail to celebrate
the Eucharist together, it means depriving our non-Christian friends of a valuable chance to personally experience God's grace and witness the living God at
work among their friends. The disunity of the church in the Eucharist is nothing
but a scandalous hindrance for its mission and must be overcome urgently.

The ecumenical movement has often discussed structural union; but structural union is not the point. The urgent question is whether the people of God
are able to come together to the Lord's Table and become one there. If eucharistic union is achieved, structural unity will become redundant. Eucharistic unity
is the goal that we desperately need to achieve as long as we aspire to be true
witnesses of God's redemption with our whole being.

Finally, we need to reflect on the question of what kind of worship is adequate
today. Typical Protestant worship has a serious weakness. Traditionally, it has at
its centre elements that depend on the rational factor: the reading of Scripture,
the sermon, verbal prayers, and hymns. Sermons are often quite long, the
Eucharist celebrated only occasionally, and with little symbolism. It is rational
worship.

But today's young people are raised in an increasingly audio-visual culture.
Many of them hardly have patience to listen to their college lectures attentively.
They are not attracted by the idea of going to church to listen to another lecture
on Sunday. It is understandable that so many churches where the sole stress is
on the rational factor lose the younger generation. The situation is made even
worse by the fact that this approach tends to exclude children, since full participation presupposes the ability to comprehend the sermon intellectually.
Foreigners, mentally impaired people, and some older people are similarly
restricted.

It is a situation that calls for renewed attention to liturgy and to non-verbal
symbolism. As Charles Ryerson of Princeton Theological Seminary writes:

> Myth, symbol, and ritual are, as you know, very powerful in both
> creating and sustaining a belief system. Protestants went too far
> with the Enlightenment and stressed rational factors, like the ser-
> mon, to the detriment of a meaningful liturgy. In most Protestant
> churches, for example, the music is only added entertainment, not
> an integral part of the worship.[11]

This observation suggests an urgent need for today's churches to rediscover
symbolic, non-rational factors in worship and overcome an impoverishment
inflicted by the Enlightenment emphasis on reason and knowledge.

In this connection, Maita Church, a Kyodan (United Church of Christ) church
in Yokohama, is a successful example. While many Protestant churches in urban

Japan have fallen into stagnation in recent years, this congregation has kept drawing in new people of different generations. Under the leadership of Rev. Akira Imahashi, Maita's former senior pastor, a professor of liturgics in a seminary in Tokyo, it has combined liturgical renewal with education over a period of years. Imahashi has long insisted that worship is mission, and has little by little incorporated into the Sunday service a range of symbolic enrichment, with many visual elements and careful attention to the calendar, the lectionary and new hymnody. As an educationalist, he has never forgotten to help the congregation understand the meaning of these liturgical elements. The enrichment has made Maita's worship attractive and enjoyable and helped its members develop a strong sense of belonging and identity as Christians. Maita is today a centre of the liturgical renewal in the Protestant churches in Japan.

This example tells us how powerful liturgy is. It is quite likely that many Japanese actually have a deeply hidden longing for mystery while they appear on the surface secular and post-religious. With its rich symbolism, liturgical worship is capable of communicating the divine mystery to such longing hearts and minds as a vehicle of the Holy Spirit.

It has, of course, its own dangers. When the church forgets the meaning of liturgy and its symbolism and simply clings to formal observance, then worship is soon mummified. Its life, therefore, has to be renewed constantly with ceaseless prayer attentive to the Holy Spirit, as well as continuous reflection on the mystery of God's redemption to which the church and its liturgy point.

6. Education as Mission: Perspectives on Some New Opportunities

Gerald J. Pillay

How this century will turn out is quite likely to be very different from anything that we can imagine – even among the most prescient among us. Few at the beginning of the last century could have imagined that two periods of global conflict lay ahead; yet those two world wars were radically and indelibly to change the shape, destiny, and values of Europe and many other parts of the world. In 1908, when people were still getting used to the notion of flight, who could have foreseen the technological advances that would shrink the world in distance and time, and place a man on the moon? Who could have imagined, even fifty years ago, the opportunities that the World Wide Web, internet, and email would bring in terms of global communications and how differently individuals would interact with each other?

Our imaginings at this early stage in a new century, therefore, should be modest in scope and reach. In the context of these essays, when trying to en-visage the role of Christian higher education institutions in this century we should perhaps only attempt to understand our present predicament as Christian educators, and seek how we as part of academe may continue to sing the Lord's song in the increasingly strange land of academe. We may venture only to imagine what may be our purpose as Christian educators for the period of our own lives and, even then, should expect that there will be some surprises.

What, then, is the missiological role of Christian educational institutions in these uncertain times? The suggestions offered here are based largely on personal experiences in particular parts of the world. The question we face, not only in the West but wherever globalisation propagates secular liberalism, is, What is the abiding role of Christian educators in societies that have adopted a distinct antipathy to religion? Secularism is an ideological determinant that has influenced the habits, discourse, and language of the public square in which Christians co-exist with others. And there, Christian institutions find themselves at the margins.

An established cultural mandate

In spite of the familiar arguments for constraining public religious influence and identifying religion as a source of divisiveness and human conflict, any fair reflection on the thousand-year-long history of the formation of Europe must view Christianity as a civilising influence, shaping the best of European culture. Pre-literate Europe received its education through the efforts of the church. The more sophisticated Byzantine Greek Christian culture of the East, and the blossoming and intellectually dynamic Muslim culture were far ahead of the primitive West in Charlemagne's time. It was the establishment of the cathedral school and the teaching of Latin to illiterate priests under the visionary prompt- ings of people like Alcuin of York that secured the viability of the Western European culture and education that today we take for granted. Latin gave it wholeness and connectedness. These cathedral schools were the forerunners of the medieval university. The first universities were church foundations, steered by theologians whose discipline laid claim to being the then queen of the sciences. (The much older Buddhist universities in the East at Toxila and Nilanda were also inspired by religious faith.)

Whatever we make of the temporal preoccupations of the medieval church, its power-brokering and political intrigue, the cultural flowering of the European Renaissance benefited greatly from the patronage of a church commit- ted to building the Kingdom of God on earth. 'Renaissance', the word that describes one of the great creative moments of early European civilisation, derives from the Christian notion of 'being born again'. It was the rebirth of a whole culture inspired by the rediscovery of classical Greece and Rome. Its humanist motifs, nevertheless, remained viable within a religious consensus about society now much more optimistic than in the previous, darker, centuries.

The Enlightenment, often pictured as liberation from church control and often viewed, especially in Anglo-Saxon circles, as fundamentally anti-Christian, had some devout Christians at its helm. Descartes, the father of modern mathe- matics and philosophy, was a devout Catholic. Newton was as interested in the doctrine of the Trinity as he was in the principles behind the physical world. The European Enlightenment is distinctly not as anti-religious as the contemporary prophets of secularisation portray it. They have aided and abetted the narrow- ing of the purview of the university and the tendency to privatise faith or to exclude it from the public or academic domain. These caricatures of religion are relatively recent – largely the product of the twentieth century.

It is now clear that those prophets of secularity were wrong who argued that by the end of the twentieth century religion would be disappearing. Peter Berger, for example, has reflected on why he changed his mind regarding the future of religion. It is true of course that the church is no longer a leading influence on public attitudes or a prime opinion-former. Christendom, as it was conceived of before the eighteenth century, no longer exists. Yet these develop- ments are not necessarily lamented by Christians, for the message of Christ is often most vital in contexts where there are no privileges under political aegis, such as the Dutch Reformed Church received in apartheid South Africa. Persecuted minority Christian communities have often shown the greatest resilience and creativity as the past century has witnessed under communist rule in Russia and China.

The view that the world as it progresses will eventually come to adopt European secularism also appears now to be largely incorrect. Africa and Asia accommodate religion and progress together in ways that Europe cannot conceive. There has been no equivalent of Christendom in European history, no adoption of Christianity as part of the state, no established religion, with its capacity to foster the persecution of others. Christian communities in Africa and Asia do not now behave or think like their former teachers from Europe. They have very different histories of co-existence with other Christians and other religions. Christians in India, for instance, have co-existed as a Christian minority alongside majority religions for many centuries and have achieved a measure of cultural integration with people of other faiths that seems impossible in many parts of Europe.

Within Europe, however, the Christian educationist has a well-established cultural mandate. Christianity preceded Europe as we know it today, influencing the tribes and fiefdoms before the formation of the large monarchies and nations. Europe is the product of the cultural engagement of the Church; and this from the time of the early Celtic missionary enterprises that created scholarly oases in the wilderness to the high culture of medieval Europe that witnessed some of the finest flowering of its art, literature, and music. It is impossible to unscramble the European cultural amalgam, permeated as it is by Christianity.

In the company of a global alliance of Christian minority communities

We may well have to conceive of this new century as a time of co-existence and interconnectedness of living Christian minority faiths across cultures and continents. Like-minded Christian educational institutions across the globe, vulnerable within their own settings, may well receive sustenance from each other because they share a common missiological purpose. Their strength and confidence will be nurtured within this global family. Their number and global presence will make them difficult to ignore. The Christian minorities in what have hitherto been the 'Western heartlands' of the faith are moving with time to the periphery of world Christianity. The Christian faith in Europe may be returning to a pre-Constantinian stage where it has no dominance or official status, no patronage of government and in some cases may be open to discrimination or persecution. (A BBC poll undertaken in March 2007 revealed that one in three Christians in the UK claimed to have experienced some form of discrimination because of their faith.)

However, we must return to the issue of Christianity's abiding interest in education as a civilising force, for it is in this area that the greatest missiological opportunities may exist for Christian faith. It is true that in reaching out to all people the churches, through their schools, have made contact with many new communities without necessarily making large numbers of converts. The early outreach by the Catholic and Methodist Churches, for example, to the indentured Indian labourers who first arrived in Natal in the nineteenth century brought them in touch with Hindus, Muslims, and only a very small Christian community. The Christian community did not grow in any significant way during the first fifty years of their work even though their Hindu and Muslim beneficiaries greatly appreciated the work of the Christian missionaries. Many local people were introduced to Christian faith through Christian educational institutions but these schools were not necessarily very successful in making Christians of their pupils. These schools had a wider and deeper social and political benefit not easily measured through the numbers of converts. Many of the children of indentured labourers were able to escape their parents' lot through these schools. Similarly, almost all of the first generation of the leaders of the new African states received their educational opportunities through the church schools. Despite the small size of the Christian population in India, substantial numbers of Hindu and Muslim leaders have benefited from church schools and colleges.

At the beginning of this new century, the Christian faith has had to engage with other cultures and other religions more directly and more closely than ever before. Large and rapidly developing economies such as India and China now constitute equal partners who often rival Western countries in areas that were hitherto the preserve of the developed countries. We are all now becoming equal players in the global village. Even small countries rebuff the haughtiness of the large and mighty. The West is no longer the initiator of contact nor the dominant player in international relations as for much of the twentieth century. The 'orientalism' of former times has been disembowelled. Where it lingers it only exposes backwardness of thought and understanding.

In our post-colonial, post-imperial times we have lived through what mission historians have identified as a 'shift of the centre of gravity' of world Christianity, from the North to the South and from the West to the East. Christianity has ceased in our time to be a predominantly white or European religion. It is now a world religion in the fullest sense, with the majority representation coming from cultures outside of Europe and North America.

The implications of this fundamental shift are already becoming clear for the church in its catholic, ecumenical, and global scope. Western bishops are now outnumbered and the balance of power has shifted in ecclesiastical conferences. Denominational affiliations have become less important and Christian alliances against unbelief and for the furtherance of justice and peace have commensurately become easier to facilitate.

When the state of the Christian faith is not viewed through Eurocentric spectacles, it ceases quite phenomenally to be a story of decline. A changed vantage point, from India or Africa for example, reveals a story of growth and vitality. The Diocese of South Kerala, for example, has 800,000 members and 625 churches; on average, a new church is established every month. Although Christians still form a minority, the Christian community is outward looking and confident.

The global implications of that vibrancy have already been felt in the lands that once sent missionaries to other parts of the world. Now these lands in effect receive missionaries from the lands to which they once sent them. Amid the declining statistics of church attendance in the United Kingdom, the vitality of Afro-Caribbean congregations in London tells a different story. So do the Polynesian congregations in Auckland or the Chinese and Korean churches in Australia or USA. The numbers attending Mass in the north west of England have grown largely due to the presence of several hundred nurses from the Philippines working in the region's hospitals. Warrington, in Merseyside, once predicted to shrink in size, has grown in recent years largely due to immigration. Many of the 2000 Poles who have settled there are devout Catholics. They have made necessary a Polish language service on Sunday afternoons. The religious implications of Britain's opening itself to all of Europe have never been fully factored into the predictions of sociologists, let alone the global migrations of people from the East to the West and from the South to the North. There is no reason to believe that these movements of peoples will cease because of attempts by modern states to control them. Europeans once populated the Americas and Australasia; now migrations are following a different pattern.

A further imponderable is the influence of ecumenical relationships. The concentration of Catholics in north west England has led to the establishment of over 35 Catholic high schools that are open to those of other faiths or none. These schools constitute a major feeder into higher education and, potentially, to church-related universities and colleges. Demographic predictions show that the population of this region is not growing in proportion to the movement southwards for work. There is thus an unexpected opportunity for Christian educational institutions that would not have been envisaged even five years ago. These schools constitute a major missiological opportunity for the Catholic archdiocese to influence tens of thousands of students and their families. The same is true of Anglican schools and of the second ecumenical academy in Merseyside, in which the Catholics and Anglicans are collaborating. A quarter of a century ago there was much intolerance towards church schools in Britain and a widespread belief that the state sector could offer educational provisions for the whole society. The mood of the 1960s and 1970s militated against the establishment of more church schools. Today the Christian schools help to prop up the nation's educational system. They have become indispensable. In contrast to the scepticism about many state schools, there is recognition of the quality and care provided in church schools. It is widely known that families will sometimes contrive church affiliation in order to gain admission for their child.

The same is true of many non-Western societies. One of the great legacies of the missionary period in India has been the schools and colleges, which serve a largely non-Christian population. Christians make up barely 4 per cent of the population, yet in the top ten university colleges in India, six are church foundations of the calibre of St Loyola College, Madras Christian College, Chennai, St Xavier's in Mumbai, and St Stephen's in New Delhi. While the church schools have a constitutional right to admit up to 50 per cent of their students from the Christian community, in practice the majority who are admitted are not

Christians. The high quality of these institutions and their distinctive ethos of personal care and nurturing have resulted in great competition for places. Several of them over the years have become centres of excellence.

In the United States too, state schools have varying degrees of acceptability and the church sector would be the first choice for many parents who cannot afford to send their children to private schools. The church sector in many parts of the world provides a viable and sought-after alternative to expensive, self-funded schools or elitist colleges on the one hand, and the state sector on the other. In general, church foundations maintain a good quality of education and retain the confidence of the communities they serve.

The challenge facing Christian schools and colleges in Britain is to maintain their sought-after quality and educational values in the context that argues for the secularisation of education; to maintain viability and integrity in a post-Christendom context where loud voices argue against the very existence of distinctively Christian institutions.

Lesslie Newbigin spoke about the need for Christians in our times to acquire a 'proper confidence' in the face of cynicism about religion. One source of this 'proper confidence' must surely be the entrenched cultural goodwill that the churches possess by virtue of serving society for so long.

In the university sector in Britain, there is a small but not insignificant group of church colleges and universities. Many of them pre-date the establishment of the so-called 'red brick' universities which emerged in the later nineteenth and early twentieth century. For instance, the founding college of what is now Liverpool Hope University was established in 1844, when there were only six universities in England, two of them the medieval establishments of Oxford and Cambridge. Very little by way of expanding the opportunities for higher education was attempted for the bulk of the population before the time that these church colleges were established.

At the beginning of the present century, the British government established criteria whereby university colleges could apply for university status. Of the first eight that were granted university title by the Privy Council, six were church foundations. In a sense, they were rewarded for their resilience (some have survived for over 150 years).

The educational institution as a means to widening participation

Governments in both the developed and developing world are being increasingly judged by their ability to address the problems of inequity and unfairness. The issues of poverty and economic development, stark in the developing world, exist in developed countries as well. The big cities and metropolitan areas have engendered their own underclasses and these are not confined to immigrants and ethnic minorities. Britain, for example, still struggles with the deep-seated effects of a class structure built over centuries. This is the background to the question of raising educational aspirations in large sections of its population.

The last twenty years have seen an effort to engender what has been termed the 'massification' of higher education to subvert the traditional elitism of the university system. In the 1960s several of the then Colleges of Advanced Technology (CATs) were granted university status. Forty years on, several of these are among the best-regarded universities. In 1992 the Conservative government granted university status to over thirty polytechnics in an attempt to create more opportunities for those hitherto excluded. Under the present Labour government, all universities are regularly reviewed as to their progress in social inclusion. 'Widening participation' has become a badge of honour for universities as they try to convince the funding agencies that they are progressing in this area. However, the traditional inbuilt elitism of the educational system in the United Kingdom means that the post-1992 institutions outdo the older universities in attracting students from poor and deprived postcode areas and bring more 'non-traditional students' into higher education.

For Christian educational foundations, this interest in the excluded and socially disinherited is part of their mission and calling. They too do better on average in attracting and caring for students who are the first entrants to higher education in their families than many other universities in the country. Liverpool Hope University, for example, was the result of the coming together of three colleges, two of which were founded in the mid-nineteenth century. Several church colleges were established to address the educational needs of the poor. It was only in 1832 with the Education Reform Bill that it was formally accepted that the children of working-class English people should be educated. Three years before had seen the Catholic Emancipation Act (1829) allowing Catholics, in principle, the same civic rights as other citizens. The church colleges were among the first to address the situation of large numbers of poor Catholics among the working classes of England. Little wonder that in the colonies the British government often failed to understand the educational needs of indigenous peoples; it had barely begun to grapple with the education of the working class at home. By contrast it was the church schools that often provided the first real educational opportunities for the indigenous peoples.

The rich protect themselves from integration with the rest of the population by creating economic zones that only they can afford to live in. With them come private schools for their children – independent schools for which they pay high fees. It is in this context that the Christian institution has a special role, that does not originate in government edicts about widening participation for the under-privileged or even in a general wish to do good to the poor. The Christian institution has the overriding obligation of obedience to Christ who taught that service done to the least is service done to him. It is part of its nature and its mission. Widening participation at institutions such as my own is an ever-abiding responsibility.

Christian institutions must dare to be different, to transcend the functional, and the proclivities of the privileged and the values of 'the way we live now'. It is significant that one of the first acts of the apartheid government in South Africa when it came to power was to take over church schools, converting them into state-funded institutions under the state's educational department. The reason was simple: the church schools constituted a threat to the state ideology; they seemed hotbeds of liberal ideas. The best compliment they could receive was that they were considered subversive: places that fostered the liberation of the individual and of society.

Alternative communities

To be an alternative community is difficult, costly, and hard to sustain. Many church educational foundations are tempted to underplay their Christian credentials in order to ensure successful recruitment. By mimicking the secular university they hope to increase their own academic credibility. This may well be the shortest route to their downfall. If church foundations are just small or medium-sized versions of the large inner-city secularised universities, they have little new or different to offer. It is precisely when they become creative, alternative communities that Christian foundations offer something of value. It is inconceivable that the tens of thousands who now deliberately choose a church school over a state school should have, after high school, no real alternative to the secular university.

The freedom to establish independent, private schools and to fund them through church communities and benefactions is a tradition well established in the USA but not in the Anglo-Saxon world, where there is an assumption that education, like health care, is a government responsibility. It could be argued that the freedom to establish self-funding schools is very limited in countries that once were 'welfare states', where higher taxation ensured that education remained a public good, funded or at least subsidised by the taxpayer. Once again, within the global village, church educational institutions in nations such as Britain may find their allies less in their own country than among like-minded institutions in non-Western societies. It is even more likely that there would be mutual benefits in the coming together across continents and the association of like-minded church foundations forming a global alliance to support their mission and values. There have been several attempts by Western universities to establish themselves in the East or to form consortia and formal alliances. Christian foundations, on the other hand, have a natural basis for co-operation in their common mission. They could form real and sustainable partnerships because of their common purpose.

This opportunity to be an alternative community extends also to the heart of the intellectual responsibility facing Christian institutions that are marginalised and feel themselves on the periphery of the intellectual public square. In the absence of large endowments and benefactor support, they often remain modest in ambition as well as size.

There is a contrivance in the university world that privatises faith and allows dogma to dominate the purview of the university. What does not fit a positivist or empirical base is judged inadmissible or is undervalued in terms of prestige or funding grants. In the eighteenth century Kant wrote about the conflict of the faculties, and made the case for philosophy and theology within the university. There is hardly a basis for this conflict to be described today. Dogma has so dominated the academy that the conflict is subsumed not resolved. Theology ends up in the seminary or if it survives at universities runs the danger of being transmuted into the phenomenology of religion. This narrowing of the intellectual frame of reference is an epistemological fashion evidenced by the preoccupation with methodology even in the humanities and social sciences. The credibility of the disciplines becomes dependent on demonstrating that it has a 'scientific' base. Very often, it is not science that is the determinant but 'knowledge transfer' or, still more often, 'technology transfer', which increasingly drives universities' financial interests, so that the basic sciences give way to the applied.

By the end of the twentieth century universities had come to model themselves on business enterprises. A strong managerial mood dominated the sector. With this 're-engineering' came a new robustness about managing the university's resources. Something was lost in the process. In the absence of the great conventions that have motivated universities and old disciplines over long periods has come a disposition to manage quality, audit processes, and assess performance, with an accompanying fascination with league tables.

It is in this context that the Christian foundations in higher education and Christian academics have a responsibility to restore wholeness to the notion of *universitas* by nurturing living communities of scholarship and learning. One of the unintended consequences of the drive for 'productivity' and 'efficiencies', has been the erosion of community and collegiality on which the university depends. Community is not created by quality audits and performance indicators, important as these may be, but by the depth and quality of the fellowship of students and scholars making a safe place for enquiry and learning. Church foundations understand these ideas at a deep level, for their ultimate derivation is theological and ecclesial. They need to clarify the role of the humanities at the university and the role of theology within the humanities. They need once more to nurture philosophy, science, and faith alongside one another, ensuring that no one of them dominates or colonises the intellectual space that constitutes the university. In the speech that Pope Benedict made at Regensburg, with its unfortunate and controversial citation of a medieval opinion on Islam, the central point was a timely argument for why faith cannot be separated from reason, a position lucidly stated in that under-utilised encyclical of his predecessor, John Paul II, *Fides et Ratio*.

There is a need for Christian scholars working in secularised universities and, above all, for church educational foundations to rediscover their confidence; and to help reframe intellectual pursuits in line with the broader quest for truth, purpose, and meaning, and the development of a humane society. The death of Christendom means there are no added political benefits or patronage. The Christian intellectual community must now articulate afresh its role and mission within a secularised society. Its best allies are institutions that share its nature and purpose in non-Western societies, and these institutions and these academics are often imbued with a freshness and zeal about their faith that may well assist Western Christian intellectuals to recover confidence. We may have to relearn a language, to articulate faith in our times in new ways that overcome the self-consciousness and defensiveness among Christian academics alienated within their societies.

We need, then, to create a broader intellectual basis that goes beyond the kind of rationalist contrivance under which we still labour; to establish a global alliance with the institutions that share a common purpose; to be alternative intellectual communities that refuse to be intimidated by the globalised secularity. The vitality that the Christian community had in the pre-Constantinian phase of the faith must again be renewed, on a global scale, in its new post-Christendom phase.

7. Discipleship: Marked for Mission

Tim Dakin

... mission ... is prior to the church, and constitutive of its very existence.[1]

Introduction

Bevans and Schroeder have written 'the book after Bosch' on mission. Their volume, subtitled *A Theology of Mission for Today*, provides an overview of mission theology and mission history. It identifies six key constants of Christian faith (Christ, church, eschatology, salvation, anthropology, and culture) while considering the variety of ways in which faith is expressed in changing historical and geographical contexts (though three enduring perspectives are identified, called, simply A, B, and C types but corresponding loosely to so-called 'conservative', 'liberal' and 'radical' theologies).

In this chapter I bring the five marks of mission into conversation with Bevans and Schroeder's six constants of Christian faith and relate these to the particular tradition which is where, I propose, the three enduring but changing A, B, and C perspectives are sited. Discipleship is therefore the key site for working out our faith *in contextual practice*.[2] My proposal is that we are 'marked for mission' in so far as our discipleship commits us to the kind of daily lifestyle which the five marks of mission outline and only in this lived expression are the constants of faith and traditions of truth and unity truly known. Using Bevans and Schroeder's three types this would offer three different ways in which the five marks of mission could be used as identifiers of true discipleship. The question for Anglicanism is whether it has sufficient clarity about its own tradition of truth and unity for it to be able to say what is recognisably a 'holy' discipleship and what might therefore be outside the range of acceptable diversity. I affirm the positive role that the proposed Anglican Covenant could play in answering this question, making some suggestions about how the draft could be revised.[3]

Mission first

Bevans and Schroeder do not compromise on the priority they give to mission. It is striking that two Roman Catholic theologians should use the kind of phrases with which this chapter begins or that they should also write 'Mission might also be called the "mother of the church"' (p. 11)! This mission-first agenda sets the tone for the whole book: 'All theology ... must be *missionary* theology' (p.1). In its ecumenical breadth and critical depth, *Constants in Context* offers a great encouragement for all Christians seeking to engage with the 'new mission' agenda of the twenty-first century. This mission-first agenda is the chief marker of discipleship in today's world and, vice-versa, makes clear that all mission should have discipleship as its intended (even if indirect) outcome.

From this perspective the five marks of mission gain a significance which helps to place them in the right relationship with other dimensions of Christian existence. This is necessary because, notoriously, the five marks do not refer, for example, to Christ or to the church. In other words, the five marks necessarily require a broader framework in which to explore how they can be used to become the markers for those who, as disciples, follow Christ in the fellowship of the church. But once given this framework the markers can also then help to give shape to the Christian life in a way that allows discipleship to be wider than the church and encourages followers to express a mission spirituality rooted in the ultimate significance of Jesus for the whole world.

The constants of mission

The constants of mission that Bevans and Schroeder identify can be interpreted as providing two sets of three constants: Christ, eschatology, and salvation; and church, anthropology, and culture. The first set determines the theological existence of Christian life; the second set seeks to explore what that might look like in context. Given that it is in Christ's mission that we see the mission of God revealed and enacted, and taking for granted that the church is given to Christ in the Spirit for God's mission, these two sets of constants become critical for enabling the five marks of mission to be effective in identifying the life of Christian discipleship.

For example, eschatology and salvation are important for the motivation and therefore the expression of mission and its outcome in discipleship. To illustrate this point, take the way that the variety of views on the 1,000-year reign of Christ, as found in the book of Revelation chapter 20, have influenced mission.[4] For post-millennialists the reign of Christ would begin after 1,000 years (or more) of a golden era of church history. They were optimistic about the unfolding of Christ's Kingdom; mission is all about drawing people into this Kingdom culminating in Christ's return. For pre-millennialists Christ's 1,000-year reign is yet to start and it will begin with judgement and only those who have responded to what Christ has done on the cross will be saved. Mission is about getting as many as possible into the Kingdom through preaching the

Gospel. These two different perspectives would affect any outworking of the five marks in the life of discipleship, encouraging on the one hand a more holistic approach to Christian existence and on the other an urgency to get the message of the Gospel across in preaching and teaching. Without unearthing some of these deeper theological constants, the five marks lack credibility as markers of genuine discipleship.

On the other hand, an understanding of anthropology and culture are important for showing how mission can take a variety of forms as the church becomes inculturated in the life of a people and in a place. Here the relationship between education and mission comes to mind.[5] For some Protestant British mission perspectives the education of those who had not yet heard the Gospel was essential in order that they might understand it properly. In other words, the view of humanity that underlay this approach, deemed it necessary for people to develop more fully a rational capacity in order for them to become truly Christian. Such a view presumes the pre-eminence of the culture from which the missioners are coming. It was the breakdown of such cultural prejudices that the encounter with other cultures gradually made possible as both sides of the translation of the Gospel from one culture to another slowly contributed to the process of the Gospel being truly inculturated. Without an awareness of this kind of concern, once again, the five marks of mission can be used in a pragmatic manner to affirm all kinds of mission practice and therefore fail to become markers of true discipleship. Unconsidered views of humanity and culture need to be unearthed so that the process of discipleship becoming a contextual practice allows for the fullness of Christ to be seen trans-culturally and in diverse local human contexts.

A, B, and C perspectives

The three perspectives which Bevans and Schroeder identify (drawn largely from the typology developed by Justo Gonzalez) each get established early. Type A is associated with Carthage and Tertullian, Type B with Alexandria and Origen, and Type C with Antioch and Irenaeus. Each type evolves but each has an enduring perspective that has been projected into modern times; representatives of each type would be John Paul II, Rahner, and Gutierrez, respectively. Each type adopts a variety of angles on the six constants. For example, Type A maintains throughout its history a high view of Christ in which the humanity of Jesus and the historical Jesus take second place to the divine and eternal. With regard to the church, Type A gives preference to the institutional and the hierarchical, drawing a close relationship between sacramental practices and the clergy in the outworking of mission. The law, order of the church, is how the Kingdom of God is known and how the revelation of Jesus is to be interpreted for salvation.

In relation to two other constants, Type B theology offers another perspective. For example, the eschatology of Type B tends towards a realised eschatology: the Kingdom has arrived, we just need to discover more of what this fullness of life is about. There is a high value given to reason and so to the 'analogy of being' or its modern equivalent of the analogical imagination. This is then seen to imply, in the constant of anthropology, that humanity is always educable as grace builds on and perfects nature, and as mission engages with the depths of a culture in the development of a society. Bevans and Schroeder suggest a connection here with Henry Venn's three-self approach to mission, a connection that is strengthened as this model also develops to include the fourth self of self-theologising (p. 60).

Then in Type C, in relation to the constants of salvation and culture, we see another perspective. For this theological perspective salvation is about more than saving the person for a future state of new creation, it is also about the healing of creation as a whole. Salvation is the reconciliation of all things with all things in being reconciled with God. Questions of injustice arise here, so that it is no surprise to find that, in relation to culture, Type C prefers a counter-cultural mission that challenges any form of captivity of culture to sin. So mission is a praxis of liberational action that unmasks the ambiguous nature of culture and explores what a just or truer society might be.

Without working through the details of each of the constants in each type, with their variety of historical and geographical expressions, it is not possible to appreciate the subtlety of Bevans and Schroeder's unfolding overview. So in what follows I offer their outline summary of what the three types have to say about the nature of Christian mission as each perspective endures but develops in relation to each constant.

- **Type A – key word, Law:**

  > *Mission* within the context of Type A theology, therefore, might be characterized as the effort to save souls and extend the church. Without the saving knowledge of Christ, offered by the church, human beings cannot be saved; without structures of the church, the reign of God on earth, men and women cannot avail themselves of the means of salvation. Salvation is found not in the transformation of the world or its enhancement of the human, but in recognition of the world's transitoriness and the value of eternal life. Culture, although it has no *religious* significance per se, might be used to make Christianity clearer, to better communicate the gospel or to help Christians better express their faith. But it might also be regarded as something to be exorcised, even eliminated altogether, so that Christ might establish his 'new creation'. (p. 49)

- **Type B – key word, Truth:**

  > Summarizing its implication for mission, we might say that mission is carried out in search for God's grace that is hidden within people's cultural, religious and historical context; it is a call to people to fulfil their deepest potential as human beings allowing Christ to be the answer to their deepest human desires. Mission, in other words, is an

invitation to discover the Truth. In that Truth lies human salvation, already realized and present in human experience and human culture. The church in mission is the great sacrament of what being human is about; it is a community in which one has access to the mystery and community of God. Contemporary concerns with the inculturation of theology in various contexts find their roots in the confidence in human experience to which Type B theology witnesses. (p. 61)

- **Type C – key word, History:**

  Mission, therefore, from the perspective of Type C theology is the commitment of Christians towards the liberation and transformation of humanity, indeed, of the world. Christians proclaim Christ as the true liberator and 'transformer of culture'. And the church is the community of liberated humanity that finds its identity in its commitment to a liberated world; it is community-in-mission. The salvation the church proclaims is a salvation already inaugurated in the saving work of Christ, yet not fully established as the church works with God in confronting the evil of systems and structures, purifying and perfecting human culture and working for the reconciliation of the entire creation. (pp. 71f.)

The five marks from three perspectives

It will be clear by now that the five marks of mission cannot stand alone as a way of describing the nature of mission. There is a lot more to mission because mission, the mission of God, is that which characterises the Christian life overall. Whether it be in the revelation of Christ or in the life of the church, mission is constitutive and *a priori*. The most effective way to explore the five marks would therefore be to engage with them from this thicker and richer description of mission: to consider how there might be three different approaches to the five marks from the three perspectives on mission identified by Bevans and Schroeder. These three different approaches might be the basis for different patterns of discipleship which are recognised as such because they exhibit the acknowledged marks of mission with the depth of an authentic perspective.

The Type A version

The five marks, from this perspective, are clearly subordinate to an overarching view of mission that emphasises the authority for what has already been given and been made clear in Scripture and in the tradition of the church. This authority is 'the law' of mission: it provides the raison d'être of mission, the limits of salvation, and an interpretation of the means of mission. Thus the first mark is clearly to be interpreted in terms of saving souls: the good news is that people can be saved and become part of God's Kingdom. The overall purpose of mission is therefore to enable this to happen most effectively. The second mark is connected with the importance of the church as the community which, in its planting and upbuilding (through, teaching, baptising, and nurture) identifies the extent of God's saving Kingdom in the world. In relation to the third mark, the purpose of responding to human need is to show the love of God, whose service to the world in the death of Christ is his response to human need and therefore the basis for fellow human response to need. The fourth mark acknowledges the place of wider society, but in this type all cultural and social human forms are necessarily going to exhibit the sin which characterises humanity, making necessary God's rightful judgement of injustice and the importance of Christian witness to an alternative social order. The last mark opens mission to the widest reality of existence yet in this perspective the ambivalence about the transitory nature of creation and the hope of a new creation make commitment to environmental mission a matter of symbolic action rather than the coming of the Kingdom of God.

The Type B version

In this perspective the first mark of proclamation is more like a dialogue in which proclamation is one side of a conversation with experience, other faiths, or uncertainty, all in the quest for truth. There is confidence that somehow God's Kingdom is already present and it just needs to be unveiled through the catalyst of sharing the good news about Jesus. The second mark of mission is therefore in this same vein, so in this perspective there would be a more open approach to who is in, or out, of the church; and the church itself would not identify the limits of salvation. The third mark, of loving service, would be interpreted as connecting to the real depths of human need – which is the fulfilment of desire in the hope that the relief of human suffering would lead to personal and social development and transformation. The fourth mark would, in this perspective, be seen as an opportunity to advocate for truth: to reveal false consciousness and to encourage right action in the face of injustice so that a society, more in keeping with the sacramental expression of humanity in the church, might result. The last mark of mission would be interpreted as a way of highlighting the sacramental nature of the whole of creation in revealing the truth about the nature of God's love and commitment to restore the whole creation, and our part in co-operating with him in this, the widest expression of the *missio Dei*.

The Type C version

For Type C, proclamation is about making known God's ongoing transformation of the world in history, making clear that this transformation touches the whole of reality and is not just about personal salvation but the ultimate significance of Jesus-the-transformer of all things. The second mark is therefore to be understood in terms of helping believers to become a community of reflective practictioners who, in relation to marks three, four, and five, seek to live a life of praxis that reflects the transformation seen in the life of Jesus and now continued through the Spirit in the lives of his followers. This means that serving human need, engaging with culture, and seeking to safeguard the environment are valuable expressions of the mission of God so that the restoration and reconciliation of the whole of creation, already begun, will be completed in the culmination of history in the coming of Christ.

Marks and discipleship in Anglicanism: 'Holy' mission

These three different perspectives on the five marks of mission not only show the need for a framework for the marks of mission, but in their diversity also highlight the need for them to be grounded in a tradition of discipleship that offers guidance about *priorities* and *limits*. The Anglican way of being a follower of Jesus may, at first sight, be an unlikely candidate for providing this kind of help. However, the first thing to note is that any interpretation of discipleship with the kind of range of perspectives outlined in the three types is going to have to be a generous one! In this sense, Anglicanism qualifies, having within itself representatives of all three types – all as serious as each other in pursuing an expression of discipleship that is sincere in its quest for holiness.

So while there may not be an agreed common way to describe the Anglican approach to discipleship, let me suggest that there are some commonalities in the quest for *grounded holiness* that, if connected to a strengthening of the way the Anglican Communion is living as a family of churches, may be useful. This approach depends on an understanding of Anglicanism that would allow it to be seen as traditions of diverse spiritualities and theologies that, even in their divergence, share enough constants of faith to offer mutual recognition and respect. That the current climate in Anglicanism seems to show little evidence of this reality, belies the fact that there is still a serious engagement across significant differences which are being sustained in Anglican conversations in a way that might not be possible in other communities.

In *Love's Redeeming Work: The Anglican Quest for Holiness* Geoffrey Rowell, Kenneth Stevenson, and Rowan Williams have explored the resources for sustaining an Anglican approach to holiness. They propose that there exists across the centuries, among the proponents of the different doctrinal perspectives in Anglicanism, a common concern, i.e. that for those who have contributed and developed this Anglican practical holiness 'thinking about God was closely bound up with thinking about how human beings became holy, came to show in their lives the grace and glory of God'. This seems to imply that 'If holy lives are recognizable, there is a prima facie case for believing that some kind of unity in doctrine is being taken for granted; and the job of theology will be to draw out what that might be, rather than to clear up all possible controversies before anyone is allowed to recognize holiness.'[6]

This practical optimism about an organic unity is, however, fed by some interesting resources. Firstly, the authors suggest there is an Anglican emphasis on scepticism which has its roots in the Reformation understanding of fallen humanity but also in an uncertainty about the institution of the church. Such scepticism has resulted in a reticence: spiritual truth always has a certain hiddenness even in the most exuberant form of spiritual renewal. Given this, those who dedicate themselves to foster and nurture such hiddenness are a welcome part of the church community: the monastic and mendicant orders and the evangelical associations for renewal and mission. Yet such emphasis on the empirical nature of discipleship has also found itself co-opted into a form of liberalism cut loose from its moorings in the discipline of community and prayer. This was made possible when, what authority the church had in relation to providing a spiritual centre to the nation, began to fade, as church and state each developed their uses for Enlightenment thought. Yet when empirical liberalism becomes experientialism the possibility for recognising holy lives is lost – the constants of faith are denied and the diversity of perspective becomes an intolerant requirement.

This has led many to suggest that the Western contribution to Anglicanism has run its course and that any hope for the future of the Communion now lies with the South: 'There is a widespread perception that the Anglican Communion needs to grow beyond its historic ethos into a more consistently biblical and evangelistic identity; though there are other voices in the Communion that argue for a new reformation infinitely more radical, a revitalizing of the entire tradition, perhaps even of conventional language of belief in a God independent of the universe or of the thinking mind. There seems no obvious way of bringing two such diverse perspectives together.'[7]

The authors of *Love's Redeeming Work* are under no illusion that, 'Without the structures of both discipline and doctrine, "spirituality" can be vacuous and indulgent.'[8] In other words, if there is an abandonment of what can commonly be recognised as holiness in the constants of faiths, then there is a fundamental shift beyond the range of different perspectives. It is their hope that in bringing the rich resources of the historic tradition of Anglicanism into conversation with the multi-cultural environment of the Communion, there might some kind of mutual *ressourcement* – an interchange in which there is a building up of the Body of Christ for its edification in mission. Their hopes are grounded in a genuine fact: that the Anglican approach to holiness fuelled the mission societies and churches which planted and fostered the Communion and which still seek to sustain the Communion in mission today.[9] Thus the Evangelical revival and the Oxford Movement were spirituality traditions that, though taking different perspectives, led to vital and transforming mission and, in today's context, find themselves sharing a common concern for holiness with those who might be called liberal or radical Anglicans who also share the Anglican tradition of holiness.

The Anglican covenant: truth and unity in mission

However, it is clear that in a tradition of spirituality like Anglicanism more is required than holy reticence and mutual recognition of holy lives. This recognition has emerged 'accidentally' through the crises that have sometimes beset the family of churches that have become the Anglican Communion. Following the Colenso crisis in South Africa in the mid 1800s, which, interestingly, emerged out of the mission context where the range of diversity of doctrine was in question, a pattern for handling disputes around truth, and a simple framework for Christian unity, emerged. The *pattern* was the gathering of bishops at

Lambeth to hold counsel with each other under the leadership of the Archbishop of Canterbury – what we now call the Lambeth Conference. The *framework*, for how Anglicans and others could recognise each other as ecclesial communities, was the Anglican Quadrilateral, which proposed that churches which accepted the authority of Scripture, the tradition of the Apostles' and Nicene Creeds, the centrality of Baptism and Holy Communion in the life of the church, and the leadership of the historic episcopate locally adapted, could recognise each other.

It seems that the range of diversity in discipleship, now being proposed in Anglican churches, requires a further development in this tradition of truth and unity. This further development is the proposed Anglican Covenant. Fundamentally, what this Covenant does with the *pattern* and *framework* of Anglicanism is to develop the conciliar nature of the Communion.[10] In other words, where there is a tradition of holy reticence that relies on mutual recognition of holy lives, there must also be a way of stating the centre and limits of truth and unity. The great advantage and the weakness of Anglicanism, is its ability to adapt to any context and therefore to express a range of theological viewpoints in a variety of patterns of discipleship. But without a way of addressing the truth of discipleship and the discipline of unity, there is the grave danger that the constants of faith are abandoned in the process of contextualisation.

The Anglican Covenant seeks to go beyond the Quadrilateral's minimalist requirements and also seeks to clarify the nature of conciliarism. These developments are an attempt to sustain the faithfulness of Anglican commitments to the constants of faith that, if abandoned or so reworked in contextual expressions, become sub-Christian. The ultimate significance of Jesus for salvation and for the future of the world is unquestionable; and the place of the church as God's fellowship for restoring humanity and redeeming culture cannot be denied. A Covenant which affirms these kind of constants would be a great utility to a tradition, like Anglicanism, whose way of discipleship is resourced by holy reticence and a mutual recognition of holy lives.

For this to happen, however, the Covenant would need to have a pattern that does indeed have a mission-first architecture. God's mission and the five marks of mission need to be the chief concerns that the Covenant seeks to promote. In support of this, there needs to be a clear affirmation of the constants of faith and an outline of the conciliar way of dealing with the local expression of discipleship in context. The current draft of the Covenant (see Appendix 1) could be revised to make this mission-first agenda clear. In simple design terms, the Introductory Statements about the narrative of God's mission in the world as revealed in the Lord Jesus Christ and sustained by the Holy Spirit need to be incorporated (something like this was in the original draft but needs integrating in the Preamble). Secondly, the layout of the Covenant should be altered so that Section Four, on the Five Marks, is swapped with Section Two, which is about some of the constants of faith. This would then allow the positive and visional aspects of the Covenant to become the key foci, offering a generative and missional centre for life in the Communion. The commitment to truth and unity, in later sections, would then be seen to serve the purpose of mission while allowing for a range but a limit to diversity. These simple proposals make possible the rediscovery of the resources of Anglican discipleship as these have emerged and are developing in an inter-cultural context.

Discipleship that is consistently biblical and has an evangelistic identity will need to be resourced in a new way in the emerging Anglican Communion. The contributions of this book are one offering in that direction, representing a new era in which there is a remaking of Anglicanism for the new mission of the twenty-first century. The five marks are helpful but they will no doubt need further clarification during this period when world mission is undergoing rapid change and the world-wide church is growing.

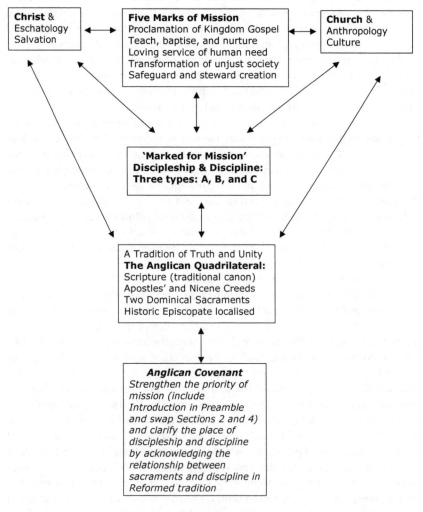

Discipleship: marked for mission

Appendix:
A Revision of the Draft Text Giving Greater Emphasis to Mission[1]

COVENANT FOR COMMUNION IN MISSION

INTRODUCTION

The Lord wants to bring all things to himself in Christ (Ephesians 1:10) for their recreation by the Spirit (Romans 8:20f.), that all might share in the divine nature (2 Peter 1:3). The church is called to participate in this ministry of reconciliation and glorification (2 Corinthians 5:18; 3:18) through the proclamation, worship, service, and teaching of God in his mission. A *Covenant for Communion in Mission* expresses this calling for the Anglican Churches.

A Covenant for Communion in Mission

The mystery of God has been revealed through his mission in all times and places, but supremely in the Lord Jesus Christ. In seeking communion with humankind, despite our rebellion and sin, the Holy Scriptures tell us that God made covenants with Noah, Abraham, Israel, and David. His aim was to bless all nations as they responded to his invitation to live in communion with him, so that he might restore his image in them.

In Jesus there is now another covenant: 'this is my blood of the new covenant, poured out for many for the forgiveness of sins' (Matthew 26:28). In this covenant we find a renewed communion with God as we share with others the forgiveness of sins through Jesus. We discover our communion with others in mission through Christ, and our mission is to spread the communion of Christ, ultimately with the whole of creation.

So the church is called to be the people of God's mission. The calling of the church is to spread God's communion: 'Christ is our peace. We are reconciled to God in one body through the cross.' In this calling the church has, in many different contexts and cultures, made known the Gospel. The fullness of Christ has been seen as people from all nations, tongues, and classes have been drawn into the communion of God's church.

The Covenant is for envisioning and shaping expressions of God's communion in mission in Anglican Churches. The Covenant encourages (but limits) both *expressions of uniformity* (but not those restricting diverse expressions of true communion) and *expressions of diversity* (but not those that fail to maintain the unity of the faith).

> The **Preamble** to the Covenant provides a summary of the nature of the mission to which the Churches of the Communion are called as a Communion in Mission. The subsequent sections follow on from this perspective to the declaration in **Section 7**.

Anglican Mission and Tradition

In the amalgam of Celtic and Roman mission to the British Isles a church developed and was later 'Reformed'. In the eighteenth and nineteenth centuries, under God, but in the context of a growing colonialism, this church reached out with the Gospel through its mission societies. And by these means, and with those from others churches planted by such mission (e.g. in newly liberated America), further evangelistic mission was carried out so that over two or three hundred years Anglican Churches were planted worldwide.

Section 2 reviews the Anglican vocation to Gospel mission as inherited from this tradition and expressed through the variety of contexts where churches witness. The five marks of this mission are set in the framework of Christ and his church.

Essential to Anglican mission has been the vintage but vernacular tradition of liturgy. Anglicans believe what they pray – so they like to pray in their own language but also in fellowship with 'all the saints'. Our unique way of doing this, like our mission, has been somewhat historically conditioned, and even accidental, and is still developing! Yet in each context there is a recognisable shape to the life of mission so that the faith expressed is in accordance with the vision and values of Scripture and tradition in the calling to be a blessing and of service to others in diverse cultures and communities.

Section 3 therefore unfolds the way in which the faith has been handed on and handled faithfully throughout the ages via: a pattern of moral discipline, eucharistic practice, interpretation of Scripture, and leadership appropriate to a pilgrim people.

The Anglican Communion has also developed to become a family of conciliar Churches within the greater church. While this conciliar pattern is not the primary way in which the Churches of the Communion interact in their common mission, it has become important for the way in which the Communion makes decisions. There is therefore a commitment to what the early councils of the undivided church have set forth concerning the fundamentals of the faith.

But there is also a commitment to use conciliar methods for developing a common mind on the contemporary responsibility of the church in the 'administration of the mystery' as revealed in the Gospel.

Section 4 concerns the way in which Anglicans are faithful to conciliar understandings of the triune God, the church, the Scriptures, the call to make Christ known in each generation and nation, and the institution of the sacraments.

The mission of the Communion is sustained in its unity through structures that help to promote this common way of life. These include the historic episcopate and four Instruments of Communion, focusing the relationships of the interdependent but autonomous member Churches. These structures are integrated into the conciliar nature of Anglicanism.

Section 5 sets out the place of Anglican understandings of episcopacy and the importance of the four Instruments of unity in the mission of the church.

The Communion has also recognised that in the development of its mission the traditions of the church have to be interpreted and adapted in different times and contexts. This has led to changes in the expression of patterns of faith and order. It has become clear that for there to be coherence across the Communion certain matters of interpretation require a common mind and therefore a singular view. The Communion has recognised that the Primates uphold the common mind of the Communion. Where there is dispute they seek to discern, after due process, what this common mind is. In stating this, the Covenant is itself therefore an instrument for affirming the unity of faith in the mission to which the member Churches are called.

Section 6 sets out some of the details of the ways in which the Anglican Churches commit themselves to develop a common mind and exercise discipline for the sake of their common participation in God's mission to the world.

1. Preamble

We, the Churches of the Anglican Communion, who have been called by God to share in the unsearchable riches of Christ and to bring his blessing to the world, solemnly covenant together in these articles, in order that we may:

- Proclaim more effectively in our different contexts the manifold Grace of God revealed in the Gospel;
- Be channels of God's love in response to the needs of the world;
- Maintain the unity of the Spirit in the face of all that would divide us;
- And grow up, together with all God's people, into the full stature of Christ, in whom people from every tribe and tongue and people and nation are brought into the life of God's eternal kingdom.

2. The Life We Share with Others: Our Anglican Vocation

(1) **We affirm** that Communion is a gift of God: that his people from east and west, north and south, may together declare his glory and be a sign of God's Kingdom. We gratefully acknowledge God's gracious providence extended to us down the ages, our origins in the Early Church [or Church of the Fathers], the rich history of the church in Britain and Ireland shaped particularly by the Reformation, and our growth into a global communion through the various mission initiatives.

(2) As the Communion continues to develop into a worldwide family of inter-dependent Churches, we also face challenges and opportunities for mission at local, regional, and international levels. We cherish our faith and mission heritage as offering us unique opportunities for mission collaboration, for discovery of the life that the whole Gospel offers and for reconciliation and shared mission with the church throughout the world.

(3) We acknowledge that our common mission is a mission shared with other churches and traditions which also belong to the catholic church. It is with all the saints that we will comprehend the fuller dimensions of Christ's redemptive and immeasurable love.

(4) **We commit** ourselves to answering God's call to share in his healing and reconciling mission for our blessed but broken and hurting world, and, with mutual accountability, to share our God-given spiritual and material resources in this task.

(5) In this mission, which is the Mission of Christ through his Church, **we commit ourselves**

1. to proclaim the Good News of the Kingdom of God
2. to teach, baptise, and nurture new believers;
3. to respond to human need by loving service;
4. to seek to transform unjust structures of society; and
5. to strive to safeguard the integrity of creation and to sustain and renew the life of the earth.

3. Our Commitment to Confession of the Faith

As we engage in the mission of God, in our various contexts, we commit ourselves to:

(1) uphold and act in continuity and consistency with the catholic and apostolic faith, order and tradition;

(2) uphold and proclaim a pattern of Christian moral discipline that is based on

the teaching of Holy Scripture and the catholic tradition, and that reflects the renewal of humanity and the whole created order through the death and resurrection of Christ and the holiness that God gives to, and requires from, his people in consequence;

(3) seek in all things to uphold the solemn obligation to sustain Eucharistic communion, welcoming members of all other member Churches to join in our own celebrations, and encouraging our members to participate in the Eucharist in another member Church in accordance with the canonical discipline of that host church;

(4) ensure that biblical texts are handled faithfully, respectfully, comprehensively, and coherently, primarily through the teaching and initiative of bishops and synods, and building on the best scholarship, believing that scriptural revelation must continue to illuminate, challenge, and transform cultures, structures, and ways of thinking;

(5) nurture and respond to prophetic and faithful leadership and ministry to assist our Churches as courageous witnesses to the transformative power of the Gospel in the world.

(6) pursue a common pilgrimage with other members of the Communion to discern truth, that peoples from all nations may truly be free and receive the new and abundant life in the Lord Jesus Christ.

4. The Life We Share: Common Catholicity, Apostolicity, and Confession of Faith

We recognise in all the Churches of the Anglican Communion, with whom we share in the mission of God:

(1) The one, holy, catholic, and apostolic church, worshipping the one true God, Father, Son, and Holy Spirit.

(2) Profession of the faith that is uniquely revealed in the Holy Scriptures (which contain all things necessary for salvation and are the rule and ultimate standard of faith), which faith is set forth in the catholic creeds, and borne witness to by the historic Anglican formularies.

(3) Loyalty to this inheritance of faith as their inspiration and guidance under God in bringing the grace and truth of Christ to this generation and making him known to their societies and nations;

(4) Due administration of the sacraments of Baptism and the Supper of the Lord ordained by Christ himself, ministered with the unfailing use of Christ's words of institution, and of the elements ordained by him.

5. The Structures by which our Common Life and Mission are Maintained

(1) **We affirm** the importance of the structures of the Anglican Communion in assisting in the discernment, articulation, and exercise of our common mission and shared faith.

(2) **We affirm** the historic episcopate, locally adapted in the methods of its administration to the varying needs of the nations and peoples called of God into the unity of his church and the central role of bishops as leaders in mission and, as such, custodians of faith, and visible signs of unity.

(3) **We affirm** the role of the four Instruments of Communion, which serve our participation in God's mission by enabling us to discern our common mind on Communion issues, and fostering our interdependence and mutual accountability in Christ. While each member Church orders and regulates its own affairs through its own system of government and law and is therefore described as autonomous, each Church recognises that the member Churches of the Anglican Communion are bound together, not juridically by a central legislative or executive authority, but by the Holy Spirit who calls and enables us to live in mutual loyalty and service in order that the mystery of Christ may be more powerfully proclaimed.

6. Unity of the Communion in Mission

We commit ourselves:

(

1) in essential matters of common concern, to have regard to the common good of the Communion in the exercise of its autonomy, and to support the work of the Instruments of Communion with the spiritual and material resources available to it;

(2) to spend time with openness and patience in matters of theological debate and discernment to listen and to study with one another in order to comprehend the will of God;

(3) to seek with other members, through the Church's shared councils, a common mind about matters of essential concern, consistent with the Scriptures, common standards of faith, and the canon law of our Churches;

(4) to heed the counsel of our Instruments of Communion in matters which threaten the unity of the Communion and the effectiveness of our mission. While the Instruments of Communion have no juridical or executive authority in our Provinces, we recognise them as those bodies by which our common life in Christ is articulated and sustained, and which therefore

carry a spiritual, pastoral, and doctrinal authority which commands our respect;

(5) to submit matters in serious dispute that cannot be resolved by mutual admonition and counsel to the Primates so that (in accordance with the responsibilities given to them by the Lambeth Conferences of 1988 and 1998) they can offer guidance on how they may be resolved, either on the basis of the existing position of the Communion, or after the development of a common mind through consultation with the local Churches of the Communion and their bishops by means of the other Instruments and their councils;

(6) to refrain from intervening in the life of other Anglican Churches except in circumstances where such intervention has been specifically authorised by the Instruments of Communion.

(7) Acknowledging the need for the exercise of discipline within the life of the Church in order to preserve its holiness and the integrity of its mission and to ensure that those who have erred are brought to repentance, healing, and restoration, **we commit** ourselves to accept the patterns of discipline involved in serving the mission of God as part of the Anglican Covenant. In the most extreme circumstances, where member Churches choose not to fulfil the substance of the Covenant as understood by the Councils of the Instruments of Communion, we will consider such Churches to have relinquished for themselves the force and meaning of the Covenant's purpose, and we accept that a process of restoration and renewal will be required to re-establish their covenant relationship with other member Churches.

7. Our Declaration

With joy and with firm resolve, **we declare** our Churches to be partners in this Anglican Covenant, releasing ourselves for fruitful service in the mission of God and binding ourselves more closely in the truth and love of Christ, to whom with the Father and the Holy Spirit be glory for ever. Amen.

Afterword:
Christian Mission in a
Five-hundred-year Context

Andrew F. Walls

The twentieth century was an extraordinary period in human history. As far as recorded history goes, it was extraordinary in its violence (though the record of the last few years suggests that in this respect it could be outstripped by its successor). In geopolitical terms, it was remarkable in that it marked the end of a vast movement of population that had shaped world history over several centuries. In the twentieth century this movement of population reached its peak, then came to a halt and went into reverse. We may call this movement the Great European Migration, and it had religious as well as economic and political effects.

It lasted from about the beginning of the sixteenth century until the middle of the twentieth. In the course of it first hundreds and then thousands and eventually millions of people left Europe for the lands beyond Europe. Some went under compulsion, as refugees, indentured labourers, or convicts, some under their conditions of employment as soldiers or officials, some from lust of wealth or power. Most, however, were simply seeking a better life or a more just society than they found in Europe.

This movement of people brought whole new nations into being – all the nations of the Americas, for instance, Australia, New Zealand, and others. Russia, for so long bounded by the Urals, grew beyond them until it stretched from the Baltic to the Pacific, and for a time into America. It was the only participant in the Migration that expanded overland, rather than by sea. The new nations that arose as a result of the Migration adopted the languages and cultural traditions of Europe. Those of the original inhabitants (often a majority) unable or unwilling to adopt those traditions were effectively dispossessed and forced to the margins of a society that now lived by European cultural norms.

The Great European Migration enabled the powers of Europe to redraw the patterns of world trade to their advantage. Sometimes the result was baleful, most notably in the case of the Atlantic slave trade, which (with the co-operation with some African states) generated immense wealth, and the China opium trade. A huge part of the population of Africa was moved to the Americas to meet the Migration's labour needs. Smaller-scale operations moved people from India and China to South Africa or the Caribbean; an Indian population was imposed on Fiji in the interests of economic development. Resistance to the desired trade patterns could be met with force; the Western powers blasted their way into China and Japan for the sake of the liberalisation of trade.

Economic involvement led imperceptibly to the extension of political control. Some of the earliest and most complex examples of this took place in India and Indonesia but by the end of the nineteenth century almost all Africa, much of Asia, and all the Pacific had been divided between the European powers. In the early twentieth century the process was extended to the Middle East as the Ottoman Empire, once ruled by the caliph or deputy of the Prophet, gave place to territories ruled by Western powers, or to newly invented states such as Iraq with Western-appointed rulers. At the beginning of the nineteenth century the great Muslim ruler was the Sultan by the Bosphorus; by its end it was Queen Victoria, with more Muslim subjects than the Sultan ever had. By the 1920s it was hard to find an independent Muslim ruler who was not the client of a Western power.

The later twentieth century, however, saw the beginnings of the break-up of the world order that had been established by the Great European Migration. In the first place, by the middle of the century the Migration had itself ceased or been reduced to a trickle; the state of Israel was its last great artefact. In the second, the European maritime empires were dismantled, and the Russian land-based empire substantially reduced. Patterns of trade became more complex, their relation to the power of nation states less evident. The rise of Asian powers, India and especially China, began to hint at new patterns of hegemony. To adopt the language of the Book of Daniel, the great beast who has occupied the centre of the stage for a long period, while still roaring and lashing its tail, seems to be in process of removal. It may be that beasts of another stripe are to occupy the stage and have their day before the books are opened and the Son of Man comes with the clouds of heaven.

But the twentieth century was also notable for the beginning of another movement of population which may turn out to be as determinative of world history as the Great European Migration itself. In mid-century the Great European Migration not only came to an end, it went into reverse. Numbers of people from Africa, from Asia, and from Latin America began to move to Europe and North America, and to set down roots there. Numbers have steadily grown, and, as United Nations population studies indicate, the process looks set to continue. On the one hand the pressures for movement from the non-Western world are inexorable; on the other, though the nations of the West may not want more immigration, they can sustain their economies in no other way.

The Great Reverse Migration alters the dynamics of cultural and religious relations. Africa and Asia are now part of Europe, part of North America, where once they lay at the end of a long maritime journey. Latin America is part of North America too. Their religious traditions have also come; Islam and Hinduism have become religions of the West in a period when Christianity has become more a non-Western than a Western religion. And the Migration has brought substantial numbers of Christians from Africa and Asia and Latin America to the West, often bringing with them Christian forms and expressions new to the West. There are people in this Migration well placed to be cultural brokers and mediators; there are academics and theologians who could open new channels of understanding.

Christendom and the Great European Migration

When the Great European Migration began, Europeans described the territory in which they lived as Christendom, a word that simply means 'Christianity'. The historical roots of the application of the name of Christianity to a geographical area lie in the period of Europe's conversion to Christianity, the centuries (and the process took many centuries) in which the various people groups of Europe communally adopted the Christian faith. They did so, generally speaking, by accepting it as the basis of law and custom. It is of the nature of law and custom that no one may opt out; law and custom bind everyone in the community. Thus all were now regarded as Christians, and were baptised into the faith in infancy. In principle, each family lived within a geographical unit served by church and clergy committed to teaching the faith, and the laws governing society were to be conformable to the law of God. No idolatry, blasphemy, or heresy should be found in Christian territory; it was the duty of the ruler, no less than of the church, to secure this, for Christian rulers were the servants, indeed the vassals of the King of kings.

The immediate neighbour of Christendom to the south and east was the Muslim territory of Dar al-Islam, in many ways the mirror image of Christendom and strengthening the identification of faith with territory. From the larger world of peoples, European Christendom, the western end of the great Eurasian landmass, was largely cut off until the trans-oceanic voyages of the late fifteenth century ended the long isolation and opened the possibility of the Great Migration.

By 1500, European Christendom had reached its broadest geographical extent; the last pagan peoples in Europe (other than those of the far north) had been brought into it, and Muslim rule in southern Spain, after six centuries of presence there, had been brought to an end. But Europe had also become more Christian in another sense. Over the centuries interaction of the Christian message with the languages and cultures of Europe had produced a powerful symbiosis. European art, music, literature, and philosophy were all dominated by Christian symbols and readily directed to Christian purposes, so penetrated by Christian themes that it was impossible to understand them without some knowledge of the faith. And not only was Europe Christian territory, it was, or so it seemed to people of the time, the *only* Christian territory. Many of the older Christian centres in Asia and Africa had now been eclipsed, or lay under Muslim rule; others, such as Ethiopia and South India, were outside the practical knowledge of Europeans. Europeans thus could readily think of themselves as the representative Christians, and their form of the faith, if not exactly the only, at least the only authentic form of it. When, therefore, their isolation ended and they met representatives of the old Christianity of Asia and Africa, they often decided that the latter were deviant.

In Africa and Asia and in that huge landmass in the Atlantic that they first identified as India but later named America, European Christians also met non-Christian peoples, and desired that they too should be part of Christendom. One or two African kingdoms responded, and became states of Christendom. But where there was no such response, European Christendom had an established institution intended to extend Christendom, or to reclaim territory lost by it. The idea of crusade, the use of force to extend the territory under Christian law, had been first developed with the idea of reclaiming formerly Christian territory lost to Islam, but subsequent crusades had been fought against northern pagans and Christian heretics. A particularly successful crusade had, as recently as 1492, culminated in the Muslim surrender in Spain. Columbus, setting out on his famous journey, witnessed the surrender. In years to come the Spanish were to apply the principles of crusade, if not the name, in the lands which Columbus opened to them. Mexico became New Spain, with the laws and customs of Old Spain. Whole populations were baptised, and were compelled to take Christian instruction. Thus Mexico and Peru entered Christendom, through the gate of crusade.

But in most of Africa, and especially in Asia, the scope for crusading was limited. Portugal, the representative power of Christendom, was a small country, with no hope of successful warfare against the great Asian empires. It never abandoned the rhetoric of Christendom, but after the early years its attempts to extend Christendom across Asia were largely confined to the small enclaves that Portugal actually ruled. The extension of Christendom ranked well behind military survival and commercial success. The Dutch, who succeeded the Portuguese in the leadership of the Migration, maintained the rhetoric of Christendom (in Protestant instead of Catholic language), while the British, their successors, did not even trouble with the rhetoric. Under the British East India Company, it was clear policy that religion must never interfere with business. Colonialism forced the powers of Christendom to choose between their economic and political interests and their religious profession. It was perhaps the beginning of the secularisation of Europe.

But there was always within Christendom a seminal minority seeking a truer Christian discipleship, and while the governments of Christendom might abdicate responsibility to spread the Christian faith, these radical Christians could not do so. They must find other ways of proclaiming Christ. It was among such Christian radicals that the missionary movement was born.

The crusading mode and the missionary mode are sharply differentiated means of extending the Christian faith. They grew up in the same area, in the same era, among people who shared the same basic theology; but in concept and in spirit they differ fundamentally. The crusader may first issue his invitation to the Gospel but, in the end, he is prepared to compel. The missionary, even if his natural instinct is to desire compulsion, cannot compel, but only demonstrate, invite, explain, entreat, and leave the result with God. But there is a further implication. If there is no power to compel, the business of demonstrating and explaining requires the missionary to win a hearing. To do so usually involves learning a language and securing a place of acceptance, a niche within the society. None of these matters need trouble the crusader, who demands submission to his terms; the missionary has to live on terms set by other people.

The missionary movement from the West originated in the Reformation era in Catholic southern Europe, among people who remained in allegiance to Rome but had been affected by the forces of renewal characteristic of the period. The renewed church had retained the religious orders which had in medieval times been the natural home of Christians seeking radical discipleship, and the forces of renewal had created new orders and societies as well as reforming old ones. These provided the infrastructure for the earliest missionary movement; it took Protestants almost two centuries to develop an alternative structure. It was therefore Catholic missions that first wrestled with the difficulties of translation, and who first worked out what it meant to live on others' terms. The latter could mean seeking to be a Christian exemplar of the Hindu ascetic or *sannyasi*, taking the diet and the dress, exploring a new language for deep Christian communication. To live on others' terms could lead to the recognition that to be a scholar in China must mean knowing the Chinese classics as a Chinese scholar knew them. Then would follow the labour of doing just that, while seeking to convey Christian teaching.

The missionary movement, first Catholic, then Protestant, then both at once, makes up a single story that arises out of the Great European Migration and covers the period of its existence. Yet it was always a semi-detached part of the Migration. It arose among the radicals of Christendom, and it remained the sphere of the radicals, the enthusiasts, people usually of minor significance in the church, rarely the holders of ecclesiastical power or the leaders of ecclesiastical thought. It survived periods of immense frustration, periods not just of failure, but of utter disaster. It was semi-detached because ultimately its mainspring lay not in the Migration, or in the forces that produced the Migration, but in the Christian Gospel. Whatever else missionaries held they should be doing, the final reason for their existence was to point to Christ. With all the failures, contradictions, and ambiguities that belong to the human condition, missionaries were migrants for Christ's sake.

Religion and the Great European Migration

The religious effects of the Great European Migration were mixed. The spread of the Christian faith soon, as we have seen, ceased to be a priority for the powers of Europe. Migration often loosened the religious allegiance of the migrants themselves; Australia, New Zealand, even Canada, became more rapidly and determinedly secular than Britain, from which most of their early migrants came. (The United States followed a different pattern; the christianisation that it underwent was perhaps the most notable success of the missionary movement during the nineteenth century.) Other religions flourished as a result of the imperial aspects of the European expansion. Hinduism as we know it today, a coherent, confident formulation unafraid of modernity and the scientific world-view, is a product of the British Raj in India. The Raj also produced the conditions for the emergence of Pakistan as the first modern Islamic state. Colonial rule, often deliberately, produced a vast increase in the number of Muslims, while at the same time policy in the Middle East ensured that Muslims felt aggrieved and offended. The strangest religious aspect of the Migration was in the position of Christianity. When the Great European Migration began in the sixteenth century, Christianity was the religion of Europe and a largely European religion. By the end of the twentieth century, a massive recession in the West, especially in Europe, and a massive accession in the rest of the world, and especially Africa, had transformed the cultural and demographic distribution of Christianity. Christianity had once more become, as in its beginnings, a non-Western religion. And – though it was by no means the only cause of the change – the missionary movement, the despised semi-detached appendix to the Great European Migration, had played a significant role.

When the Great European Migration began, Europe was Christendom, Christian territory. Even in the nineteenth century, any informed person, if asked what defined Europe, what all Europeans had in common, would be likely to point to the experience of Christianity. And this answer would come from believers and unbelievers alike. The influence of Christianity in shaping European civilisation, its impress on laws, social organisation, public ritual, art, literature, and music was beyond question. In the first decade of the twenty-first century the issue of a draft constitution for the European Union caused Europeans to revisit the question of what makes up 'Europeanness'. On this occasion they decided, after due debate, to make no reference to Christianity at all, even as a historical influence in the making of Europe. Old Christendom is no longer an operating concept.

Even its landmarks are changing. A walk round the centre of my own city tells a story. The most striking older buildings reflect the traditional dominance in Scottish civic life of Christianity in its Reformed expression. At the corner where the principal street begins is the college where the ministry of the church was once trained. It still bears plaques on its walls commemorating some of the eminent theologians who once taught there; but it has now been converted into a smart restaurant, with a notice indicating one of its special attractions: 'Babylon – the ultimate night experience'. A little up the street is an imposing church building, once famous for the notable preachers who occupied its pulpit. It is now a casino, the signboard with its new name, 'Soul', giving a poignant hint of its original function. Nearby is another church converted into a nightclub under the name of 'The Ministry'. To continue the walk would be to pass church building after church building with architecture and design that bespeak old Christendom, but now fulfil a new function as a night spot, a drinking hall, a restaurant, a store, an apartment block. And the reason is that no one needs them as churches any longer.

The country that once sent missionaries across the world stands in desperate need of mission. It is too late for revival; the need is basic, primary evangelisation, cross-cultural evangelisation such as missionaries once sought to carry out in other continents. Old Christendom has been succeeded by an essentially non-Christian culture. Our god, if we have one, is Mammon, and Mammon's altars are as gruesome as Moloch's.

Here is the strangest development of the Great European Migration. The Christian faith declined sharply and so rapidly in what had long been its heartland, the apparent centre of its strength, in lands where it had permeated culture and moulded law and custom, while it spread into lands beyond. It was not the first time in Christian history that what seemed to be the heart of the church wilted, and it may not be the last. Christian history is marked by such collapses in the locations of apparent Christian strength, which have coincided with rapid growth at what seemed to be the margins. The majority of those who profess the Christian faith are now Africans, Asians, Latin Americans, and Pacific Islanders; and they substantially outnumber the professed Christians of Europe, the old Christendom, and its North American outcrop. What is more, the trends that have produced this transformation appear to be continuing; in every recent year there have been fewer Christians in the West, and more in the rest of the world. Even in the United States the downward trend is clear, clearest, perhaps, in those areas from which the European decline accelerated: the cities, the universities, the intellectuals. That the American decline is not sharper seems due to the impact of the Great Reverse Migration: the arrival of Christians from Africa, from Asia, and especially from the Hispanic world.

How long these trends will continue is beyond our knowledge. Nor can we tell whether we are currently living in the last days, or in the era of the Early Church. But if the trends were to continue much longer, it would not be unreasonable to expect that two thirds of the world's Christians will be from the non-Western world. What is already certain is that Christianity is now a predominantly non-Western religion, the profession principally of African and Asian and Latin American people, and that it is currently moving progressively in that direction.

The high-water mark of the missionary movement

How has this come about? Certainly not according to the predictions of the best informed people. And here another visit to Scotland, this time to Edinburgh, may be instructive. What is now the Assembly Hall of the Church of Scotland was in 1910 the venue for the World Missionary Conference, perhaps the high-water mark of the missionary movement. It was called to discuss 'the missionary problem of the world', in other words, how the work of Christian mission could be so organised that the Gospel would reach the whole world. This vision seemed attainable. We have spoken of the awesome violence of the twentieth century, but in the century's first decade this feature had not yet been revealed. Few in the Assembly Hall could have heard the beating wings of the Angel of Death. Despite Great Power rivalries and colonial flare-ups, the world appeared stable, and there were very few areas absolutely closed to the Gospel. Full mobilisation of the resources of Christendom, organised international co-operation in the work of mission – these seemed in 1910 to be the instruments of world evangelisation. And the resources to be mobilised were to be those of Europe and North America, with such marginal assistance as Australia, New Zealand, and the White community of South Africa could afford. The benches of the Assembly Hall were packed with European and American missionaries and mission executives. A small number of Asian delegates, from China, Japan, India, and Korea made up an important symbolic presence; but no African was present, and it had been agreed in advance that the Conference would not discuss Latin America.

The mode of procedure was to study and debate reports, the fruit of careful research prior to the Conference. The first report surveyed the existing state of evangelisation. As regards Asia it was upbeat in tone, especially as regards Japan, China, and India, the countries in which missions had invested most resources. Korea, where Protestant missions were still new, received only a short notice. On Africa, the report strikes a sober note. The gist of what it says is that, in general, the situation is not as discouraging as might have been expected. But it adds that the evangelisation of the interior of the continent had hardly begun. And another part of the report offers a 'worst-case' scenario of Africa as a Muslim continent. The Conference ground rules ensured that Latin America would feature only marginally in the report.

The tide moves out

For those present, the Conference was an inspiring, and for some a transforming, experience. It ended on a note of high commitment. 'The end of the Conference' announced John R. Mott in his closing address, 'is the beginning of the conquest.' And with this in view the delegates dispersed, pledged to full mobilisation of Christian resources and to international co-operation.

Then came the First World War, sinking many of the immediate hopes of international co-operation. Before long, the government of one Christian nation was interning the missionaries of another. Then came the Angel of Death, and much of that young life that was to be mobilised for the evangelisation of the world drained away in the trenches of France and Flanders. Then came the Depression, eroding the economic base on which missions had operated for a century. Then more war, more destruction, the appearance of weaponry of a power unimagined before, the dismantling of the European empires that in 1910 had seemed a pledge of political stability and missionary accessibility. Finally came the most shattering realisation: that the lands once thought to be evangelised, the home base of missions, the treasure house that was to yield the dedicated resources of the Christian world, themselves needed to be evangelised afresh. One by one, all the props that upheld the world of 1910 were taken away; all the assumptions underlying their vision of the world and of world evangelisation were undermined.

But the vision that was granted at Edinburgh, the vision of a world-wide church and a world-wide spread of the Gospel – that was a true vision. And the event took place; but it took place in ways that no one at the Edinburgh conference could have predicted.

Among the surprises is the little Asian country that the survey of 1910 passed over so quickly. Korea had a very unusual Christian history in the twentieth century. It also developed a quite unusual sense of missionary vocation, so that hundreds of Korean missionaries operate in every continent, even in places regarded as inaccessible to missions in 1910. Another surprise has been the emergence of a whole chain of churches stretching from the Himalayas deep into south east Asia. In 1910 – and indeed, long after – Nepal was regarded as a 'closed land'. Now it has a thriving church. In the early twentieth century mission reports from north east India talked darkly of headhunters; now more than 90 per cent of the population of Mizoram professes the Christian faith, and from there and from other north east states comes a mission force whose presence is felt across the Indian sub-continent. Across the artificial frontier with Myanmar created by the British Raj, people of similar ethnic origin and culture have also turned to the faith, leading to a large increase in Christian numbers since the expulsion of Western missionaries in the 1960s. Across other national borders, with China in one direction and Thailand in another, the Christian churches among people of the same stock continue. Along this chain – shall we call it Himalayan-Arakan? – a Christian community has come into being that is very much a product of the twentieth century; before 1900 the signs of it were unimpressive. Its homelands lie in various nation states, and in each of those nations Christians are a minority, in some a small minority; taken together the Himalayan-Arakan Christian constituency is significant.

The story of Christianity in China did not follow the path to which the most favourable signs that were visible in 1910 were pointing. Estimates of the numbers of Christians in China today differ widely, not to say wildly, but most agree that the number now is many times what it was when Western missionary activity ceased in the middle of the twentieth century. It is impossible to predict what part Chinese Christianity will play in the new global configuration of church and world, but it is unlikely to be peripheral. The twentieth century was more turbulent, perhaps, for China than for anywhere else in the world. And there can be few parallels in Christian history of churches that have undergone so much and emerged as the Chinese church has done. Nor should we forget that Chinese Christianity is not confined to China. The 1910 report had little of substance to say of the huge overseas Chinese population across Asia and beyond; the Christian portion of this is now substantial, another development of the twentieth century.

But the most astonishing difference in the Christian world between 1910 and the present lies in Africa. The report read at Edinburgh spoke of the evangelisation of the interior of Africa as hardly begun, yet during the twentieth century the expansion of the churches of sub-Saharan Africa was phenomenal. The century saw the emergence of sub-Saharan Africa as a Christian heartland, with Africa quietly slipping into the place in the Christian world once occupied by Europe. At the same time, many of those churches have endured fiery trials, having to cope routinely with war, violent disruption, famine, disaster, and displacement. Many have seen movements of renewal or developed new forms of church life. It is as though sub-Saharan Africa has crammed several centuries of

Christian history and experience into the single century that separates us from the World Missionary Conference of 1910.

Latin America's Christian history has been different. Incorporated, as we have seen, into European Christendom at an early period of the Great European Migration, it effectively took on a Christianity made in Europe, effectively omitting the sixteenth century in the process. It adopted the provisions of the Council of Trent – a response to essentially European religious situations – without having had to work for them. Only in the twentieth century did the sixteenth century catch up with Latin America, bringing with it all the passion and ferment and upheaval that European Christianity experienced in that earlier era. Movements of renewal, Catholic and Protestant, emerged; indeed, a specifically Latin American version of Protestantism was born. A powerful current of theology, engaging with issues of local society, broke new ground, threw off its Europe-derived character, and, paradoxically, began to influence the world beyond Latin America as it became distinctively Latin American. Another theological and pastoral current engaged with the social and religious realities of the original inhabitants, uncovering issues never faced in the imposed European model of Christianity that came with Christendom. Latin America has the capacity to release into the world church swirling cross-currents full of the Bible, full of social reality, that reflect the theological intensity and pastoral seriousness that Europe knew in the era of its great Reformations.

Early in the nineteenth century George Canning, British Foreign Secretary of the day, realising that movements in the Americas would alter the traditional European politics of the balance of power, made a policy shift. 'I called' he said, with rather too much grandeur, 'the New World into existence to redress the balance of the Old.' In the twentieth century God called a New church into existence to redress the balance of the Old.

Mission from anywhere to anywhere

For the balance of the church has shifted; it has, as in other periods of church history, been redressed. Lands that were once at its heart are now on the margins, others that were on the margins are now at its heart. It has no single centre; above all, the idea of a 'home base' in Europe and North America, such as the Edinburgh fathers took for granted in 1910, is long past. The church now has not one but many centres; new Christian impulses and initiatives may now be expected from any quarter of the globe. Christian mission may start from any point, and be directed to any point.

The global character of Christianity, now so obvious, is not a new feature. In principle the faith has always been global, and earlier centuries saw it spread across the whole Eurasian land mass and deep into East Africa. The exceptional period of Christian history, when Christianity seemed to belong essentially to the West, is the one from which we have just emerged: the period of the Great European Migration and that immediately preceding it. With its return to a non-Western religion, Christianity has reverted to type.

In the multi-centric Christian church there can be no automatic assumption of

Western leadership; indeed, if suffering and endurance are the badges of authenticity, we can expect the most powerful Christian leadership to come from elsewhere. The same may be true of intellectual and theological leadership; multi-centric Christian mission has the potential to revitalise theological activity and revolutionise theological education. Theology springs out of mission; its true origins lie not in the study or the library, but from the need to make Christian decisions – decisions about what to do, and about what to think. Theology is the attempt to think in a Christian way, to make Christian intellectual choices. Its subject matter, therefore, its agenda, is culturally conditioned, arising out of the actual life situations of active Christians. This means that the normal run of Western theology is simply not big enough for Africa, or for much of the rest of the non-Western world. It offers no guidance for some of the most crucial situations, because it has no questions related to those situations. The reason is that Western theology – whether of more liberal or more conservative tendency is irrelevant – is heavily acculturated. It is substantially an Enlightenment product, designed for an Enlightenment view of the universe. The Enlightenment universe is a small-scale one; witchcraft or sorcery, for instance, do not exist within it, its family structures have no place for the ancestors, the living dead of the family. The frontier between the empirical world and the realm of spirit, the natural and the supernatural, is closed. There is no place for those 'principalities and powers' that Paul sees as world rulers routed by the triumphal chariot of the cross of the Risen Christ. (The Bible is not an Enlightenment book.) Much of humanity lives in a larger, more populated universe, with constant activity across an open frontier between the empirical and the spirit worlds, and faces issues for which Western theology has no resources. For assured Christian living, Christ must fill the world as people see that world, and this is the province of theology. Christian mission in and from Africa is likely to widen the theological agenda; the consequent benefit could be of more than African significance. A wider theology of the principalities and powers might deepen our theology of evil, illuminating the nexus between personal sin and guilt on the one hand, and systemic, structural evil on the other that has stalled much Western theological discussion. The engagement of biblical thinking and the Christian tradition with the ancient cultures of Asia and Africa could open an era of theological creativity to parallel the encounter with Hellenistic culture in the second, third, and fourth centuries. That early encounter, by following up issues raised for Christians within the culture, and using the intellectual materials to hand, gave us the great creeds and the beginnings of classical theology. Who can say that the encounter with Africa and Asia will not be equally enriching?

Church and mission are multi-centric, but the different centres belong to a single organism. Christian faith is embodied faith; Christ takes flesh again among those who respond to him in faith. But there is no generalised humanity; incarnation has always to be culture-specific. The approximations to incarnation among Christians are in specific bits of social reality converted to Christ, turned to face him, and made open to him. All our representations of humanity are partial and incomplete; complete humanity is found only in Christ in his fullness.

The relation to each other of the different pieces of converted social reality was central to the life of the New Testament church. Cultural diversity was built into the church for ever when, so early in the church's life, the decision was taken to abandon the Jewish proselyte model which in effect would have made every Gentile follower of Jesus into a Jew. From that time on there were two converted lifestyles in the church. There was the converted Judaism of the Old Believers of Jerusalem, of whom the old apostles themselves were representative; and there were the New Believers following the Hellenistic way of following Christ that we see under construction in Paul's letters. The Epistle to the Ephesians shows how the two have been made one through Christ's cross. Here are not simply two races, but two lifestyles, two cultures, and, different as they are, they belong to each other. Each is a building block in a new temple that is in process of building; nay, each is an organ in a functioning body of which Christ is the brain. The Temple will not be completed, the Body will not function, unless both are present. Moreover, Christ is full humanity, and it is only together that we reach his full stature.

There are now not two, but an infinite number of segments of partially converted social reality within the church. They include representatives of some of the richest and some of the poorest peoples on earth. Their human relations are shaped by the events of the Great European Migration; the conditions of the Great Reverse Migration bring them as close together as the representatives of the two converted lifestyles in the New Testament hurch. Like them, each is a building block belonging to a new temple still in process of construction. Like them, each is an organ necessary to the proper functioning of a body under Christ's direction. Only together will they reach the fullness of Christ which is the completion and perfection of humanity.

Notes

Section One

Chapter 1 (ii)

1. That there are no references in the text should not be construed to mean that all the ideas originate with me! I am not able to acknowledge all those books and people that have impacted my thinking and practice in proclaiming the good news of the Kingdom of God. However, I want to acknowledge those friends and colleagues that contributed stories at my request: Keturah Turyakira at the Kampala Diocese office; Brian Muhame of All Saints Cathedral, Kampala; Kirk Wolf of Christ Church, Overland Park; and Nick Wayne-Jones of Christ Church, Beckenham.

Chapter 2 (i)

1. This is a term used to describe African nationalism expressed through the church. One of the most significant works on this subject is *Bantu Prophets in South Africa* by B. G. M. Sundkler (Oxford: Oxford University Press, 1961).
2. Andrew F. Walls, 'The Gospel as Prisoner and Liberator of Culture' in *The Missionary Movement in Christian History: Studies in the Transmission of Faith* (Maryknoll: Orbis, 1996), p.10.
3. An address by E. A. Ayandele, in Edward Fasholé-Luke, Richard Gray, Adrian Hastings and Godwin Tasie (eds), *Christianity in Independent Africa* (London: Rex Collings, 1978), pp. 611–612.
4. This is a coinage by Prof. G. O. M. Tasie in his inaugural lecture, 'The Vernacular Church and Nigerian Christianity,' University of Jos, 1997. He further alludes to instances of fanciful European names like George, Best, Dick, Harry, Jack, Napoleon, Limejuice given as baptismal names to native converts!
5. David L. Edwards, *Christianity: The First Two Thousand Years* (London: Cassel, 1997), p. 541.
6. See G. O. M. Tasie, *Christian Missionary Enterprise in the Niger Delta 1864–1918* (Leiden: Brill, 1978), pp. 44–45; Originally quoted in F. W. Smart to CMS Secretary, 10 November 1875, CA3/M3.
7. 'Mission and Ministry: A Theology of Lay Ministry' in *The Truth Shall Make You Free: The Lambeth Conference 1988* (London: Church House Publishing, 1988), p. 51.
8. Rick Warren, *The Purpose-Driven Life* (Grand Rapids: Zondervan, 2002), pp. 120–121.
9. Andrew F. Walls, *The Cross-Cultural Process in Christian History* (Maryknoll: Orbis Books, 2004), pp. 10–11.
10. M. Olusina Fape, *Where Are The Anglican Youths?* (Ibadan: Golden Wallet Press, 1999), pp. 80–81.
11. Andrew F. Walls, op. cit., p. 12.
12. Ogbu Kalu, *Christianity Today/Christian History Magazine* Issue 79, Spring 2003, Vol XXII, No 3, 7.

13. Philip Jenkins, *The Next Christendom: The Coming of Global Christianity* (Oxford: OUP, 2002), p. 37.

14. Roland Allen, *Missionary Methods: St. Paul's or Ours* (Grand Rapids: Eerdmans, 1962), p. 81.

15. Kwame Bediako, *Theology and Identity: The Impact of Culture upon Christian Thought in the Second Century and in Modern Africa* (Cumbria: Regnum Books, 1999), p. 7.

16. This scenario of contradiction is constantly replayed in my experience with rural churches trying so hard to sing English hymns (sometimes translated) and tunes with foreign instruments. Whenever at some point in the worship, the opportunity is offered to switch to the native tune, the animated transformation among the same people is incredible.

Chapter 2 (ii)

1. Eleanor Johnson and John Clark (eds), *Anglicans In Mission: A Transforming Journey* (London: SPCK, 2000), p. 20.

2. ibid., p. 20.

3. ibid., p. 30.

4. PEAC, *Kitabu Cha Sala kwa Watu Wote* (Rethy: R.D. Congo, 1998), pp. 149–150.

5. *The Encyclical Letter from the Bishops together with the Resolutions and Reports*. Lambeth Conference 1958. (London: SPCK, 1958).

6. Paul Avis, *The Anglican Understanding of the Church: an Introduction* (London: SPCK, 2000), p. 24.

7. Paul Avis, *Christians in Communion* (London: Geoffrey Chapman Mowbray, 1990), p. 34.

8. Quoted in Joseph Healey and Donald Sybertz, *Towards an African Narrative Theology* (Nairobi: Paulines Publications, 1996), p. 149.

9. Ande Titre, *Authority in the Anglican Church of Congo*, The University of Birmingham, PhD Thesis, 2003, unpublished, p. 162.

10. Skevington Wood, *The Burning Heart: John Wesley, Evangelist* (Grand Rapids: Eerdmans, 1967), p. 212.

11. See Manfred Waldemar Kahl and A. N. Lal Senanayako (eds), *Educating for Tomorrow: Theological Leadership for the Asian Context* (India: SAIACS Press, 2002), p. 134.

12. Paulo Freire, *Pedagogy of the Oppressed* (London: Penguin Books, 1996), p. 62.

13. Laurenti Magesa, 'Theology of Democracy' in Laurenti Magesa and Zablon Nthamburi (eds), *Democracy and Reconciliation: A Challenge for African Christianity* (Nairobi: Acton, 1999), pp. 117–134.

14. Theresa Okure, quoted in *Perspectives Missionnaires, Revue Protestante de Missiologie* no 45–46, 2003.

15. T. Tuma, *A Century of Christianity in Uganda* (1977), XV.

Chapter 3 (i)

1. Walter Wink, *Naming the Powers* (Philadelphia: Fortress Press, 1984).

Chapter 3 (ii)

1. *UN Global Study on Violence Against Children*, October 11, 2006 – accessed from the UN website, 2 April, 2007 (http://www.unicef.org.nz/media/news/news 1160684054.html).

Chapter 4 (i)

1. In his small article entitled 'Shalom', Jim Punton, in *The Lion Handbook of Christian Belief* (Tring, UK: Lion Publishing, 1982, pp. 314–315), tries to highlight the significant meaning of this Hebrew word which means much more than peace. 'Shalom', he says, 'is wholeness, completeness, unbrokenness, full health, comprehensive well-being'. He also stresses the collective and societal dimension of shalom as well as affirming in which hands it rests and finds full meaning. Shalom is 'a gift of God', he affirms and stresses its all-encompassing reality: 'Shalom encompassed all reality, structural as well as personal. It speaks of the state of affairs where everything works and works together as God originally designed.'

2. Stephen Neill, 'Creative Tension: The Duff Lectures', 1958 (Edinburgh: House Press, 1959), p. 8.

3. John Stott, 'The Biblical Basis of Evangelism', in *Let the Earth Hear His Voice*, ed. by J. D. Douglas (Minneapolis: World Wide Publications, 1975), p. 69.

4. In all the synoptic gospels we find the names of those who were called to follow Jesus (Mark 3:13–19; Matthew 10:1–4; Luke 6:12–16).

5. The whole of chapter 10 of Matthew contains Jesus' instructions to the twelve; they are very similar to the ones given to the seventy in Luke 10:1–12.

6. A kind of contemporary version of the orphan, the widow, and the stranger, as seen stressed in the prophetic tradition of the OT.

7. Tracy Kidder, *Mountains Beyond Mountains. The Quest of Dr. Paul Farmer, a man who would cure the world* (New York: Random House Trade Paperbacks, 2004).

8. WL stands for 'White Liberals'.

9. Kidder, *Mountains Beyond Mountains*, p. 40.

10. ibid., pp. 100–101.

11. Nicholas Wolterstorff, *Until Justice and Peace Embrace* (Grand Michigan: Eerdmans, 1983), p. 22.

12. *Economics of Religion in Brazil*, Project of the FGV and co-ordinated by Marcelo Neri. www.fgv.br/cps/pesquisa.

13. Abstract of the research, *Economics of Religion in Brazil*.

14. 'Católicos: ritos de fé', in *Jornal da Globo*, 10 May, 2007.

15. Data from IBGE/2000.

16. The study, *Poverty, Inequality and Stability: The Second Real* (Project of the FGV, co-ordinated by Marcelo Neri. See the summary report (6), at www. fgv.br/cps/pesquisa) indicated that during the years 2003 to 2005 the poorer segments of the population increased their annual income by 8.4 per cent, against 3.7 per cent of the rich as a tentative indication of some social changes in our society. These changes are due to the implementation of policies of macro-economic stability as well as many public policies, like the official distribution of non-perishable food, and community kitchens, established by the government.

Chapter 4 (ii)

1. See Sampie Terblanche, *A History of Inequality in South Africa, 1652–2002* (Pietermaritzburg: University of Natal Press, 2002).

2. A regional structure of the South African Council of Churches that was affiliated to the World Council of Churches.

3. *Kairos Document* (Johannesburg: Skotaville, 1986).

4. Itumeleng Mosala and Buti Tlhagale (eds), *The unquestionable right to be free* (Johannesburg: Skotaville, 1986).

5. Allan Boesak, *Farewell to innocence: a socio-ethical study on Black Theology and power* (Maryknoll, NY: Orbis Books, 1977) and Allan Boesak, *Black and reformed: apartheid, liberation and the Calvinist tradition* (Johannesburg: Skotaville, 1984).

6. Steve Biko, *Steve Biko: no fears expressed* (Johannesburg: Skotaville, 1987).

7. José Bonino, *Toward a Christian political ethic* (London: SCM Press, 1983).

8. Gustavo Gutierrez, *A theology of liberation* (London: SCM Press, 1974) and Gustavo Gutierrez, *We drink from our own wells: the spiritual journey of a people* (Maryknoll, NY: Orbis Books, 1984).

9. See Per Frostin, *Liberation theology in Tanzania and South Africa: a first world interpretation* (Lund: Lund University Press, 1988).

10. Gayatri Spivak, 'Can the subaltern speak?' in *Marxism and the interpretation of culture*, Cary Nelson and Lawrence Grossberg (eds) (London: Macmillan 1988), pp. 271–313.

11. Donna Landry and Gerald MacLean (eds), *The Spivak reader: selected works of Gayatri Chakravorty Spivak* (New York: Routledge, 1996).

12. See Gerald West, 'Contextual Bible study in South Africa: a resource for reclaiming and regaining land, dignity and identity', in *The Bible in Africa: transactions, trends and trajectories*, Gerald West and Musa Dube (eds) (Leiden: Brill, 2000), pp. 595–610.

13. See Beverley Haddad, 'We pray but we cannot heal: theological challenges posed by the HIV/AIDS crisis', *Journal of Theology for Southern Africa* 125, 2006, 80–90 and Tinyiko Maluleke, 'The challenge of HIV/AIDS for theological education', *Missionalia* 29(2), 2001, 125–143.

14. UNAIDS, '2006 AIDS epidemic update', http://www.unaids.org/en/HIV_data/epi2006/.

15. See Thomas Rehle, Olive Shisana, Victoria Pillay, Khangelani Zuma, Adrian Puren and Warren Parker, 'National HIV incidence measures – new insights into the South African epidemic' in *South African Medical Journal* 97(3) 2007, 194–199.

16. UNAIDS, '2006 AIDS epidemic update', op. cit.

17. See Tessa Marcus, *WO! Zaphela Izingane It is destroying the children: living and dying with AIDS* (Pietermaritzburg: University of Natal, Pietermaritzburg, 1999).

18. *Forum Review:* Religious Organisations in Reproductive Health No 4 December 2001.

19. Daniela Gennrich (ed.), *The Church in an HIV+ world: a practical handbook* (Pietermaritzburg: Cluster Publications, 2004), p. 65.

20. Gerald West, 'Reading the Bible in the light of HIV/AIDS in South Africa', *Ecumenical Review* 55(4), 2003, 336.

21. David Korten, *Getting to the 21st Century: voluntary action and the global agenda* (Hartford, Connecticut: Kumarian Press, 1990).

22. The Treatment Action Campaign (TAC) is an activist movement made of mostly HIV positive people who have worked tirelessly in lobbying the South African government on issues of HIV/AIDS policy, including access to treatment.

23. The Ujamaa Centre for Research and Community Development is attached to the School of Religion and Theology, University of KwaZulu-Natal. It has pioneered the contextual Bible study methodology and has worked for nearly two decades in the social transformation of poor and marginalised communities in South Africa.

24. PACSA. 'Churches and HIV/AIDS: Exploring how local churches are integrating HIV/AIDS in the life and ministries of the church and how those most directly affected experience these', Research report, Pietermaritzburg, December 2004.

25. See Gerald West, 'Reading Job "positively" in the context of HIV/AIDS in South

Africa', *Concilium* 4, 2004, 112–124.

26. I am indebted to Canon Gideon Byamugishya for this term.

27. Anna-Louise Crago, 'Women and AIDS in Africa', *Z Magazine Online* 19(6), 2006.

Chapter 5 (i)

1. Donald Worster, *Nature's Economy: the Roots of Ecology* (San Francisco: Sierra Club Books, 1979), p. 37.

2. University of Athens website: http://www.cc.uoa.gr/theology/html/english/cac/sections.htm.

3. Commentary on Genesis 2:15, from John Calvin's *Commentary on Genesis* (first Latin edition, 1554; first English edition, 1578). English translation of 1847, reprinted by Banner of Truth Publishers, Vol. I, Chapter II.15, 1965.

4. William Blake, 'Jerusalem' 15:14–20. In *The Complete Poems*, ed. W. H. Stevenson (London: Longman Annotated English Poets, 2nd rev. edn, 1989).

5. A consequence of this re-conception is that the great deposits of carbon that have been sequestered by mires, marshes, and moors – and their related stores of coal are 'fossil fuels'. Viewing these deposits as our teachers on the workings of the great economy, however, would tell how green plants in the distant past removed excessive carbon dioxide from the atmosphere thereby making earth more habitable.

6. For a more comprehensive treatment, see my 'Biogeographic and Trophic Restructuring of the Biosphere: The State of the Earth Under Human Domination', *Christian Scholar's Review* 32 (2003) 347–364.

7. Camille Parmesan and Gary Yohe, 'A Globally Coherent Fingerprint of Climate Change Impacts Across Natural Systems', *Nature* 421 (2 January 2003) 37–42.

8. Jeremy B. C. Jackson et al., 'Historical Overfishing and the Recent Collapse of Coastal Ecosystems', *Science* 293 (2001) 629–637.

9. Consider, for example, the Orange Roughy. Discovered in 1889, this fish now is consumed, lives at depths of 2500 to 5000 feet, is thought to live up to 150 years, and reproduces when it is 25–30 years old. It is caught when it is concentrated on its spawning grounds. Its population is declining and we do not understand its place in the sea's food web.

10. Abbreviations here for various Bible translations are: NIV, New International Version; DBY, Darby Version; KJV, King James Version; and YLT, Young's Literal Translation.

11. Third Edition of *Webster's Third New International Dictionary of the English Language Unabridged* (Springfield, Mass.: Merriam-Webster, 1981), p. 720.

12. Parallel translations in the King James Version (KJV) and the Septuagint (LXX) show a consistent correspondence of the Hebrew *'eretz* with the Greek *ge* as in Isaiah 34:1, LXX.

13. Andrew F. Walls, *The Missionary Movement in Christian History: Studies in the Transmission of Faith* (Maryknoll, New York: Orbis Books, 1996), p. 26.

14. Kevin J. Vanhoozer, *The Drama of Doctrine: A Canonical Linguistic Approach to Christian Theology* (Louisville, Kentucky: Westminster John Knox Press, 2005), pp. 137–139.

15. John Milton, *Paradise Lost*, Book V, lines 185–191.

16. Andrew Walls writes, 'The mission of the church is not simply to add to itself but to bear witness that by his cross and resurrection Christ bought back the whole creation and defeated the powers that spoiled it.' *The Missionary Movement*, p. 255.

17. Vanhoozer, p. 223.
18. Augustine writes, '… they did not recognise Him, as is shown by Luke's narrative, until the breaking of the bread took place … The deeper significance of all which is this, that no one should consider himself to have attained the knowledge of Christ, if he is not a member in His body – that is to say, in His Church …' *The Harmony of the Gospels*, Book III, 72, S. D. F. Salmond, transl.
19. Rowan Williams, *Archbishop's Larkin Stuart Lecture*, 'The Bible Today: Reading & Hearing' (Toronto, Canada, 16 April 2007). [This lecture is accessible at: http://www.archbishopofcanterbury.org/sermons_speeches/070416.htm.]
20. Irenaeus, writes, 'He took from among creation that which is bread, and gave thanks, saying, "This is My Body." The cup likewise, which is from among the creation to which we belong, He confessed to be His Blood.' *Against Heresies*, 180 AD, 4,17,5.
21. Summarizing Committee Report of the World Evangelical Theological Commission and *Au Sable* Institute Forum, In Mark Thomas (guest ed.), *Evangelicals and the Environment: Theological Foundations for Christian Environmental Stewardship* (special issue), *Evangelical Review of Theology* 17(2), 1993, 122–133.

Chapter 5 (ii)

1. Quoted in David Bosch, *Transforming Mission* (Maryknoll: Orbis, 1992), p. 489.
2. Nazmul Chowdbury, Bangladesh, quoted in *The Climate of Poverty* (London: Christian Aid, 2006).
3. 'The Stern Review: The Economics of Climate Change', November 2006. See www.hm-treasury.gov.uk/media/A/8/stern_speakingnotes.pdf (page 3).
4. From interview with Pastor Tri Robinson on 'Tending the Garden – A Documentary of Environmental Ministry', available via www.letstendthegarden.org/media.htm.
5. Jeff McIntyre-Strasburg, 'Evangelical Minister Proclaims – Let's tend the Garden', 9 December 2006, see www.treehugger.com.
6. 'Why Christians are called to Environmental Stewardship', see www.letstendthe garden.org.
7. *A Rocha* is Portuguese for 'The Rock', see www.arocha.org.
8. Peter Harris, *Under the Bright Wings* (London: Hodder & Stoughton, 1993; reprinted Regent Books, Canada, 2004).
9. Peter Harris, speaking on short film 'Introduction to *A Rocha*' 2006, available from *A Rocha* UK, 13 Avenue Road, Southall, UB1 3BL or other national *A Rocha* offices.
10. ASSETS – The Arabuko Sokoke Schools Eco-Tourism Scheme, www.assets-kenya.org.
11. Southall Regeneration Partnership report to London Borough of Ealing, 1999.

Section Two

Chapter 1

1. This question is taken from the title of Lamin Sanneh's book: *Whose Religion is Christianity? The Gospel Beyond the West* (Grand Rapids: Eerdmans, 2003). The title of Sanneh's book, with which I identify, indicates the perspective from which I intend to explore the 'opportunities and challenges' that now face African Christian scholarship. An earlier version of this paper was given at a doctoral sem-

inar in the School of Religion and Theology, University of KwaZulu-Natal, Pietermaritzburg, South Africa, on 16 November 2005.

2. Kwame Bediako, 'Africa and Christianity on the threshold of the third millennium – The religious dimension', *African Affairs*, Vol. 99, No. 395 (April 2000) 303–23 (303).

3. See Kevin Ward, 'Africa', in Adrian Hastings (ed.), *A World History of Christianity* (Grand Rapids: Eerdmans, 1999), p. 235: '… at some point in the twenty-first century, Christians in Africa will become more numerous than Christians in any other continent and more important than ever in articulating a global Christian identity in a pluralist world'.

4. See Philip Jenkins, *The Next Christendom – The Coming of Global Christianity* (New York: Oxford University Press, 2002). For Jenkins the emergence of this 'next [South-based] Christendom', 'which carries the potential of enabling us to see Christianity again for the first time', 'looks like a very exotic beast indeed, intriguing, exciting and a little frightening' (p. 220). Emmanuel Katongole's observation on Jenkins' analysis is apposite here: 'The Next Christendom is bad news for Christians, not simply because it assumes the existing North-South dichotomies shaped by the economic and political realities of late capitalism, but because it seeks to secure this current vision of the world against any interruption. In this way, its assumptions and objectives obscure and even resist the possibility of any social interruption.' Emmanuel M. Katongole, 'Hauerwasian hooks and the Christian social imagination – Critical reflection from an African perspective', in Gregory Jones, Reinhard Hutter and C. Rosalee Velloso Ewell (eds), *God, Truth and Witness – Engaging Stanley Hauerwas* (Grand Rapids: Brazos Press, 2005), p. 143.

5. See the recent article by Tim Stafford, 'A historian ahead of his time', *Christianity Today*, Vol. 51, No. 2.

6. John Mbiti, 'Theological impotence and the universality of the Church', *Lutheran World*, Vol. 21, No. 3 (1974); republished in Gerald Anderson and Thomas Stransky (eds), *Mission Trends 3: Third World Theologies* (New York/Grand Rapids: Paulist Press/Eerdmans, 1976), pp. 6–18. For a discussion of Mbiti's idea, see Kwame Bediako, *Christianity in Africa – The Renewal of a Non-Western Religion* (Edinburgh/Maryknoll, NY: Edinburgh University Press/Orbis Books, 1995), pp. 154ff.

7. Andrew F. Walls, 'Structural problems in Mission Studies', in his *The Missionary Movement in Christian History, Studies in the Transmission of Faith* (Edinburgh/Maryknoll, NY: T & T Clark/Orbis Books, 1996), pp. 143–59 (146).

8. Adrian Hastings (ed.), *A World History of Christianity* (London: Cassell, 1999), p. 1.

9. Lamin Sanneh, *Piety and Power – Muslims and Christians in West Africa* (New York: Orbis Books, 1996), p. x.

10. On this subject, see my *Christianity in Africa, The Renewal of a Non-Western Religion*, Chapter 6 on 'The primal imagination and the opportunity for a new theological idiom', pp. 91–108.

11. On this subject, see the insightful treatment by Gillian Bediako, 'Christian faith and primal religion – Soul-mates or antagonists?', *Journal of African Christian Thought*, Vol. 3, No. 1 (June 2000) 12–16.

12. Kwame Bediako, *Theology and Identity: The Impact of Culture on Christian Thought in the Second Century and Modern Africa* (Oxford: Regnum Books, 1992; 1999).

13. Johannes Verkuyl, *Contemporary Missiology – An Introduction* (trans. & ed. Dale Cooper, Grand Rapids: Eerdmans, 1978), p. 277.

14. For one attempt to respond to the question from an African perspective, see Kwame

Bediako, *Jesus in Africa, The Christian Gospel in African History and Experience* (Akropong/Yaounde: Regnum Africa/Editions Clé, 2000), in a chapter entitled: 'How is Jesus Christ Lord? Evangelical Christian apologetics amid African religious pluralism', pp. 34–45.

15. For a representative sample of Turner's work, see H. W. Turner, *History of an African Independent Church – Church of the Lord, Aladura* (Oxford: Clarendon Press, 1967).

16. H. W. Turner, 'The contribution of studies on religion in Africa to Western Religious Studies', in Mark Glasswell and E. W. Fasholé-Luke (eds), *New Testament Christianity for Africa and the World, Essays in Honour of Harry Sawyer* (London: SPCK, 1974), pp. 169–78.

17. Bediako, *Christianity in Africa – The Renewal of a Non-Western Religion*, pp. 253–58.

18. Turner, 'The contribution of studies on religion', op. cit., p. 170.

19. Turner, 'The contribution of studies on religion', op. cit., p. 178.

20. Turner, 'The contribution of studies on religion', op. cit., p. 177–78.

21. Katongole, 'Hauerwasian hooks and the Christian social imagination', p. 137.

22. Stanley Hauerwas, *With the Grain of the Universe: The Church's Witness and Natural Theology* (Grand Rapids: Brazos Press, 2002).

23. Katongole, 'Hauerwasian hooks and the Christian social imagination', p. 137–38.

24. Kwasi Wiredu, *Philosophy and an African Culture* (Cambridge: Cambridge University Press, 1980).

25. Kwame Gyekye, *Essay on African Philosophical Thought – The Akan Conceptual Scheme* (Philadelphia: Temple University Press, 1995), p. 69. See also his sustained treatment in his, *Tradition and Modernity, Philosophical Reflections on the African Experience* (New York: Oxford University Press, 1997).

26. Bediako, *Christianity in Africa*, p. 104.

27. Kwesi Dickson, *Theology in Africa* (London: Darton, Longman & Todd, 1984), p. 42.

28. Dickson, *Theology in Africa*, p. 46.

29. Tahir Sitoto, 'The ambiguity of African Muslim identity with special reference to Christianity', *Journal of African Christian Thought*, Vol. 7, No. 2 (December 2004), 8–15.

30. Bediako, *Christianity in Africa*, p. 265.

31. Sitoto, 'The ambiguity of African Muslim identity', 12.

32. Harold W. Turner, 'The way forward in the religious study of African primal religions', *Journal of Religion in Africa*, Vol. 12, Fasc. 1 (1981), 1–15 (13).

33. The literature on post-coloniality, or post-colonial discourse, as an intellectual framework of analysis is already vast and is not to be lightly dismissed. In relation to the field of Christian studies, see the seminal collection of essays, *The Bible and Postcolonialism, 1: The Postcolonial Bible*, edited by R. S. Sugitharahah (Sheffield: Sheffield Academic Press, 1998). In his introduction to the second volume, *The Bible and Postcolonialism, 2: Vernacular Hermeneutics* (Sheffield: Sheffield Academic Press, 1999), p. 16, the editor, R. S. Sugitharahah implies that there already has to be a larger framework. In positioning oneself as post-colonial, one is handicapped to understand one's indigenous heritage.

34. Bengt Sundkler, *Zulu Zion and Some Swazi Zionists* (London: Oxford University Press, 1976), pp. 318–19.

35. Bengt Sundkler, *Bantu Prophets in South Africa* (London: Oxford University Press, 1948).

36. G. Tasie and Richard Gray, 'Introduction', in Edward Fasholé-Luke *et al.* (eds), *Christianity in Independent Africa* (London: Rex Collings, 1978), p. 4.

37. See, for an example of this, Mercy Amba Oduyoye, *Beads and Strands, Reflections of an African Woman on Christianity in Africa* (Akropong/Yaoundé: Regnum Africa/Editions Clé, 2002), pp. 94–97.

38. Walbert Buhlmann, *The Coming of the Third Church* (Slough: St Paul Publications, 1976). (First published in German as *Es kommt die dritte Kirche – Eine Analyse der kirchlichen Gegenwart und Zukunft*, 1974.)

39. Buhlmann, *The Coming of the Third Church*, p. 23.

40. Andrew F. Walls, 'Africa in Christian history, Retrospect and prospect', *Journal of African Christian Thought*, Vol. 1, No. 1 (June 1998), 2–15 (14); reprinted in Andrew F. Walls, *The Cross-Cultural Process in Christian History* (Maryknoll, NY: Orbis Books, 2002), pp. 85–115 (115).

41. Note the quip of a South American theologian reported by Emmanuel Katongole, 'Hauerwasian hooks and the Christian social imagination', p. 150: 'Liberation theology opted for the poor, but the poor opted for Pentecostalism [a theology of prosperity]'.

Chapter 2

1. Han van Dijk *et al.*, 'Population Mobility in Africa: An Overview', in *Mobile Africa: Changing Patterns of Movement in Africa and Beyond*, ed. Mirjam de Bruijn *et al.* (Boston, MA: Brill Publishers, 2001), pp. 9–26, p. 14.

2. Stephen Castles and Mark J. Miller, *The Age of Migration: International Population Movements in the Modern World*, 2nd ed. (NY: The Guilford Press, 1998).

3. W. R. Böhning, 'International Migration and the Western World: Past, Present, Future', *International Migration* xvi, no. 1 (1978), 13.

4. Of these, 60 per cent (or 33 million people) settled in the United States alone; and 85 per cent settled in just five countries (Argentina, Australia, Canada, New Zealand, and the United States).

5. Cited in Castles and Miller, *The Age of Migration: International Population Movements in the Modern World*, p. 54.

6. See Böhning, 'International Migration and the Western World: Past, Present, Future', p. 15.

7. W. M. Spellman, *The Global Community: Migration and the Making of the Modern World* (Stroud, England: Sutton Publishing, 2002), p. 121.

8. ibid., p. 116.

9. Today, the U.S. is home to the largest Chinese community outside mainland China.

10. Andrew N. Porter, *Religion Versus Empire?: British Protestant Missionaries and Overseas Expansion, 1700–1914* (New York: Manchester University Press, 2004), p. 194. Though it has to be said that Hudson Taylor's China Inland Mission, perhaps the best-known example of faith missions, was made possible by the 'unequal treaties' imposed on China by European military aggression and commercial ambitions. Also, faith missionaries, in West Africa and China, were hardly free from the arrogance and paternalism which characterized the Western missionary project in general.

11. Castles and Miller, *The Age of Migration*, p. 23.

12. Cf. David Held *et al.*, *Global Transformations: Politics, Economics and Culture*, (Stanford: Stanford: Stanford Univ. Press, 1999), p. 43.

13. The colonies and former possessions of the British Empire in Africa, the Caribbean and Asia were constituted into a British Commonwealth (later 'Commonwealth of Nations'), and possession of a British passport granted their citizens unhindered

rights to enter Britain.

14. The backlash to the influx of these new immigrants was fierce. Shunned by the wider population and labeled 'ethnic minorities', they crowded into Britain's declining towns and created a distinctive underclass. In particular, the growth of black communities triggered the rise of racial violence and riots in cities like Birmingham and Nottingham.

15. Cf. Ataullah Siddiqui, 'Muslims in Britain: Past and Present', (1995). See www.islamfortoday.com/britain.htm.

16. ibid.

17. David Masci, 'An Uncertain Road: Muslims and the Future of Europe' (The Pew Research Center, 2005), p. 5.

18. 'Muslims in Europe: Country Guide' (BBC News, 2005).

19. 'Human Development Report' (2001), p. 19.

20. Cf. Castles and Miller, *The Age of Migration*, p. 79; Held *et al.*, *Global Transformations*, pp. 303–305.

21. 'World Population: More Than Just Numbers' (Population Reference Bureau, 1999), p. 1.

22. Cf. Paul Kennedy, *Preparing for the Twenty-First Century* (New York: Vintage Books, 1993), p. 24; 'World Population: More Than Just Numbers', p. 2.

23. 'World Population: More Than Just Numbers', p. 1.

24. See Saskia Sassen, *Guests and Aliens* (New York: The New Press, 1999).

25. Hania Zlotnik, 'Trends in South to North Migration: The Perspective from the North', *International Migration* xxix, no. 2 (1991) 318.

26. ibid., 319.

27. ibid., 319–320. Zlotnik limits his analysis to five European countries: Belgium, Germany, Netherlands, Sweden, and the United Kingdom.

28. ibid. As Zlotnik points out, the fact that UK data classifies immigrants by country of previous residence introduces significant bias into the assessment since it would include British citizens returning from the developing world.

29. Cf. Pippa Norris and Ronald Inglehart, *Sacred and Secular: Religion and Politics Worldwide* (New York: Cambridge University Press, 2004), p. 217.

30. 'Turkey and Europe: Coming Apart?', *The Economist*, 6 May 2006, 16.

31. Grace Davie, *Europe, the Exceptional Case: Parameters of Faith in the Modern World* (London: Darton, Longman & Todd, 2002), pp. 38f.

32. Tariq Ramadan, *To Be a European Muslim: A Study of Islamic Sources in the European Context* (Leicester, England: Islamic Foundation, 1999), p. 121.

33. 'Decline in Churchgoing Hits Church of England Hardest', *Guardian*, 14 April 2001, p. 4.; Masci, 'An Uncertain Road: Muslims and the Future of Europe', p. 6.

34. Cf. Peter L. Berger, 'The Desecularization of the World: A Global Overview', in *The Desecularization of the World: Resurgent Religion and World Politics*, ed. Peter L. Berger (Grand Rapids, MI: W. B. Eerdmans, 1999), pp. 1–18, pp. 7f.

35. David B. Barrett *et al.*, *World Christian Encyclopedia: A Comparative Survey of Churches and Religions in the Modern World*, 2nd ed. (New York: Oxford University Press, 2001), p. 5.

36. Evan Osnos, 'Islam Shaping a New Europe', *Chicago Tribune*, 19 December 2004.

37. Robert D. Putnam, *Bowling Alone: The Collapse and Revival of American Community* (New York: Simon & Schuster, 2000), p. 72.

38. Barrett *et al.*, *World Christian Encyclopedia*, p. 5.

39. Between 1750 and 1850, for instance, Europe doubled its population from 270 to

over 460 million. See Spellman, *The Global Community*, pp. 73f.

40. Cf. David B. Barrett and Todd M. Johnson, 'Annual Statistical Table on Global Mission: 2004', *International Bulletin of Missionary Research* 28, no. 1 (2004).

41. Peter W. Brierley, *U.K.C.H. Religious Trends No. 3* (London: Christian Research, 2001), p. 4. By 2050, reckons Philip Jenkins, only about one-fifth of the world's Christians will be white Caucasian. See Philip Jenkins, *The Next Christendom: The Coming of Global Christianity* (New York: Oxford University Press, 2002), pp. 2, 3.

42. For a helpful appraisal of this historic link, see Andrew Walls, 'Mission and Migration: The Diaspora Factor in Christian History', *Journal of African Christian Thought* 5, no. 2 (2002); also, Jehu J. Hanciles, 'Mission and Migration: Some Implications for the Twenty-First Century Church', *International Bulletin of Missionary Research* 27, no. 4 (2003).

43. Samuel E. Escobar, *A Time for Mission: The Challenge for Global Christianity* (Leicester, England: Inter-Varsity Press, 2003), p. 66. For more on the missionary potential of the Latin American migrant movement see Miguel A. Palomino, 'Latino Immigration in Europe: Challenge and Opportunity for Mission', *International Bulletin of Missionary Research* 28, no. 2 (2004).

44. Analysis of missionaries in the world, never fully empirical to begin with, became further complicated by the upsurge and varying definitions of 'short-term' missionaries from the 1980s.

45. Scott Moreau, 'Putting the Survey in Perspective', in *Mission Handbook 2001–2003: U.S. And Canadian Christian Ministries Overseas*, ed. John A. Siewert and Dotsey Welliver (Wheaton, Ill: Billy Graham Center, 2000), pp. 33–80, p. 34.

46. Brent Ashabranner, *The New Americans: Changing Patterns in U.S. Immigration* (New York: Dodd, Mead & Company, 1983), p. 9.

47. Cf. Diana L. Eck, *A New Religious America: How A 'Christian Country' Has Now Become the World's Most Religiously Diverse Nation*, 1st ed. (San Francisco: Harper, 2001).

48. For a full analysis, see Guillermina Jasso, *et al.*, 'Exploring the Religious Preferences of Recent Immigrants to the United States: Evidence from the New Immigrant Survey Pilot', in Y. Y. Haddad, J. I. Smith & J. L. Esposito, *Religion and Immigration: Christian, Jewish, and Muslim Experiences in the United States* (New York: Alta Mira Press, 2003), pp. 217–253, p. 221.

49. Putnam, *Bowling Alone*, p. 76.

50. Cf. Helen R. Ebaugh and Janet S. Chafetz, *Religion and the New Immigrants: Continuities and Adaptations in Immigrant Congregations* (New York: AltaMira Press, 2000), p. 14.

51. ibid., p. 14.

52. Cf. Fenggang Yang and Helen Ebaugh, 'Transformations in New Immigrant Religions and Their Global Implications', *American Sociological Review* 66 (2001).

53. Ebaugh and Chafetz, *Religion and the New Immigrants*, p. 14.

54. My own research on African immigrant churches in the US (under the 'Mobile Faith' project) confirms this trend.

55. Report of the Council of African Christian Communities in Europe (CACCE) at the 1999 meeting in Belgium, quoted in Roswith Gerloff, 'Religion, Culture and Resistance: The Significance of African Christian Communities in Europe', *Exchange* 30, no. 3 (2001) 277.

56. 'London Is Different!', *Quadrant*, January 2007.

57. Lindsay Bergstrom, 'Worldwide Baptists Survive, Reflect Century of Cultural

Change' (Associated Baptist Press), 6 January 2005.

58. Cf. Mark Sturge, *Look What the Lord Has Done!: An Exploration of Black Christian Faith in Britain* (Bletchley, England: Scripture Union, 2005), p. 93.

59. Sunday Adelaja, 'Go to a Land That I Will Show You', in *Out of Africa*, ed. C. Peter Wagner and Joseph Thompson (Ventura, CA: Regal Books, 2004), pp. 37–55.

60. See the Embassy of the Blessed Kingdom of God for all Nations website, www.godembassy.org.

61. See Steve S. C. Moon, 'The Recent Korean Missionary Movement: A Record of Growth, and More Growth Needed', *International Bulletin of Missionary Research* 27, no. 1 (2003); also www.kidok.com (use browser to translate from Korean to English, as required). While South Korea is ranked second to the US in numbers of overseas missionaries officially sent by mission agencies, its missionary output far surpasses the US when it is considered that only 26 per cent of South Korea's 49 million population is Christian. The growth of its 'official' missionary force is also un-paralleled. By 2002 approximately 1,000 new missionaries were being 'officially' sent from South Korea each year.

62. For a discussion, see Jehu J. Hanciles, 'Mission and Migration: Some Implications for the Twenty-First Century Church', ibid., no. 4, pp. 146–153.

Chapter 3

1. Gladstone, *The State and Its Relations with the Church*, 2nd edition, 1839. For a criti-cal assessment of Gladstone see Lord Macaulay (Thomas Babington), 'Gladstone on Church and State', *Essays* (London: George Routledge and Sons, 1887), pp. 490–524.

2. Lawrence Friedman, *The Republic of Choice* (Cambridge, Mass.: Harvard University Press, 1990).

3. This brings to mind the celebrated clash between king and prophet: 'but prophesy not again any more at Beth-el: for it *is* the king's chapel, and it *is* the king's court', Amos 7:13.

4. Philip Jenkins contends that 'Today, Europe provides territory in which scholars, Islamic and others, can perform on the Qur'an the same task of scholarly criticism and analysis that their predecessors did on Jewish and Christian scriptures; pro-gressive interpretations of the Qur'an.' Philip Jenkins, *God's Continent: Christianity, Islam and Europe's Religious Crisis* (New York: Oxford University Press, 2007), pp. 140–141.

5. 'A Christian Society?' p. 10. Draft unpublished manuscript essay.

6. T. S. Eliot, *Christianity and Culture: The Idea of a Christian Society, and Notes Towards the Definition of Culture* (1940; repr. New York: Harcourt, Brace, Jovanovich, 1968), p. 22.

7. ibid., p. 29.

8. ibid., p. 34.

9. 'A Christian Society?', p. 12.

10. 'A Christian Society?', p. 15.

11. Lesslie Newbigin, *Signs Amid the Rubble: The Purposes of God in Human History*, col-lected lectures, edited by Geoffrey Wainwright (Grand Rapids, MI: Wm. B. Eerdmans Publishing, 2003), pp. 53–54.

12. Henri de Lubac, *The Drama of Atheistic Humanism* (San Francisco: Ignatius Press, 1995), p. 14.

13. As George Weigel noted, that was how Rocco Buttiglione, the distinguished Italian

Catholic intellectual, was blackballed by the European Commission for the post of Commissioner of Justice merely for holding views deemed heretical by the enforcers of Europe's secular agenda. Weigel, 'The Cathedral and the Cube: Reflections on European Morale', *Commentary*, vol. 117, no. 6, June 2004, 33–38.

14. Karl Marx, 'On the Jewish Question', in *Selected Writings*, edited by Lawrence H. Simon (1994), p. 9.

15. Lesslie Newbigin, *The Relevance of Trinitarian Doctrine for Today's Mission*, C.W.M.E. Study Pamphlets No. 2 (London: Edinburgh House Press, 1963), pp. 16–18.

16. Lesslie Newbigin, *The Gospel in a Pluralist Society* (Grand Rapids: Eerdmans Publishers, 1989), p. 156.

17. ibid., p.157.

18. For a study of this theme see Ratzinger (Pope Benedict XVI), *Truth and Tolerance: Christian Belief and World Religions* (San Francisco: Ignatius Press, 2004), p. 2004.

19. 'Britain's Plans for Addressing Its Muslims' Concerns Lag', *New York Times*, 19 August 2006, A3.

20. *The Gospel in a Pluralist Society*, p. 169.

21. ibid., p. 178.

22. ibid., p. 166.

23. ibid., p. 178.

24. ibid., p. 179.

25. ibid., pp. 173–74.

26. ibid., pp. 177, 180.

27. Sherwin & Kasimow (eds), *John Paul II and InterReligious Dialogue* (Maryknoll: Orbis, 1999), pp. 28–29.

28. Lesslie Newbigin, *Foolishness to the Greeks: The Gospel and Western Culture* (Geneva: World Council of Churches, 1986), p. 146.

29. ibid., p. 147.

30. Philip Jenkins, *God's Continent*.

31. Cited in Jenkins, *God's Continent*, p. 8.

32. ibid.

33. ibid., p. 9.

34. ibid., p. 12.

35. Stephen Metcalf, 'The God Disillusion', review article of *Easter Everywhere: A Memoir* by Darcey Steinke, *The New York Times Book Review*, 22 April 2007.

36. Jenkins, *God's Continent*, pp. 265–266.

37. ibid, p. 268.

38. 'More People are Staying at Home to Worship', *Sunday New York Times*, 1 December 1991, pp. 1, 44.

39. Jenkins, *God's Continent*, p. 91.

Chapter 4

1. James Barr analyses how relativism has affected Western Christians in their view of the Bible. Cf. James Barr, *The Bible in the Modern World* (New York: Harper & Row, 1973), p. 11. According to Barr, the normativity of the Bible is rejected because the Bible is a book from the past, culturally and historically conditioned, and there seems to be no way of combining this 'pastness' with a normative role in modern society. A book produced in one cultural context cannot have decisive authority for people living in another cultural context (p. 42). The Bible has to be relativised as a book 'belonging to an environment entirely different from our own, in which the

questions and answers also were entirely different' (p. 43).

2. Archie C. C. Lee, 'Biblical Interpretation in Asian Perspectives', *Asian Journal of Theology* 7 (1993) 38.

3. Kwok Pui Lan, 'Discovering the Bible in the Non-Biblical World', *Semeia* 47 (1989) 34, holds that in Asia the concept of 'scripture' did not exist; that the notion of 'scripture' is culturally conditioned and cannot be found in Hinduism or Confucianism. According to Kwok, this explains why the Asian religions have relatively more fluidity and are able to assimilate their visions with those of other traditions. Thus the Bible is only one form of human construction to talk about God. However, by arguing that 'the various stories that contain both the liberation of women and other cultural situations must be regarded as "sacred" *as the biblical stories*' (emphasis mine), she contradicts her own argument and acknowledges the status of the Bible as a sacred book.

4. Stanley J. Samartha, *One Christ, Many Religions: Toward a Revised Christology* (Maryknoll: Orbis, 1991), p. 58.

5. ibid., pp. 58–75.

6. R. S. Sugirtharajah, 'The Bible and its Asian Readers', *Biblical Interpretation*, 1 (1993) 65.

7. Samartha, *One Christ, Many Religions*, p. 61.

8. E. Schussler-Fiorenza, 'The ethics of interpretation: De-centering biblical scholarship', *Journal of Biblical Literature*, 107 (1988), 10.

9. Samartha, *One Christ, Many Religions*, p. 61.

10. George M. Soares-Prabhu, 'Towards an Indian Interpretation of the Bible', *Biblebhashyam* vol. 6 (March 1980) 156.

11. Archie C. C. Lee, 'Biblical Interpretation in Asian Perspectives', *AJT* 7:1 (1993) 35–39.

12. ibid., 38.

13. Archie Lee, 'Cross Textual hermeneutics on Gospel and Culture', *AJT* 10:1 (1996) 45.

14. Sugirtharajah, 'The Bible and its Asian Readers', 59.

15. Sugirtharajah, 'The Bible and its Asian Readers', 61.

16. Stanley J. Samartha, 'The Asian Context: Sources and Trends', in R. S. Sugirtharajah (ed.) *Voices from the Margin* (Maryknoll: Orbis, 2006), p. 46.

Chapter 5

1. 'Towards 2010: Mission for the 21st Century, The Vision and the Process', in *Towards 2010 Online*, available from http://www.towards2010.org.uk/int_vision.htm, Internet, accessed 12 June 2007.

2. *Mission in a Broken Land: Report of ACC-8 Wales 1990* (London: Church House Publishing for the Anglican Consultative Council, 1990), p. 101.

3. Paul Avis, *A Ministry Shaped by Mission* (London: T & T Clark, 2005), p. 16.

4. Anglican Consultative Council, 'The Five Marks of Mission', in *The Anglican Communion Official Website, Mission and Evangelism* (Anglican Communion Office, 2004), available from http://www.aco.org/mission/fivemarks.cfm, Internet, accessed 12 June 2007.

5. Brian Stanley (ed.), *Christian Missions and the Enlightenment, Studies in the History of Christian Missions* (Grand Rapids, Michigan: Eerdmans, 2001), p. 17.

6. ibid., p. 8.

7. As for some examples of this type of contextual theology, see Ken Christoph Miyamoto, *God's Mission in Asia: A Comparative and Contextual Study of This-Worldly*

Holiness and the Theology of Missio Dei in M. M. Thomas and C. S. Song (Eugene, OR: Pickwick Publications, 2007).

8. Anglican Consultative Council, 'The Five Marks of Mission'.

9. Paul Avis, *A Church Drawing Near: Spirituality and Mission in a Post-Christian Culture* (London: T &T Clark, 2003), p. 183.

10. The Secretary General of the Anglican Consultative Council 1988, *The Truth Shall Make You Free: The Lambeth Conference 1988, Reports, Resolutions and Pastoral Letters from the Bishops* (London: Church House Publishing for the Anglican Consultative Council, 1988), pp. 42, 66.

11. Charles Ryerson, in a personal e-mail to the author dated 27 April 2006.

Chapter 7

1. S. B. Bevans and R. P. Schroeder, *Constants in Context* (Maryknoll: Orbis, 2004), p. 13.

2. See Bevans' book on *Models of Contextual Theology* (Orbis, 1992) as well as the final chapter in Bevans and Schroeder (op. cit.) where they discuss six components of God's mission in which the church is called to share: proclamation and witness; prayer, liturgy, and contemplation; justice, peace, and integrity in creation; inter-religious dialogue; inculturation; and reconciliation (pp. 351ff.). There is some overlap here with the five marks of mission. For a recent overview of discipleship in the New Testament see R. N. Longenecker, *Patterns of Discipleship in the New Testament* (Eerdmans, 1996) and for a classic (evangelical) account see D. Watson: *Discipleship* (Hodder & Stoughton, 1981) which roots Christian faith in daily life.

3. See the diagram at the end of this chapter which shows the inter-relationship between these aspects. See also the subsequent appendix on the draft covenant.

4. For an overview of Evangelical perspectives on millennialism and mission, see Ian Randall, *What a Friend we have in Jesus: The Evangelical Tradition* (London: Darton, Longman & Todd, 2005), ch. 10.

5. What follows is dependent upon two chapters in Brian Stanley (ed.), *Christian Missions and the Enlightenment* (Grand Rapids: Eerdmans, 2001), i.e. Jane Samson, 'Ethnology and Theology: Nineteenth-Century Mission Dilemmas in the South Pacific' (ch. 5) and Ian Douglas Maxwell, 'Civilization or Christianity? The Scottish Debate on Mission Methods, 1750–1835' (ch. 6).

6. Geoffrey Rowell, Kenneth Stevenson and Rowan Williams, *Love's Redeeming Work: The Anglican Quest for Holiness* (Oxford: Oxford University Press, 2001), p. xxiv.

7. ibid., p. xxxi.

8. ibid.

9. For more detail on this, see Mark Chapman, *Anglicanism: A Very Short Introduction* (Oxford: Oxford University Press, 2006).

10. For a detailed exploration of this development in Anglicanism see Ephraim Radner and Philip Turner, *The Fate of the Communion: The Agony of Anglicanism and the Future of a Global Church* (Grand Rapids: Eerdmans, 2006), especially ch. 9.

Appendix to Chapter 7

1. This document was a collaborative piece of work with Dr Martin Davie.